A Duel of Nations

A Duel of Nations

GERMANY, FRANCE, AND THE DIPLOMACY
OF THE WAR OF 1870–1871

David Wetzel

The University of Wisconsin Press

The University of Wisconsin Press
1930 Monroe Street, 3rd Floor
Madison, Wisconsin 53711-2059
uwpress.wisc.edu

3 Henrietta Street
London WC2E 8LU, England
eurospanbookstore.com

Printed in the United States of America

Library of Congress Cataloging-in-Publication Data

Wetzel, David.
A duel of nations : Germany, France, and the diplomacy
of the War of 1870–1871 / David Wetzel.
p.   cm.
Includes bibliographical references and index.
ISBN 978-0-299-29134-1 (pbk. : alk. paper) — ISBN 978-0-299-29133-4 (e-book)
1. Franco-Prussian War, 1870–1871—Diplomatic history.
2. France—Foreign relations—Germany.
3. Germany—Foreign relations—France.
4. Bismarck, Otto, Fürst von, 1815–1898. I. Title.
DC300.W48   2012
943.08'22—dc23
2012010178

To the memory of Ed

Contents

Illustrations

ILLUSTRATIONS

Preface

The volume these words will introduce represents the second part of what was conceived as a study, in depth, of the tension that brought France and Prussia to a crisis in July 1870 and resulted in a war between the two of them that began on the nineteenth of that month and ended, eight months later, by the Treaty of Frankfurt, on 10 May 1871.

The first part of this study, published in 2001 by the University of Wisconsin Press under the title *A Duel of Giants*, was addressed to the period preceding the outbreak of the war and the main issue over which it ostensibly developed—namely the question of the Hohenzollern candidacy for the occupancy of the Spanish throne. The present volume, picking up the story in July 1870, is addressed to the diplomacy of the war itself and the means by which the two belligerents tried to realize their goals—the French, on the one side, to win allies for themselves; the determination of the Prussians, especially of Otto von Bismarck, the prime minister, on the other, to prevent them from doing so while at the same time securing the fundamental Prussian war aims as Bismarck conceived these to be.

My attention was initially drawn to this subject by certain appreciations borne in upon me by my earlier study of the crisis of July 1870. Central to these appreciations was the recognition that, despite several valuable secondary works in French, German, and Italian on the diplomacy of the Franco-Prussian War, there was in English no general treatment of this subject tapping all the sources available today that could serve as a foundation for critical judgment. In these circumstances, there could be no alternative but to delve into the original source material and attempt, as best I could, to unravel the tangled web of what actually occurred. This book attempts to look at the diplomacy of the war in high detail, as though through some sort of historical microscope, with a view not to attempting to describe the totality of the relevant events but, as in A *Duel of Giants*, to examining the texture of the process; not to record all the significant things that happened but rather to show how they were happening; above all, by revealing by what motives and concepts the key actors were driven as they said and did the things that the record reveals. To the task at hand—the identification of the traits of the leading French and Prussian actors as they strove to conduct the diplomacy of the war of 1870–71—this process would do as well as any other, and possibly better than some.

A look at the totality of the diplomacy of the Franco-Prussian War is, then, the aim of the present work. But why precisely the Franco-Prussian War? For two reasons. First, the Franco-Prussian War of 1870–71 was without question a turning point of the utmost importance in the history of nineteenth-century Europe and was of particular importance as a factor causing Bismarck to begin, through the cultivation of a system of alliances, the quest, ultimately futile, for a new international stability. But, second and most outstandingly, the overwhelming abundance of source material and especially the enormous collection of documentary evidence once locked away in governmental archives—much of it now online—is now available to scholars through the efforts of librarians, archivists, scholars, and technicians. This book attempts to access these materials to the fullest extent possible.

Describing the manner in which the diplomacy of the Franco-Prussian War developed involved confrontation with a set of subsidiary problems to which, in the secondary literature, no satisfactory answers had been found. How and under what circumstances, for example, did Bismarck come to conceive the Prussian war aims? How were these affected by the overthrow of the government of Napoleon III and its replacement by one that enjoyed no international recognition? What were the circumstances in which there developed the League of Neutrals, and in what ways did its development shape the policy of the actors on both sides? What value is one to attach to the extravagant claims of such chauvinistic figures as Léon Gambetta to have been the defender of France's honor? Were the rulers of Russia, Tsar Alexander II and his foreign minister, Alexander Gorchakov, justified in their suspicion that their ostensible friend and ally, Prussia, was bent on expanding in central Europe in such a way as to upend and make a mockery of that allegiance and friendship? To what extent were their suspicions the product of well-considered and compelling national interest and to what extent the product of self-interest, prejudice, and intrigue? To what extent, more explicitly, were their suspicions the product of the hot-headed Pan-Slavists in the Russian court and society? Why was the counsel and advice of such an experienced and enlightened actor as Adolphe Thiers ignored for so long by the leading French authorities, and how did it finally come to prevail? In what circumstances, similarly, did the French foreign minister, Jules Favre, come to believe that the assumptions and beliefs he entertained when he took office were the wrong ones, and how and to what extent was he able to bring his colleagues to the same conclusion?

The present volume brings together the fruit of researches that led me to attempt to answer these and other questions. In attempting to answer them, I have attempted to describe what I have gleaned on the strength of the available record, to examine the evidence critically and imaginatively, to select from among the records (for they were—and always are—multitudinous in number), to try to grasp the reality behind them, and to try to depict them in a way that reveals their true meaning. But, beyond that, it is my hope that this book will serve, in addition to its strict scholarly purpose, not only to illuminate the strains of the figures charged with conducting the Franco-Prussian War but also to evoke that ineffable quality of atmosphere in the absence of which no period of history can be made real and purposeful to those who have not themselves been a part of it.

More important still is my hope that the reader who has sufficient patience to pursue to its final pages the second volume of this study will come to understand it for what it was: like the July crisis that preceded it, the story of individuals and individual behavior in the context of political history, not the operation of forces or structures beyond the play of human personality. There are no human beings, to be sure, who do not feel the setting within which they move, but all of them, or at least those whose activities are recounted here, transcend their setting and in their turn affect it; what they do both within and to it remains explicable, if not predictable. Those who argue that structures are more important than people deprive humankind of its humanity—of its power for good and evil, of its ability to think and choose, of its chance to triumph and to suffer. Concern for those in positions of leadership as the events unfolded makes the telling of what happened here intelligible, understandable, and, above all, rewarding. If the reader comes away from this story believing this to be the case, the effort undertaken in the pages that follow will not have been wholly in vain.

Acknowledgments

The number of persons from whom I have received assistance and support in the preparation of this volume is so great that space does not permit me to mention them all.

My gratitude goes out, in the first instance, to the Department of History of the University of California, Berkeley, which, though I am not a member of its permanent faculty, has supported my work in several ways, and not least by its incomparable atmosphere of understanding and consideration for all scholarly endeavors.

Among the individuals at Berkeley and elsewhere in the United States to whom I must record my debt, the following friends and colleagues richly deserve this special mention.

First and foremost, Professor Margaret Lavinia Anderson, for whose devoted interest and unselfish help on many occasions I have difficulty finding adequate words of appreciation; Professor James J. Sheehan of Stanford University, one of the leading historians of Germany in our time, from whose immense erudition, rich warmth, humor, endless curiosity, love of subject, and generosity of communication I have never ceased to benefit; Professor Paul W. Schroeder of the University of Illinois at Urbana-Champaign for his generosity in giving me, over the last ten years, the benefit of his incomparable knowledge and great experience in the field of nineteenth-century international history; Professor Theodore S. Hamerow of the University of Wisconsin–Madison for reading the manuscript from cover to cover and providing detailed commentary on various portions of the work; Professor Diethelm Prowe of Carleton College for his valuable and spontaneous assistance in uncovering some details with which to improve the concluding chapter; Professor Herbert F. Ziegler of the University of Hawaii, Manoa, a statistician as well as a historian, for his kindness in reading the manuscript and giving me valuable comments.

I am also greatly indebted to Hugo Lini, of the UC Berkeley Library, upon whose energies and good will the reviewing of the manuscript never ceased to levy its exactions.

For devoted help and gentle discipline in the final editing of the volume my thanks must go out to Sheila McMahon of the University of Wisconsin Press and to Matthew Cosby, acquisitions assistant at UW Press, who repeatedly answered, sometimes hour by hour, barrage after barrage of my questions.

Though the facilities extended to me in these instances did not go beyond those normally extended to scholars, I should like to express my appreciation to the respective archivists of the Politisches Archiv of the German Foreign Office, in Berlin; the Archives du Ministère des affaires étrangères, in Paris; and the Haus-, Hof- und Staatsarchiv, in Vienna, for the courtesies extended to me in those places.

Finally, I wish to thank my students, and particularly four members of my freshman-sophomore seminar in the fall semester of 2009—Kevin Gibson, Alex Ouligian, Andrew Hoglund, and Tristan Parker—who did so much to make those months of that year among the most rewarding and enjoyable periods of my life. This book started life in your presence, greatly benefited from your papers and feedback, and was only brought to conclusion by the inspiration, enthusiasm, and encouragement you never ceased to provide.

A Duel of Nations

1

Politics and Personalities

The declaration of war by France against Prussia on 19 July 1870 constitutes the formal point of departure for this narrative. But it was, of course, only the final phase of a crisis that had begun with the acceptance by Prince Leopold of Hohenzollern-Sigmaringen of the throne of Spain less than four weeks earlier. Before we proceed to examine the course of the diplomacy of the war, it will be useful to consider the situations that prevailed in the two capitals at the time it broke it out.

In France, the crisis of July had turned, as many higher figures in the imperial government had hoped from the start that it would, into a clash of arms with Prussia. A great many Frenchmen had dreamed of a war that would reverse the decline of French prestige that had seemed inexorable in the wake of the Prussian victory over Austria in 1866. Berlin's astonishing success and the military advantages that now flowed to it in its wake made resistance by France to further expansion on the part of Prussia an overriding imperative. France was now resisting, and finally things seemed to have been set right.

Much of the country was celebrating. In Paris, something like hysteria reigned; mobs in the street blurted out the forbidden *Marseillaise* and shouted "*Vive la guerre!*" by day and night. Unbridled joy filled the air. The chauvinistic *Le Figaro* begged its readers for contributions to a subscription fund the purpose of which was to present every soldier in the army with a glass of brandy and a cigar. Troops departed among huge and wildly enthusiastic crowds and were often given dinners and parties before they left for the front. There were, to be sure, a few whose souls were less bombastic. With barely a pause to envisage the prospect of defeat, Victor Hugo's son laid down in the *Rappel*: "The greatest danger is that of victory" because it would result even more in the strengthening of the structures of imperial power.[1] Prosper Mérimée, a leading intellectual, wrung his hands to a friend in Switzerland. Observing the sanguine mood of the population, he noted: "I am afraid the generals are not geniuses," then, a few days later: "I am dying from fear."[2] Lucien-Anatole Prévost-Paradol, newly arrived minister in Washington, expressed something along the same lines when he cautioned prophetically to his fellow citizens: "You will not go to Germany; you will be crushed in France. Believe me, I know the Prussians."[3] Shortly after this admonition, he put a gun to his head, opened fire, and killed himself. Still, these were voices crying in the wilderness.[4] The press and the public of France were in no mood to take a measured view of events, convinced that they were seeing the onset of some new and wonderful historical era, pregnant with pleasing self-sacrifice, adventure, valor, and glory.

In the meantime, popular support for war was finding its enthusiasm in the person of General Edmond Leboeuf, minister of war. This intellectually shallow but superficially impressive man, with his great flair for self-dramatization and his formidable powers of demagogic interaction with the masses, had played skillfully both on the existing social discontents and on the national sense of self-humiliation in the hectic days of the July crisis of 1870. He succeeded, by the end of July, in producing enhanced nationalistic and patriotic fervor among the senior officials of the French government. Nor was he alone. Empress Eugénie, consumed as ever with a hatred of Prussia and of Bismarck personally, met with Napoleon on 16 July and insisted that the best way to instill passion for war in the hearts of the people was for him to go to the front and take supreme command of the troops—one great army, of eight corps under imperial command with two divisions, not three, as had hitherto been planned. Napoleon agreed. At heart unsure of himself, now sick and unaccustomed to thinking things through independently, disinclined to take any personal initiative, he found it impossible to resist the anti-Prussian tendencies of such a powerful figure. As a result of this decision, the government was left in the hands of a council over which the empress herself would preside.

Yet, for all of Eugénie's influence, Napoleon's generals ascribed the decision regarding the deployment of French forces to something quite other—namely to pressure brought to bear upon the emperor by Archduke Albert of

4

Austria, who, Napoleon was told, believed that an army so organized could be more flexible and better able to join in a combined allied thrust.[5] The result was a certainty in the minds of the army chiefs, Leboeuf's most of all, that Austria was bent on intervening in the war on the French side. It was the result, too, of many misimpressions of the strength of the French army. The episode stands as a vivid example not only of the intensity of the efforts put forward by the French chauvinists to deflect policies of the Austrian government in a direction more favorable to an eventual alliance but also of the considerable success such efforts had on a mind so predisposed to credit their tendencies as was that of Napoleon III. Such tendencies found, it may be added, strong expression and support in various aspects of the French press and military publications. Outstanding among these was the *Military Almanac*, which contemptuously dismissed the warnings of Prévost-Paradol about the strength of the Prussian army, commenting that it constituted "a magnificent organization on paper, but a doubtful instrument for the defensive, . . . which would be highly imperfect during the first phase of an offensive war."[6]

This assessment of the enemy army was woefully wide of the mark. Whether on paper or in practice, the Prussian army of 1870 was a glittering piece of machinery—the mightiest engine of war that Europe had seen in half a century. At its head was William I, the first professional soldier to rule Prussia since Frederick the Great; as chief of the General Staff there stood Helmut von Moltke. It was a matter of pride to both that either could inspect eighty-seven battalions in twenty-two days. Under William's mantle, nothing had been too good for the army. Though the combined population of Prussia and the Prussian-led North German Confederation, at 30,000,000, was less than that of France, a system of universal service and of reserves organized on a regional basis that was years ahead of the time enabled the German states to produce an army of 1,183,000 men within eighteen days of mobilization. Nothing on this scale had ever been seen before. The army was issued maps of France dotted with cities not yet marked on the maps of the French ministry of war. With the invading army came a system of military government (virtually unheard of before the twentieth century) that included such refinements as a Post Office functionary dispatched to make sure that the accounts of the enemy's postmasters corresponded to their own book entries. The Teutonic "organization man" had arrived.[7]

In Prussia, news of the outbreak of war was not greeted with the same outpouring of enthusiasm as seen in Paris. But there was nonetheless a deep sense of moral earnestness and pronounced self-righteousness. It flowed from the image of the French regime—indeed, of the people—that confronted them. It was the image of unmitigated darkness—the image of a group of people seeking to dominate and rule key parts of Europe and motivated, in particular, by a relentless determination to bring the German peoples under its yoke. It was especially in north Germany that this image found, as it did in France, strong support and expression in large sections of the press. The French minister in Hamburg put it well: "The Government of the Emperor would be well advised to prepare less for a campaign on the Rhine than for . . . war to the knife, according to the newspapers. . . . The war in the North has taken on an irresistible character, all restraints and hesitations have been swept aside. M. de Bismarck has succeeded by wise maneuvers in arousing sentiments of justice and fairness so deep among the Germans that no one on this side of the Rhine could be convinced that the war was stoppable by any means."[8] But, beyond that, and more important still, there was, again in the north at least, a deeply religious element that did much to foster an anti-French impression. All the states that constituted the North German Confederation were overwhelmingly Lutheran; Lutheran hymns mingled with journalistic pronouncements to produce a solidarity of purpose necessary to successfully carry out the coming war. The records of the time reflect this sentiment. They run over with anti-French passions and contrast their own sense of earnestness and determination with that of a superficial, unctuous, and hereditary foe. In the relationship to France, there gradually emerged, by the last week of July 1870, an element of finality in what its rulers had done during the first half of that month and boiling anger for the abuse they had heaped on the tenets of accepted international behavior.[9]

The passion in the north found somewhat less reflection in the states south of the River Main. Instead of fury, there was hesitation and anxious foreboding. Shaken and horror-stricken by the flood of events, the South Germans were seized with the fear that they might be occupied by the French, as they had so many times in the past; that a French invasion was imminent; that resistance might come too late; and that they had no alternative but to bind themselves inextricably to the control of Berlin. This was music to the Prussian ears. The crown prince wrote excitedly that "even in South Germany the population is so fired with unanimous zeal for this war that Princes and Cabinets will find it impossible to stem the current much as they might wish to."[10]

But here one must note some crosscurrents. In Stuttgart and Württemberg, there were anguished and alarmed feelings of frustration and resentment about the way Bismarck had conducted his policy toward France, and some—the judiciary of Mainz, for example—were rumored to be awaiting the coming of the French Redeemers; all over South Germany the mood, it was said, "was still not properly edified,"[11] and even the official historian of the war was obliged to concede that there were figures and groups that "went their own way, grumbling and embittered out of hatred for Prussia, and even sympathized openly or in secret with the enemy."[12] But, in the end, there could be no turning back. There was a clear *casus foederis*; Bismarck reminded his minister in Munich that the first article of the treaties of 1866 made clear Bavaria's obligation to assist Prussia in a case such as the one now at hand.[13] In the end, there was no serious resistance. Mobilization was ordered in Bavaria and Baden on 16 July, in Württemberg on the following day. By 1 August 1870, 1,183,000 were marching in the German lines, embedded into the army and put on a war footing; railroads carried 462,000 to the French border to commence hostilities.

In a word: the Prussian military leaders knew what they wanted; they worked day and night to get it into effect; they gave no thought to themselves. In their seriousness of purpose, in the forthright simplicity of their behavior, in their refusal to bother about nonessentials, in their unhesitating subordination of personal considerations to the demands of the hour, in their willingness to get their hands dirty in the interests of the cause—in these manifestations of the Prussian military personality of 1870, a thousand outworn affectations and pretenses that paralyzed the progress of French arms would go crashing to the ground.

The story of the diplomacy of the Franco-Prussian War represents, like every other prolonged phase of military and diplomatic history, a fabric in which individual personalities appear, like threads, to bear for a time their share of strain, only to disappear again at some point, often quite abruptly, resigning the burden to others. In general, these personalities will be introduced and examined when they appear on the scene. But there remains the necessity of introducing those who were already on the scene at the time this story opens and would remain on the scene for the duration of the war—and even longer; unless the reader has some knowledge of their background and peculiarity of their approach to these problems, the account of their behavior loses much of its significance.

In the case of the French: the Emperor Napoleon III and his wife, the Empress Eugénie, need no general introduction to the reading public. Their respective reactions to the problems of the war and those of the members of the Government of National Defense (GND) that came into power after their downfall, on 4 September 1870, will best be left to reflect themselves in the happenings that make up the body of this narrative. In the case of the Germans, three leading figures—King William I; Otto von Bismarck, minister-president of the North German Confederation; and chief of staff of the Prussian Army Helmut von Moltke—had been at their posts throughout most of the 1860s (Moltke since 1857) and would remain there throughout most of the next two decades. They were obviously destined to play a central role in both the military and the diplomatic aspects of the Franco-Prussian War itself. They thus appeared in 1870–71 to be permanent fixtures at the Prussian end of the conflict. A few words about them will therefore not be out of place.

The figure of William I is one familiar from a multitude of historical sources and treatises. This tall, bearded, taciturn man—often compared to an ox or a bull—was a man of unshakable political conviction not often seen in public and, when seen, always in soldier's uniform. He had begun his rule in 1858, first as prince-regent of Prussia, then (after the death of his brother Frederick William IV three years later, in 1861) as king. He would continue to reign as king and emperor for the next twenty-seven years, and, during this period, his state was fated to fight three successful wars, to gain the mastery of all of Germany, and to assume a position of unrivaled domination in the configuration of the Great Powers of Europe.

When he came to the throne, in 1861, William was sixty-three years of age. He was a man set in his ways, and his mind was dominated by one overriding passion: the army. His object was to reform it, to abolish a middle-class militia called the *Landwehr*, and to extend the term of service in the regular army from two to three years. These plans met with furious opposition in the Prussian parliament when they were first introduced, in 1860. A pronounced deadlock lasting for almost two years then ensued. By September 1862, parliamentary opposition had reached a point where the assembly refused to grant further money for army reform, and William, on the advice of his war minister, summoned as prime minister the ruthlessly unorthodox Otto von Bismarck. Within fifteen months of taking office, Bismarck had involved Prussia in a war with Denmark; two years thereafter, he entered into a struggle with Austria for the mastery of Germany. With these two wars, all the unity and fervor of the opposition began to melt, and the constitutional crisis was decisively resolved in favor of the king at the battle of Königgrätz on 3 July 1866. On 20 October 1867, Albrecht von Roon, the minister of war, could write jubilantly to William that the struggle with parliament was over at last.[14] By July 1870, the entire Prussian government from the king on down could take comfort in knowing that he had succeeded in accomplishing exactly what he had set out to do—and then some.

By 1870, William was indeed the most powerful monarch in Europe. When the Franco-Prussian War broke out in that year, he was already seventy-one years old. A stiff soldier, a stout Protestant, a man of his word, William was married to Queen Augusta, a woman of superior character and intellect and a figure who remained, until her death, in 1890, one of Bismarck's fiercest opponents. The two had one child, Frederick, whom they loved deeply. William's habits and tastes were the robust and simple ones of Prussia in the middle of the 1850s. As such, they bore little affinity to the refined predilections that characterized much of continental diplomacy. William was sometimes accused of having a phlegmatic temperament, of indifference to his surroundings, of a sort of bovine stubbornness. There was a little truth in these observations—but only a little, for they were far from penetrating the complexities of this extraordinary personality.

While indeed retiring, given to burying himself in his various palaces and not in the habit of learning about the rest of Prussia—or, for that matter, the other states that made up the North German Confederation—from personal observation or from wide personal contacts with other people, William was not really as indifferent about what was occurring throughout his kingdom as was sometimes supposed; he merely preferred to learn about it in the privacy of his palace, through the reports of his leading ministers. Though a reputed reactionary during the great revolutionary disorders from 1848 to 1850, he had none of his predecessor's high-flown mysticism, and, indeed, on becoming king, in 1861, he dismissed the clique of ministers to which Frederick William had clung and proclaimed a "new ministry." But the scars he took from the disturbances at the middle of the century remained with him, and he punished ruthlessly what he saw as attempts to overthrow his dynasty or undermine the political system. He took as well—and would take throughout his reign—a keen interest in foreign affairs, and, whenever his personal sensitivities were not too extensively involved, his judgments on such matters were not devoid of perception and good sense. His sensitivities, on the other hand, his likes and dislikes—his reaction to what he saw as slights to his person or authority—could be lively in the extreme. Once aroused, they were not easily assuaged.

William I was fully aware of his power and his responsibility. His leading ministers reported to him weekly throughout most of the year. He was punctilious in receiving them, listened carefully to what they had to say, and made his decisions when he considered that the proper time had come, but he left to them the execution of those orders. He was in a certain sense politically diffident—a quality not to be confused with any lack of readiness to assert his own power. He simply liked to deal with familiar faces and disliked having to deal with unfamiliar ones. For this reason, he changed his ministers very rarely—and sometimes kept them beyond the period of their greatest effectiveness. But he never allowed them—or even the members of his own family—to forget who was king and what this meant. The numerous grand dukes who formed part of his family, some of them older and headstrong men, all learned to respect his authority. But he did not like dramatic personal confrontations and went out of his way to avoid them. Yet there were certain other individuals in his entourage to whose opinions he was particularly sensitive and whom he hesitated to controvert. When these disagreed among themselves and gave him conflicting advice, he was capable

William I, king of Prussia. (*The Correspondence of William I. & Bismarck*, trans. J. A. Ford [New York: F. A. Stokes, 1903], ii.)

(like many another absolute ruler) of vacillating, temporizing, and even act-ing deviously. He abhorred personal confrontations and went out of his way to avoid them. For all his strength and consciousness of authority, there was within him a curious streak of evasive shyness that inclined him to avoid participation in collective discussions of any sort, to deal with his ministers only individually, to make his decisions in private, and to make them known in ways that precluded objection or counterargument.[15]

If William I was the most powerful monarch in Europe when the Franco-Prussian War opened in the summer heat of July 1870, then Otto von Bis-marck, foreign minister of Prussia and minister-president of the North Ger-man Confederation, was beyond question the commanding figure on the scene of European diplomacy. His stormy advancement of the position of Prussia in Central Europe and the final creation, in the wake of the war of 1870–71, of the German empire were observed by the other powers of Eu-rope with mixed feelings. But Bismarck managed to bring this about without provoking a general European war, a feat all the more remarkable because the dangers of intervention in it by the Great Powers, especially Russia and Austria, were, if not imminent, certainly real. That Bismarck was able to conduct the war the way he did, avoiding intervention, was a reflection of his competence as a statesman of a wholly superior order.

What were the specific qualities that made Bismarck appear, to his own and later generations, to be the very model of diplomacy and that continue to excite admiration even in the breasts of those who disapprove of his methods or the results of his labors? Perhaps, if we take a moment to note these, we can gain some understanding of the reasons not only for Bismarck's success in foreign policy and for the failures of his immediate and more remote suc-cessors but also, more important for the purpose at hand, for his attitude toward the great issues to which the unification of Germany gave rise during the course of the Franco-Prussian War.

Born in the East Prussian province of Pomerania on 1 April 1815, the son of a dull, unprepossessing Junker from whom he inherited his huge physical frame, Bismarck came to diplomacy late in the day. He grew up at a time

Otto von Bismarck, chancellor, North German Confederation. (J. Julius Albert G. von Pflugk-Harttung, *The Franco-German War, 1870–71*, trans. and ed. Major-General J. F. Maurice [London: Swan Sonnenschein and Co., 1900], 3.)

when Prussia was the least great of the European powers. When brought to power on the heels of the constitutional crisis just recounted, he was forty-seven years of age. He had never been a government minister and had spent much of his uproarious early years in the Prussian bureaucracy two decades before. His diplomatic experience had been shaped by his years as the Prussian delegate to the Frankfurt assembly (from 1851 to 1859) and by two ambassadorships, the first at Saint Petersburg from 1859 to 1862 and the second at Paris from May to September 1862. A word or two about these experiences will not be out of place here.

In his first weeks as delegate at Frankfurt, Bismarck had written: "In the art of saying absolutely nothing with a lot of words I am making raging progress and if Manteuffel [the prime minister of Prussia] can say what's in them when he's read them, then he can do more than I."[16] One need merely glance at a few of the dispatches that Bismarck sent to Manteuffel to realize that this statement, like many of the brilliant but willful passages with which Bismarck's writings are replete, needs to be taken with a large pinch of salt. The noteworthy feature is rather the thoroughness and the speed with which Bismarck mastered the mechanics of his craft and the skill so vital to success in his profession: the ability to discern the essence of a situation and to draw attention to those aspects that are salient and worthy of deeper study.

Years later, the great novelist Theodor Fontane wrote: "Bismarck says in one of his letters: 'The art of landscape painting does not lie in the ability to reproduce a whole landscape faithfully, but more in being able to discover the *one* point by which *this particular* landscape is to be distinguished from all the others.' This is wonderfully true and not restricted merely to landscapes but to any given situation."[17] This ability to pinpoint the special characteristic Bismarck never lost from the onset and, despite his efforts to deprecate himself, he also possessed the skill of depicting what it disclosed to him in a way that fully vindicated the authority he later exercised of rebuking the stylistic imperfections of those who worked under him. Manteuffel can have had no difficulty in comprehending the reports of one who, had he not been a diplomat, would unquestionably have been one of the great men of letters of the nineteenth century. Sometimes his words, preserved for posterity by the written page, stand out on his lips like the little balloons of utterance from the characters in a cartoon strip. The great dispatch of May 1856 in which Bismarck portrayed Austria and Prussia as "plowing the same disputed acre" and waiting for war "to set the clock of evolution at the right hour"[18] is a perfect illustration of these qualities, as are others that he wrote before, after, and during the Franco-Prussian War.

Bismarck's literary skills can be ascribed in part to his enjoyment of travel, which he did often after his appointment to his first post at Frankfurt in 1851. How much this was so can be seen in a letter to Leopold von Gerlach of September 1855. Gerlach had taken Bismarck to task for going to Paris and had gone so far as to insinuate that the body and the mind could be corrupted by contact with the inhabitants of the French capital. Bismarck answered: "You criticize me for being in Babylon, but you surely cannot demand from a diplomat hungry for knowledge the kind of political chastity that sits so well on a soldier like Lützow or on an independent country gentlemen. I must learn to know the elements in which I have to move, and I must do so by my own observation as far as opportunities present themselves to me."[19] And, in July 1862, to Albrecht von Roon, minister of war: "I have just come back from London, and the people there are much better informed about China and Turkey than about Prussia. Loftus [the British minister at Berlin] must be writing more nonsense to his minister than I thought."[20] Such observations, emended and broadened as time went on, gave Bismarck a vantage point that could not have been afforded by immersion in ambassadorial reports, and there flowed from his musings upon them some of his most penetrating general impressions about the characteristics and attitudes of the respective Great Powers of Europe. Thus, even before he was called back to Berlin, on 23 September 1862, to assume the position he would hold for twenty-eight years, Bismarck had managed to achieve a knowledge of Europe of which few others could boast, an incredible linguistic fluency, and a flair for analysis and reporting that was nothing short of remarkable. He had acquitted himself with distinction in the handling of the essential assignments in the world of a workaday diplomat—representation, reporting, and negotiation—as only a professional can understand them, and this was of the utmost significance, for, aside from precision and the sharpness of mind that it lent to his statecraft, it also gave him a vision of what he could expect from diplomatic agencies.

Bismarck often made mistakes—and these will be treated as the narrative of our drama unfolds. But they were never mistakes that result from naïveté or faulty expectation of what the practiced diplomat could accomplish.

Apart from the professional skills described, Bismarck possessed unique qualities of mind and character that are further worthy of note. Though he read widely, people were always more important to Bismarck than books; this was shown in his social demeanor. He was a master of every refinement of diplomatic protocol, and he gained from those around him, especially from diplomats and foreign statesmen, an almost universal respect. All seem to have been impressed with his deep experience, his shrewd judgment, and the reliability of his word. No one ever questioned his honesty or integrity. Even the military men, not predisposed to uncritical thinking of diplomatic statesmen, came to think highly of him, even when expressing, as they would frequently in the course of the war, their violent opposition to his views.

In view of the scorn and disdain with which Bismarck approached his profession at the outset, one would never have expected that he could bring himself to dedicate an unfettered commitment of his resources to it. He said to his wife in May 1851: "No one, not even the most ill-disposed and cynic of a democrat could believe how much charlatanry and pompousness there is in this diplomatic business,"[21] and not long afterward he was complaining to Leopold von Gerlach that his new job was devoid of the sparkle to which he had been accustomed in his work in government and in politics. But these sentiments quickly dissolved. Soon Bismarck was taken by his new profession, and his engagement would not lessen with the passage of time. His devotion to his job would present itself to contemporaries as an almost terrifying force.

But, as part and parcel of these abilities, there always came with Bismarck the recognition of a commensurate measure of moral responsibility, about which he would not infrequently write. Bismarck, in a word, never forgot that, within the confines of a single human frame, the individual needed outside help that could only be the help of faith to make life endurable. Here we can turn to another feature that stands out on the map of Bismarck's cosmology: the importance of religion in his life.

Ludwig Bamberger once jeered: "Prince Bismarck believes in a God who has the remarkable faculty of always agreeing with him,"[22] and this jibe has sometimes been construed to mean that religion was something that was not important to Bismarck and that he used only to justify decisions and policies that he had laid down beforehand. This is certainly unfair. True, Bismarck was not outwardly devout; the religion acquired with not inconsiderable misgivings when he was young was far removed from the humanitarianism of the twentieth century, and there was in it little love except perhaps for his own family. But that is only one side of the medal. The truth was that Bismarck embraced faith because it sustained him, helped him shoulder the authority of his position, not the least of which was power over life and death, and gave him the ability to endure the cruel moments that the necessities of diplomacy can sometimes inflict upon those who devote their lives to the service of it. He wrote once: "People and men, folly and wisdom, war and peace come and go like waves but the sea remains. Our states and their power are nothing to God but ant-heaps which are trampled on by an ox's hoof or snatched by fate in the shape of a honey gatherer."[23] And again: "I am God's soldier and wherever He sends me I must go, and I believe that He does send me and that He shapes my life as He needs to."[24]

The faith upon which Bismarck drew was an intensely personal matter. It sustained him in struggles in which, despite occasional setbacks, he could have the feeling of holding his own but in which there were—for him, at any rate—few sensational triumphs. It gave him a sense of modesty, self-control, self-discipline, sensitivity to the dictates of conscience, awareness of his own imperfections and the effort to struggle against them, humility in the face of his failures, and the willingness to accept the trivia of human affairs and to deal with them in an effective manner. This is not to suggest that Bismarck was immune from the baser emotions, for he was not. That he was filled with bursts of anger was well known, and he could admit that hatred had often deprived him of sleep for whole nights. To this heritage, however, Bismarck added markedly different characteristics—restraint, moderation, the ability to peer into the minds of others, and a readiness to risk his prestige for the sake of peace and moderation. Bismarck rarely allowed his emotions to interfere with, much less overcome, his conduct of foreign policy. Bülow the elder once wrote to his younger and more famous son (and later chancellor): "Prince Bismarck is in the habit of saying indignations and rancor are conceptions foreign to diplomacy. The diplomat is neither preacher of penitence, nor a judge in a criminal court, nor a philosopher. His sole and exclusive concern must be the real and downright interests of his country."[25]

The faith upon which Bismarck often drew when faced by questions of life and death gave his not infrequently turbulent life a sense of purpose and stability when he reflected on the vagaries of human affairs. He wrote to his wife, Johanna: "I cannot conceive how a man who reflects and yet knows nothing of God, and will know nothing, can endure his life for contempt and boredom. If I lived life as I once did, without God, without you, without children, I cannot think why I should not put life aside like a dirty shirt."[26] But it was not just these observations upon which Bismarck's faith was based. The plain fact was that nasty tasks had to be performed, and those who performed them had constantly to fall back upon God's grace in the hope that it would be extended to them. He once wrote: "Had it not been for me there would not have been three great wars; 80,000 men would not have perished; and parents, brothers, and sisters would not be in mourning. But that is something I must settle with God."[27]

Had Bismarck been asked to evaluate his own qualities, he would, as Gordon A. Craig once pointed out, almost certainly have emphasized caution and patience.[28] He was convinced that true wisdom was to recognize that, as he put it, "we can set our watches, but the time passes no more quickly because of that, and the ability to wait until conditions develop is a requisite of practical policy."[29] And again: "We can all carry national union in our hearts but . . . if Germany attains her desired goal in the nineteenth century I should regard that as a great achievement, if it were reached in ten or fifteen years it would be something extraordinary, an unexpected crowning gift from God. No one can accept responsibility for a war that would perhaps only be the first in a series of *Rassenkriege* [racial wars]."[30]

Equally, there can be no question that Bismarck would have endorsed the proposition that a fundamental principle of politics—and especially international politics—is that one is seldom free to act as one wants. The path that theory would point to as the best in a specific situation is almost always rendered impossible by the force of circumstance, and the statesman finds himself obliged to choose the least disagreeable of a number of options.[31] This was a maxim that Bismarck would always observe and one by which he repeatedly instructed his ambassadors to abide—often in reports marked by mature judgment, keen powers of observation, and, not least, brilliant literary style. Bismarck despised writers and literary men, but only Luther and Goethe rank with him as masters of German prose.

Prussian and later German policy was, in the first instance, limited by important geographical constraints. Both countries lay in the center of Europe, and this demanded an assertive and watchful policy, to which Bismarck bore witness when he wrote, in 1857: "[A] passive lack of planning, which is content to be left alone, is not for us, situated as we are in the middle of the continent."[32] Equally important, it ruled out romantic and ambitious undertakings in parts of the world remote from the nation's salient area of interests, concerns, and perils. Hence Bismarck's expostulation to a colonial champion during the 1880s: "Your map of Europe is very beautiful, but my map of Europe is very different. Here is Russia and here is France and here we are in the middle. That is my map of Africa."[33]

Otto von Bismarck's facilities were, in a word, analytical and critical in character. They were analytical in the sense that he endeavored to discover what was in the minds of his antagonists when the latter led him into confrontations of one kind or another. And they were critical in the sense that, having examined the intellectual and political motivations, he tried to measure them against the situations to which he conceived himself to be reacting, as well as the results to be achieved, and to assess the adequacy of the response. His mind was one of wholly exceptional power, subtlety, and speed of reaction. He was often described as arrogant and was criticized for this, and it was certainly true, though the evidences of it often reflected primarily the influences of people around him as much as the natural impulses of his own personality. The shattering quickness and the critical power of his mind doubtless made him impatient with the ponderous, the obvious, the platitudinous, in the discourse of others.

Bismarck has often been described as a realist, the embodiment of a uniquely ruthless and amoral realpolitik. But all statesmen, even the most high-minded and idealistic, regard themselves as realists. The distinctive quality of Bismarck's realism lay in his flexibility, in his refusal to be bound by any fixed rules or preconceptions, his sense of limits, of proportions, of dimensions. His plans were robust, always allowing for the intervention of accident, of mistake, of the unforeseen—the imponderabilia, as he once

19

called it. Bismarck received extensive attention in European and American historical literature even before his death, in 1898, and the full pattern of his complicated and subtle personality continues to emerge in the light of the more intensive and detached scrutiny to which it is constantly subjected. It is my hope that glimpses of Bismarck in his confrontation with the problems of the Franco-Prussian War, as they appear in this narrative, will contribute something to the fullness and richness of this pattern.

The year 1870, marked as it was by the great event of the outbreak of the Franco-Prussian War, brought important changes into Bismarck's life. Three points are worth bearing in mind as we observe the reactions to the problems posed by it.

First and foremost, it was the fundamental aim of all Bismarck's diplomacy vis-à-vis the other powers of Europe, especially Russia and Austria-Hungary but also Great Britain and Italy, to deprive these powers during the war of any and all incentives to align themselves with France and, what was likely to follow from this, to intervene (militarily or diplomatically) in the war itself. But it was also designed to prevent any of these powers from going to war against each other, for a war of that nature, whatever form it might take, would almost always be sure to disrupt the delicate structure of intra-European relations that formed the basis of his calculations and in terms of which he thought he could see ensured a successful German war effort.

Bismarck's second aim flowed logically from the first: the prospect of foreign intervention would be significantly increased every day the war dragged on. Once a decisive victory had been achieved and German war aims, as he construed them, had been attained, it was time for hostilities to cease. Bismarck was only too keenly aware of the speed by which the crisis with France over the Spanish throne had escalated into war between the two sides, and the possibility that it could be widened into a general European conflict stood at all times at the height of his concerns and priorities.

Third, while Bismarck had around him other highly competent, intelligent, and reasonable officials, he determined that he would at all times be the center of Prussian diplomacy. In this sense, he had no colleagues, only subordinates. But he determined never to allow himself to become isolated and was (as we shall see) roused to violent, defensive action against those he conceived to be the authors of such attempts. He sometimes liked to play the threatened party, thinking in this way to nip in the bud tendencies that, if allowed to develop, could truly threaten his position, as he conceived this position to be. And there were those in positions of power in the Prussian military who, in part because of the differences they had had with him over the conduct of the war with Austria in 1866, were bent on keeping politicians like Bismarck from interfering with their operations.[34]

Of these, Helmut von Moltke, since 1857 chief of staff of the Prussian Army, was by far the most prominent, the most brilliant, and the most dangerous. Geoffrey Wawro has noted that Moltke ranks with the most innovative strategists of the nineteenth century, and one can see what he means.[35] Since Moltke's name has already come up, and since it will come up at many points in the remainder of this account, it may be well to take note now, if only briefly, of the personality and character of this most gifted and fascinating of men.

Moltke stood, in competence, in intelligence, and, indeed, in all the qualities that make for a successful military career, at the head of the leading Prussian military figures of his time. Moltke was born in 1800 to a family that was all but impoverished. His father, Friedrich, joined the Danish army, in which his relatives also had commissions and, hardly able to support his fourteen children, enrolled his son as a cadet at Frankfurt/Oder near the Polish border at the age of eleven. The young Moltke was then for three years drawn into military service, first in Silesia, then in Posen. Down and out, starved for cash, Moltke was forced to find employment in a variety of jobs—including translating Gibbon—to augment his income. In 1832, he joined the General Staff at Berlin and was soon promoted to second lieutenant, largely as the result of the influence of Prince William, at the time a lieutenant general but destined to become King William I of Prussia. Here Moltke acquitted himself with distinction in a long series of responsible and important assignments in the field of military planning and engineering. Conscious of his duties and an indefatigable worker, he began to rise to a position of preeminence in the Prussian military.

Moltke's views on military relations with civilian authorities seemed to

Helmut von Moltke, chief of the Prussian General Staff. (von Pflugk-Harttung, *The Franco-German War*, 6.)

have been formed as early as 1848, when, as a junior officer in the Prussian army, he expressed his strong opposition to the revolutionary disturbances that swept Berlin that year and enhanced his belief in the power of absolutist rule. He noted, in a letter of 21 September of that year to his brother: "We now have 40,000 men in and around Berlin; the crux of the whole German problem is right here. Order in Berlin, and we shall have order in the country. . . . They [presumably King Frederick William IV and his ministers] now have the power in their hands and a perfect right to use it. If they don't do it, then I am ready to emigrate with you to Adelaide."[36] Moltke's hope was disappointed. The king, Frederick William IV, was first inclined to use the troops to crush resistance in the capital, but, as usual, at the critical moment his resolve deserted him, and he determined to follow a moderate course of action. The years after 1848 disillusioned Moltke. The Prussian army was, in many respects, a ramshackle operation. There were no plans for an offensive strategy, and each exercise in war games revealed a serious lack of cooperation between units. It sometimes took an officer five days to receive an order after a practice mobilization had been declared.[37]

This situation was redressed only after 29 October 1857, when Moltke was promoted to chief of the General Staff. The transformation of that organization into an agency responsible for all operations of warfare and the appointment of its chief as the principal adviser to the monarch in all matters of war was, as Arden Bucholz has convincingly demonstrated, Moltke's singular achievement.[38] This he accomplished with great skill and competence, skillfully guiding his ship, often behind the scenes, toward the port to which he would bring it, seldom inviting attention to his own person. But he did not accomplish it overnight. In the years immediately after his appointment, Moltke's plans seem to have taken a back seat to those of Count Roon, the minister of war, to whom he was still responsible but with whom he hardly ever corresponded. It was during the last phase of the Danish war of 1863–64 that Moltke's skill as a commander began to catch the eye of the king. In the operation against Alsen, which brought the war to a close, Moltke's hand was visible at every turn, and William I saw fit to reward him with repeated invitations to the critical crown councils that considered the policies to be taken with respect to Austria and the war that broke out in June 1866.

During that war, Moltke's position with William I was enormously strength-ened. On 2 June 1866, an order from William released the head of the General Staff from communicating with the king through the War Ministry and directed that henceforth the former would issue orders directly to the troops in the field. It was shortly after this time that there began a conflict of epochal dimensions between Moltke and Bismarck, the progression of which will be recounted at length in the course of this book. Here it is important to note that the conflict did not begin with the actual elevation of Moltke, for Bismarck, whatever misgivings he might have had about the arrangement, did nothing whatever to stand in the way of its implementation.

Moltke's abilities as a military commander have already been touched upon. A dedicated student of Clausewitz, whose writings he read voraciously, he was one of the few strategists in this period to note the importance of the uncertainties that attended every war and to prepare for these by conceiving of and dealing with multiplex scenarios of military action. "It is only the lay-man," he noted, "who thinks he sees in the course of a campaign the previously determined execution of a minutely detailed and scrupulously observed plan."[39] A plan had, for this reason, to be both flexible enough to envisage a whole set of different outcomes and specific enough to enable the quick deployment of soldiers to their appointed destinations. But, beyond this, and more important still, Moltke was one of the few men of his time who wished to take advantage of the intensive program of railway construction that had taken place in Prussia in the middle decades of the nineteenth century. The impact of the railroad on the face of war was, he grasped, nothing short of revolutionary. The railroad at once changed two key ingredients of modern warfare: its tempo and its dimensions. Understanding this, Moltke was able to qualify significant salient strategies in a way that allowed for rapid concentration of troops and for superior lines of interior communication. It was clear to him that this new technology, if used properly, would allow troops to move separately before coming together quickly and delivering devastating hammer blows to the enemy. Such a strategy would take advantage of time and would more than compensate for the numerical superiority an enemy might be expected to enjoy.[40]

Of Moltke's distinction as a strategist there can be no doubt. His name continues to dominate books addressed to this subject. But, the reader should not fail to note, Moltke's character contained some unfortunate and defective elements, as well. Of all the senior officials in Prussia, Moltke seems to have taken from the start the firmest and most uncompromising anti-French attitude. Of course, as leader of the army charged with defeating the enemy, this was understandable. But his hatred of France continued long after it was clear that Prussia would win the war, and, as we shall have repeated occasion to note, this hatred was at bottom the fundamental expression of his belief that the fighting should not cease until France had been pulled down from the ranks of the Great Powers and driven back into the inferiority from which it ought never to have escaped. An incident in his early life had contrived to symbolize in a curiously prophetic way the basis of his attitude. In 1805, the forces of Napoleon Bonaparte had burned down the house in Lübeck in which he was living with his family. Either by way of reaction to this or as a consequence of some ensuing complication unknown to the historian, there was aroused (or perhaps there matured) at this time in the steady and quiet disposition of Moltke an aversion and resentment toward France for which there seems to have been no parallel in the entire history of that general's attitude toward foreign powers. The historian can only emphasize the violence of this aversion. A powerful emotional nerve had been in some way touched and offended—so painfully offended that it would never cease to hurt. From that time on, hatred of France would become, for this otherwise astute military strategist, an unreasoning and uncontrollable emotional fixation. This disposition on Moltke's part was, especially as the war dragged on, a matter of common knowledge in all well-informed circles. Although Bismarck could not remain long unaware of this disposition, it seems to have taken him some time to understand the full depth of Moltke's hatred.

With these personalities, destined all to play important roles in the further unfolding of our tale, in mind, we are ready to turn to the tale itself.

2

The Position of the Powers

When the Prussian and French armies took to the field in the summer of 1870, they not unnaturally hoped to receive assistance in one form or another from the other powers of Europe. And the point at which our narrative has now arrived—just after the inauguration of hostilities between the two powers—is perhaps not a bad one to look at some of the ulterior preoccupations and to see how the Franco-Prussian War was being affected by them. This exercise—addressed as it is to the 1870–71 period—will necessarily have to reach back in time through the period treated in the previous volume, but this is necessary to throw light on the events still to be described.

We have already seen, in the preceding pages, something of the way in which the fears of possible foreign intervention and hopes of the French for it affected the thinking of Bismarck during the early days of the war. The French, for their part, had reason to believe that foreign intervention would be forthcoming. Both their reasons for believing this and Bismarck's attempts to prevent it therefore merit a glance.

On the French side, negotiations had been put in hand in the last months of 1868 and the first ones of 1869 for an alliance that would involve Austria-Hungary. France's proposals were complex, but what they essentially boiled down to was this: a demand for Austrian intervention against Prussia and a promise to assist Austria against Russia in a war over the Near East. The French offer rested on a sound assumption. For the Austrians, there was, over the whole period from 1866 to 1870, no bilateral relationship more significant than that they were obliged to entertain with their new neighbor to the west, the newly formed North Germanic Confederation under the indisputable domination of Prussia. At no time does there seem to have been any determination on the part of the Austrians to initiate an armed conflict with Prussia with a view to recovering their position in Germany, from which, as the principal result of the war of 1866, Austria had been excluded. But neither was there any disposition to be reconciled to this exclusion or their intention to end it someday, one way or another. This intention did not preclude the possibility that recovery of this position might one day be achieved by force of arms, but it also did not commit the Austrians to the initiation of such a contest over any particular issue or at any particular time. Still, the Austrians had reason to hesitate. In view of what they had learned in 1866 about the power of Prussian arms, any conflict with that power had to be regarded as at best a risky undertaking. Should it lead to an Austrian defeat, there could be no hope for the political survival of those who had inaugurated it, and it was indeed doubtful if the monarchy itself (in which the Hungarians had now become partners) could withstand such a blow.[1]

For these and other reasons, the Austrians were decidedly unhappy with the French offer. France, argued Friedrich von Beust, the chancellor of Austria-Hungary, was putting the cart before the horse. Austria's immediate interests were bound up in the Near East. An alliance involving this region must be concluded first; discussions about Prussia and the Rhine would have to follow. Besides, he pointed out, France had interests in the Near East, as well; there was trouble brewing in Romania, whose king had been placed on the throne at Napoleon III's insistence. And had it not been France that was the principal author of the Treaty of Paris, which had ended the Crimean War—the last war in the Near East? Did not France have a paramount interest in seeing to it that this treaty was defended?[2] Turning to the situation in Western Europe, Austria's overriding objective, Beust continued, concerned the states of South Germany. Its principal anxiety was that a war between France and Prussia would end in their destruction—as indeed turned out to be the case. With this last point, Beust laid his finger on the dilemma that barred an understanding between the two powers. Neither the German Austrians nor the Hungarians of the Habsburg monarchy could bring themselves to regard Napoleon III as the defender of South German independence, though it was precisely that independence upon which France's security as a Great Power largely depended. Napoleon's behavior in the years that followed the war of 1866, notably his attempts to seek compensation from Prussia in

Germany precisely at the expense of the South German states, made this all too clear.[3]

The negotiations thus broke down; they were revived only by the entry onto the scene of a third power: Italy. The prospect of any agreement between Austria and France, however remote, haunted the corridors of Italian foreign policy, as it had haunted them in 1859, when Napoleon III abandoned Piedmont-Sardinia (later Italy) at Villafranca. Italy had no quarrel with Prussia and little reason to quarrel with Russia, apart from being a rather unenthusiastic member of the Crimean coalition (1854–56) against it. All the same, Italy could ill afford to be excluded from a Franco-Austrian alliance. Moreover, Italy's king, Victor Emmanuel II, wished to cement his creaky throne against republican agitation by concluding a pact with two emperors. He hoped to gain the Tyrol from Austria, Rome (which had, since 1849, been occupied by French troops), and perhaps even Nice from France by binding himself to Napoleon III and the Habsburg emperor Francis Joseph. For these prizes, the Italians offered two hundred thousand men; this could, extensive examination revealed, only be sixty thousand, and the poor railway lines between Austria-Hungary and Italy rendered it difficult to put even these to effective use.[4] The major Italian offer was neutrality—this would allow Austria to operate without fear of attack on its southern borders and thus escape a war on two fronts, which had proven so ruinous in 1866. On this meager but useful understanding, matters were to rest until 1869.[5]

In December 1868, the Italians made a formal proposal to Beust: neutrality in a war between France and Prussia or in one between Russia and Austria-Hungary, south Tyrol for Italy in return.[6] Beust was in a quandary. Only three days earlier, he had had an alarming interview with Gyula Count Andrássy, prime minister of Hungary, and, as we shall have occasion to note, a powerful actor in the Dual Monarchy. Andrássy could not deny the unsatisfactory state of relations in which Austria-Hungary found itself with Russia as a result of its siding with the enemies of the latter during the Crimean War. Nor could he deny that the unhappiness of this relationship would force the Austrians to strengthen their relations with other powers. Beust was initially encouraged, but he soon developed doubts. In the end, he decided that the Italians were asking for too much and referred them to Paris. There now appeared on the horizon a project of which Napoleon III had long dreamed: a triple alliance that would secure European tranquility and for which the French would have to pay nothing. Beust's decision was therefore music to his ears. But the leading members of Napoleon's cabinet wanted the alliance to have a more specific and decidedly anti-Prussian cast. Who would pay the price for this—Italy or Austria—was a matter of indifference to them. Bringing in Italy would have a great advantage. It would be tied to France and to Austria-Hungary, erasing the line between the Near East and the German question. The alliance would be followed by a general Congress of Europe, at which the aggressive impulses of Prussia and Russia would be put to an end.[7]

In the end, Napoleon III got his way, at the cost of much anguished effort and great strain on his nerves and health. On 1 March, a triple alliance against Russia and Prussia was initialed in Paris. Its terms were simple: France would commit forces to the Rhine in case of an Austro-Russian war; likewise, Austria-Hungary would station a corps of troops in Bohemia and take up arms if the Russians came to the assistance of Prussia. Should either conflict arise, Italy was obliged to contribute two hundred thousand men. It would also be handed the Tyrol, and its two allies would help it compose its differences with the pope.[8] Yet, no sooner was the draft treaty sent to Vienna than Beust began to hesitate. He wrote to Richard Metternich, his minister in Paris: "We know very well that the moment we have to place an observation corps on our frontier as a result between a conflict between France and Prussia, we can soon be driven to give up the neutrality we have so carefully proclaimed."[9] It now fell to the French to complain. Napoleon's foreign minister, Charles La Valette, expostulated: "How do you ever expect me to defend to the Chamber a treaty which so one-sidedly favors Austria?"[10] There followed a conflict of epochal dimensions between La Valette and his colleagues. In the end, Paris decided to propose something of a more general nature: the three powers would undertake to maintain a defensive and offensive alliance in the event of a European war. The Austrians were secretly told that they could maintain neutrality; the Italians were not. The French would have their army of two hundred thousand men.[11]

This bargain suited the Austrians. They would have Italian support in the event of a war in the Near East; yet they would not be tied to a war against Prussia that would offend pro-German sentiment in the monarchy. But the Italians would have none of this. So long as a Franco-Austrian alliance was a realistic prospect, they were eager to become a third; now the alliance was no longer in the cards, and they saw no reason why they should furnish two hundred thousand troops whenever it pleased the French or the Austrians to take up arms. They therefore demanded hard cash; probably they had been waiting for payment all along. In June, they told the French that they could not sign the alliance as long as French troops remained in Rome protecting the papacy of Pius IX. This situation had been tolerated in Florence, the Italian capital since 1864, but never fully accepted. There were numerous attempts to dispose of it, the most famous being an agreement known as the September Convention of 1864. This provided that the French would withdraw from Rome after a period of two years; the Italians, on their side, promised not to attack the city. And the government remained true to its word. But the Italian radicals, led by Giuseppe Garibaldi, could never be reconciled to the surrender of Rome, and nationalist feeling drove them on. In the spring of 1867, Garibaldi attacked the papal army at Mentana. Though Garibaldi's forces were defeated, the result was the return of the French army. Still, in Italian eyes, this did not preclude the possibility in any way that the city might one day be theirs, and they now felt it essential give a formal registration to this demand. On 25 June 1869, King Victor Emmanuel told the French ambassador that the alliance could never be signed as long as the French refused to withdraw their army.[12]

For Beust, a Protestant, this demand posed no real problem. He liked the prospect of turning Italian eyes on Rome and thereby averting them from the Tyrol. But it was an impossible condition for the French to fulfill. The Second Empire was passing through difficulties at home, and clericalist support was the necessary condition of its survival; certainly this support was rated by Napoleon more highly than any diplomatic arrangement. In such circumstances, the emperor found himself against a wall. He had to content himself with the belief that the alliance had been *"morally signed,"*[13] and on 24 September he wrote to Francis Joseph that, if Austria-Hungary "were threatened by aggression, I shall not hesitate to put all the forces of France at her side"; moreover, he promised not to enter into negotiations with a foreign power "without previous agreement of the Austrian Empire."[14] But Francis Joseph was not so easily caught. He would not, he replied, make an alliance without first informing Napoleon but was silent on what Beust later referred to "as the voluntary engagement"[15] undertaken by France. Victor Emmanuel went one better; he simply expressed his desire to make an alliance once the September Convention was again in place—that is, after Napoleon had withdrawn his troops from Rome.

The great dream of a triple alliance thus turned to smoke. With respect to Austria-Hungary, the alliance failed for three reasons. First was the reluctance of many Austrians to take a position against Prussia that would have aroused the objections of the Hungarians. The Hungarians owed their existence as an independent country in the Dual Monarchy to the victory of Prussia over Austria in 1866. They saw in the situation created by this victory no occasion for a change of policy on the part of the Austrians, and their opposition to such a change, of course, redounded to the advantage of Prussia. Closely aligned with this was another factor: the divided loyalties of the Austro-Germans, who, though Catholic, still looked toward Berlin. It was plainly unlikely that they could support a policy that aimed at the weakening of a people whose blood and speech were the same as theirs. This faction was composed of people who were reasonably content with Austria's German position, who wanted to see tranquility preserved in Austria's relations with the German states, and who favored, for this reason, cultivation of friendly and peaceful relations with Berlin—a faction that included Andrássy and Kaiser Francis Joseph. Finally and decisively, though resentful of Prussia and the North German Confederation, the immediate concern of the Austrians was to protect their interests in the Near East. At bottom, their only interest in the alliance was to guard against a French victory; they wanted to be sure that, should such occur, they would not be robbed of the spoils. As Francis Joseph put it rather piously: "If the Emperor Napoleon entered southern Germany not as an enemy but as an ally, I should be forced to make common cause with him."[16] The Austrians were looking for an ally that would confront the Russians in Eastern Europe, especially in Romania, and against what they correctly perceived as a threat to their interests to the southwest, to the Balkans, and the Straits, as a theater where they envisaged a dramatic expansion of Russia's power and influence. In a nutshell, France sought an ally against Prussia; Austria, one against Russia, and, in the end, despite repeated attempts yet to be recounted, these two deep-seated desires could never be reconciled.[17] The French would have been well advised to take a bit more seriously than they did the caveats that Beust and Victor Emmanuel expressed in the fall of 1869. But these caveats were lost upon those on whose shoulders rested responsibility for the tragic circumstances of July 1870.

The importance of Russia as a factor in any future Franco-Prussian war was even more apparent to Bismarck than it was to Napoleon III, and he wasted no time, in the years preceding the onset of hostilities between France and Prussia in 1870, in attempting to make sure he had a cast-iron guarantee of Russian friendship and support in the event hostilities should arise. Before I explain how he tried to accomplish this, a word or two of background with respect to Bismarck's attitude toward Russia will perhaps not be out of place.

First, Bismarck was a man who had a deep-seated interest in, and knowledge of, Russian affairs, if only as a result of his having served as ambassador to Petersburg for three years, from 1856 to 1859. The dark and violent history of that country constantly occupied his mind. Like many others, including his master, William I, he felt a profound sympathy for the tsarist autocracy as he knew it and a violent antipathy for the revolutionary movements just now making their appearance on the Russian political scene that sought to overthrow it. Throughout this whole period of his career, he would do nothing that could be construed as damaging to relations between Prussia and Russia—though the Russians, one may add, did not always see his actions this way. Still, Bismarck's reasons for wanting good relations with Russia were logical and obvious ones. He saw in Russia a bar to closer Austro-French cooperation. He wanted to retain any and all levers that would permit him to obstruct the conclusion of a Franco-Russian alliance. Pursuant to these intentions, he was eager to avoid unnecessary anti-Russian agitation and to keep tensions to a minimum. As he later put it in a message to an Austrian chancellor who complained about the problems he was having in putting together a conference with the Russians: "The natural defect of the Russians will not be cured in accordance with the practices of Austrian psychiatry. Russia is more an elementary force than a government, more a mastodon than a diplomatic entity, and she must be treated like bad weather until things are different."[18]

In March 1868, Bismarck managed to secure what he wanted: a promise of Russian cooperation with Prussia against France. The background of how he did so is well known and requires no extensive recapitulation. In a nutshell: in January 1868, the suspicions of Tsar Alexander II were aroused not only by the fact that there had been an improvement in relations between Prussia and France following a nasty dispute over Luxembourg during the previous year but also by rumors to the effect that Beust was attempting to conclude an alliance with France that would operate against Russia in the Balkans (as just described). The tsar did not wait for official confirmation of these rumors before taking action. The Russian minister in Berlin was at once authorized to inform the Prussian government that the Russians were ready to conclude an alliance with Prussia against Austria-Hungary; Prussia should do the same thing in the event of conflict between Austria-Hungary and Russia in the Near East. Bismarck was prepared to accept most of this language but not all. He was concerned lest the specific obligation to support Russia in such a manner led Austria into just what the tsar feared most: an alliance with France. In the end, he succeeded in introducing a significant modification into the original Russian proposal, making it more elastic and wider. Russia and Prussia bound themselves to support each other if either found itself in a war with two other powers. If France attacked Prussia, Tsar Alexander would pin down Austria-Hungary by placing one hundred thousand men on its frontier.[19] William I gave a similar promise to the tsar; in the event of an Austro-Russian war, he would place armies on the Rhine—the figure not given, but it was generally assumed to be about the same number of troops as the tsar had promised to commit against Austria-Hungary.[20]

As Stéphanie Burgaud, to whose magisterial account of the relations of Bismarck with the Russians during the wars of unification every student of this period is indebted, has remarked, the alliance was something of a comedown as for Russia: "Prussia now deserved to be treated as an ally and no longer as a secondary partner."[21] No doubt this reaction sprang from the resentment of the Russians over the upheavals in central Europe that flowed from the Prussian victory over Austria in 1866 and from the effect these had on upending the status quo in that part of Europe. But Burgaud also sees this alliance as a reflection of the weakness of Russian power. "On the cardinal points—status quo in the Near East, status quo in Germany—Russian policy was defeated, thwarted, held in check."[22] Solid evidence that the alliance did nothing to contain Russia's congenital suspicions of Bismarck is to be found in the papers that Burgaud has examined.

It is interesting to note that the agreement that Bismarck concluded was purely a verbal one, but not for a minute did this detract from its significance. Monarchical solidarity in those days, like democratic principles in ours, was taken seriously. The pact was not a sentimental statement of intentions, and in the diplomatic circles of Europe those who knew of its existence were by no means confined to the highest echelons of government. An Austrian representative in Petersburg anticipated: "One of my colleagues, whose wisdom I do not question, gave his impressions of the factors that will, in the event of conflict, bind the Russian government to us. In case of war between France and Prussia, the attitude of Russia would depend on that of Austria. If Austria moves to act, Russia will too; but if Austria remains on the sidelines, Russia most likely will refrain from action."[23]

The pact of March 1868 was, one hastens to add, an achievement of the first order for Bismarck, for it separated two spheres of possible war—one in the east between Russia and Austria-Hungary and one in the west between France and Prussia. A conflict in one of these areas would not inaugurate a conflict in the other. As it turned out, Russia's Balkan policy, so active and so central to all its other concerns, remained during the first half of 1870 inactive and sterile—a situation that suited Bismarck excellently, since the last thing he wanted to see was Russia again involved actively in that part of the world. But it represented too a certain temporary abnormality in the general pattern of Russian policy. The Balkans and the Near East generally were too intimately related to Russia to be the object of such neglect. But Bismarck, as we shall see, did not fail to give heed to this reality, and when the day came he would show that he was not unaware that it was of determining importance in the functioning of Russo-Prussian relations.[24]

Outside the ranks of Russia and Austria-Hungary, there was no power with whom relations were more important for both Prussia and France than Great Britain. French interests crossed those of Great Britain at many points, particularly in Luxembourg and Belgium. Prussian interests crossed them at few. For both powers, relations with Britain had an important, though not a decisive, influence on the dispositions and decisions taken by the two sides during the Franco-Prussian War.

Most of the conflicts that troubled Anglo-French relations in the period in question were those that dealt with northwestern Europe. Of these, the most serious was the acute British unhappiness over the persistence of the French in their behavior toward Belgium. The suspicions of the British had been stirred by schemes of French aggrandizement in 1866 and during a crisis over Luxembourg the following year. But relations reached their lowest point at the opening of 1869, when a French railway company acquired an important Belgian railroad. The British and Belgian governments suspected, though wrongly, that this was a deliberate plan to gain control of Belgium, in one way or another, on the part of Paris. The Belgians passed a law forbidding the transaction; the British threatened to join Russia and Prussia in an alliance against France, and the French backed down.

These irritants would have sufficed to ensure a seriously troubled state of Anglo-French relations. But, beyond them, there was one more source of conflict, more important at this time than any of the others, and this was the French behavior during the crisis of July 1870. This last, in particular, rubbed the British the wrong way. They saw in the elements of French policy resulting in their declaration, on 19 July 1870, of war against Prussia a mixture of components united by a spirit of active—sometimes exalted—nationalism, envious of Bismarck for the success he had achieved in the war against Austria in 1866, eager to see French prestige elevated by exploits of a similar magnitude and impressiveness, and inclined to look to the southwest, to the Rhine and the states of South Germany, as the area for a decisive growth of French influence and power.[25]

All these seemed to show that Anglo-French relations would remain strained for some time to come, and this could only redound to Prussia's benefit. Still, there was one aspect of British policy in the middle of July that Bismarck took as a cause for alarm. This was the decision on the part of London to protect French citizens living in North Germany. Though the British undertook to protect Prussian citizens living in France, the manner in which this was done aroused Bismarck's anger, the more so because the British presented their decision to him as a fait accompli. The decision was made by Prime Minster William Ewart Gladstone's cabinet on 16 July;[26] Bismarck learned of it only two days later. This development was disturbing in its own right. But it acquired a new level of seriousness with the arrival in Berlin, in the course of July 1870, of a flurry of reports concerning the confidential attitude of the senior figures of the British foreign office toward the two belligerents. Particularly galling was the decision of the British government to agree to look after the affairs of France in Berlin and its desire to do the same thing for Prussia. Bismarck noted: "Lord Granville's [the foreign secretary's] attitude was not—as it seems to me—as benevolent with respect to us as we would have expected. . . . I don't see how the British can be impartial if they try to represent French interests in Prussia, and now look after the affairs of Prussia in Paris."[27] Instead, Bismarck saw to it that this assignment was given to the United States—he was on good terms with the American secretary of state, Hamilton Fish—and Fish accepted the undertaking on 19 July. Bismarck was unable to understand why the British were acting the way they were. And yet he was obliged, from the middle to the end of July, to endure another disturbing development in what was—or appeared to be—British policy.

This was the decision of the British government to allow its subjects to trade with both belligerents—though expressly forbidding any trafficking in contraband. Though on paper this appeared to be evenhanded, in reality it was anything but. The French possessed, after the British, the most powerful navy in the world. In the last days before the onset of hostilities, Napoleon III had improvised a plan for a diversionary amphibious operation in the Baltic area with a view to blockading the Baltic coast of Prussia. If this plan was successful, it would mean that the French could trade with the British while the Prussians, possessing only a tiny navy locked away behind the blockade, could not. Indeed, during the whole course of the war, French commerce would flourish; the French had access to markets all over the world—quite unlike the Prussians.[28]

Then there was the issue of contraband itself. Though the British could not engage in contraband trading *on the seas*, nothing prohibited the export of contraband—horses, coal, weapons, and munitions—abroad. In practice, the French were free to charter British ships in Newcastle for the delivery of coal to their shores and to barter with the merchants of Birmingham for cartridges needed for their prized chassepots. This last stuck particularly in Bismarck's craw. Why were the British permitting it? Repeatedly, he caused the question to be put to the British representatives themselves. And he went further. He authorized attacks on the hypocrisy of British neutrality in the North German press. At his urging, King William wrote a peremptory letter to Queen Victoria asking for an end to such practices.[29] At London, Albrecht count von Bernstorff, the North German minister, in an interview with Granville on 30 July, pointed out: "The way the British government has conducted its neutrality has . . . given rise to all sorts of alarms in Germany as has the failure of the government to say one word about the injustices of the French." Granville, expressing skepticism about the extent of the trade, replied that the British government had absolutely no invidious intent toward Prussia: "We are neutral and will try to remain wholly neutral [but] if we pursued a lopsidedly unfriendly attitude toward France with respect to trade we would ruin British industry and cause the French to turn to America."[30]

Natural as this might be, it was equally natural that the increasing evidences of British favoritism toward France in the matter of trade should be highly disturbing to Bismarck. It was in these circumstances that he determined to do something to change British policy decisively, and this was the release to the British public of a draft of a secret treaty put to him in the wake of the Prussian victory over Austria in 1866, calling for the annexation of Belgium. According to the terms of this treaty—it was only a draft written by the hand of Vincent Benedetti, at the time French minister to Berlin—Prussia would assist France in this acquisition, and the French would not stand in the way of the union of the North German Confederation with the states of South Germany. Bismarck saw to it that this draft treaty was published in *The Times* on 25 July, though, as Eberhard Kolb has shown, his motives for doing so have been misunderstood.[31]

The overriding reason for the draft's publication had nothing to do with protection or contraband or the issues to which each gave rise but rather reflected Bismarck's desire to see the French pinned down to war. France had, it is true, declared war against Prussia on 19 July, and the great armies were now in the process of mobilizing. But suppose Napoleon suddenly had had a change of heart and decided to make peace? Sick, weak, vacillating, he could have used Belgium as a bargaining card to get out of the war after a first

French victory as he had done in the Italian war in 1859. Publication of the Benedetti treaty was an announcement to the world that Prussia considered Napoleon an aggressor whose appetite for conquests knew no bounds. Belgium as an escape hatch to avoid a Franco-Prussian confrontation was now a dead dog, as Bismarck observed when he said on 20 July 1870: "Turning back is no longer possible."[32]

In any case, on 9 August 1870, there took place in London the signing of a convention between Prussia and Great Britain guaranteeing the independence of Belgium not only during the period of hostilities but down to the conclusion of peace. A similar convention between the French and the British followed the next day. With these signings, the issue was settled. Still, Bismarck could not get over his dislike of seeing Prussia being treated the same way as France. It was the French, not the Prussians, who had pressed for the Benedetti treaty; it was the French, not the Prussians, who had tried to acquire Luxembourg in 1867; and it was the French, not the Prussians, who had put in hand the negotiations of 1869 the purpose of which had been to acquire a railway that, had they been successful, would have left Belgium to the mercy of Paris. In every case, Prussia had been the rock blocking the French path. What more did the British want? Prussia's behavior during the years in question was evidence in itself; the idea that Prussia had designs on Belgium was an absurdity of the first order. As it turned out, Bismarck's anger, though not unjustified, was quickly displaced by news from the battlefront. By the time the instruments in London were put into execution, the Prussians had scored important victories over the French in the battles of Wörth and Spicherer Berg, and a blow had been struck at the creaky character of the French high command from which it was never to recover.[33]

But to return to Great Britain: the policy of the government may be said to be one of general passivity apart from the concern over any infringement the proceedings of war were to have on the independence of Belgium. Prior to the conclusion of the conventions of 9 and 11 August, most of the conflicts that troubled Anglo-French relations were in the Americas. Though the British were frustrated and displeased by the chauvinism displayed by the French during the crisis of July 1870 and though they were conscious that it was the French, not the Prussians, who had actually declared war, they were determined to do nothing that might arouse the ire of either belligerent. Of course, in agreeing to trade with the French, to take under British protection French subjects in North Germany, and to look after the interests of Paris during the war, in their essential refusal to distinguish French ambitions with respect to Belgium from those of Prussia, they struck what seemed to Bismarck a decidedly unfriendly pose. But the truth of the matter was that the British were determined, for the moment, to avoid commitments on the continent.[34]

There was one other area in Europe where, at the outbreak of the war in 1870, the clouds were scarcely larger than a human hand but where they were destined to grow, quickly and in ways Bismarck was beginning to perceive, with great and alarming rapidity. This was Denmark. The Danes had ample reason to resent the Prussians. Apart from their defeat in war in 1864, as a consequence of which they were to lose the provinces of Schleswig-Holstein, the Danes were in a unique position to steer Russian sensibilities in an anti-Prussian direction. Though Russian policy toward Prussia was generally friendly and though Alexander II was quite fond of his uncle, King William of Prussia, there were those at Petersburg who entertained, with respect to this policy, pronounced reservations. And with respect to those reservations one thing is certain: they met with no discouragement at the hands of Alexander's wife, the beautiful, if unhappy, Empress Maria Aleksandrova, sister of the Danish king Christian IX and aunt of the future Queen Alexandra of England. Maria Aleksandrova never interfered overtly in governmental affairs, but she had ways of making her influence felt behind the scenes, and that influence, highly colored by her personal reactions to individuals and particularly by her bitterness against Prussia and Bismarck personally because of Danish sufferings in the Prusso-Danish War of 1864, was sometimes invidious and by no means helpful.[35]

Further deserving of mention among the influential members of the Danish community in Europe is Jules Hansen, political agent and public relations adviser to the Russian embassy in Paris. The personality of Hansen has found extensive and colorful manifestation in the pages of Burgaud's volume, and it is from those pages that this sketch is primarily drawn.[36] Hansen was an extraordinary character. Having played a considerable role in Danish and European political affairs in his earlier years, he was well acquainted with Russian policy and destined to have a good deal to do with Franco-Russian relations in the coming years. Hansen was a freelance writer, both journalist and publicist, widely read and widely traveled. By conviction, he was a stout champion of Denmark and a bitter foe of Prussia. Born in Copenhagen in 1828, he was, in 1864, dispatched by a group of patriotic Danes to Paris to serve as a press agent for his country in the conflict with Prussia just then reaching its climax. This assignment he carried out with great zest and vigor. A warm sympathizer of the French government, he had functioned in the years just preceding the war as a confidant of the Russian embassy. Between 1864 and 1870, he was an active go-between in the complex rigmarole over Schleswig-Holstein. Hansen, according to the biographical sketch of Fr. De Fontenay in the Danish biographical dictionary, was "a small unprepossessing man, outwardly shy, who was generally known in Copenhagen under the nickname of 'Spidsmusen' (the Shrew) or 'the President.'"[37] There is no evidence that he was a man of bad character or sinister designs. But of his desire to promote better relations with France there could be no doubt, and in the years before the outbreak of war he threw himself into a campaign against Prussia. Particularly galling to him was the Russo-Prussian alliance of 1868, which Bismarck had worked so hard to achieve and to the destruction of which Hansen dedicated himself repeatedly. In the months following the outbreak of the war, he was constantly on the move, dashing from one place to another, seeing a most extraordinary variety of people. His extensive acquaintance with members of influential French circles and his easy access to many senior French statesmen made him a formidable figure. He used his simultaneous relationship with the French government and Russian embassies during the war to promote their mutual rapprochement. His activities were designed to promote a warmer feeling for the French in official Russian circles than that which existed. In this respect, he was at all times very much helped by Empress Maria Aleksandrova.[38]

With these personalities, all destined to play a role in the further unfolding of this tale, in mind, we are ready to turn to the complications that, in the late summer of 1870, sowed trouble for Bismarck and opened new prospects for foreign intervention in the war he was waging against France.

3

The League of Neutrals

While the events discussed in the preceding chapter and others still to be recounted were taking place in the various exchanges between Bismarck and the senior officials of the British and Russian governments, they were not, of course, taking place in a vacuum. All the governments of the Great Powers were beginning for the first time to grapple seriously with the problems of high policy that arose out of the fact that two of their members were now at war with each other and the real prospect that, unless decisive action was taken, the war was likely to expand and perhaps become general.

The most significant development on the horizons of both the French and the Prussians over the three weeks following the outbreak of war was the attempt on the part of the foreign minister of Italy, Marquis Émilio Visconti-Venosta, to form a league of neutral powers the purpose of which was to limit the war to the two belligerents. I find it impossible to give the reader an idea of the atmosphere in which the League of Neutrals came into existence without saying a word about the character of this extraordinary figure. An aristocrat by birth, connected by family with the great Italian revolutionary Giuseppe Mazzini and even at one time employed as an agent by him; well educated; a scholarly person; at first a radical but soon an idealistic intellectual nationalist who had thrown in his lot with the Risorgimento of the first Italian prime minister, Count Camillo Cavour, and had passionately believed in it and in him; a man who had seen service in the Austro-Sardinian War of 1859; an essentially cautious man who never spared himself, who was largely without a personal life; who worked eighteen hours out of twenty-four; who wrote every diplomatic note personally; whose office was the scene of a monumental scholar's disorder, with books and papers and foreign office files lying in piles all over the place; a man who worked by preference at night; a hypochondriac, a tall peering figure of a man with long whiskers and a flowing white beard; a man devoid of personal vanity whose carelessness of dress equaled the disorder of his office—but withal, a man who lived his work, who believed in it passionately, who pursued it with a seriousness, a dedication, a self-denial, and an eloquence that put many of the foreign ministers of his day to shame: this was Visconti-Venosta, and a more appealing character from the ranks of Italian statesmen during this period cannot be found. Visconti-Venosta believed, in my opinion, many of the wrong things, but he believed in them for the purest of motives. And when one tries, as one must, to follow the progress of the political cause he represented, one's sympathies are often with him, even if they are not always with it.[1]

The first act of Visconti-Venosta was to seek assistance from the British government, and this he did on 15 July, when he held a series of secret discussions with Sir Augustus Barclay Paget, the British representative, about the "future policy of Italy and the other Powers not now involved in the war."[2] The effort to avert hostilities having turned to smoke, Visconti-Venosta believed that "every endeavor should now be directed to limiting the war to the two Powers immediately engaged."[3] It was his view that "the possibility of succeeding in this attempt depended essentially upon Austria." If, contrary to his regret and sorrow, Austria came in on the French side, "it was to be apprehended . . . that Russia would join the other side, and with these four colossal Powers engaged, what other Power could be sure of being able to maintain its neutrality?"[4] Another meeting between the two men was held the next day. At this meeting, Visconti-Venosta made a declaration that may stand as the most responsible Italian statement on the crisis during its entire first month. He began by recounting the highlights of the situation that existed during the two days that had elapsed since he had last seen a few of his friends in the cabinet. He discussed the reactions to the French calls for aid, which he found to be "untenable," and those of the Prussians. Britain appeared to him to be the most important of the neutral powers. The British government, he declared, was most averse to seeing the war widened. He was well aware that the policy of the British government was "to avoid mixing up Great Britain in conflicts on the continent, but in keeping too much aloof might not the unavoidable result be that England would ultimately find herself drawn into the strife?"[5]

As for Russia, the war was testing its ties to Prussia. In Petersburg, conditions were "favorable to the Italian initiative." Or were they? Visconti-Venosta was seriously disturbed by events then taking place in the great Russian capital. While he evidently allowed himself to be reassured of Russia's interest in a league of neutrals for the formation of which Russia had, some days earlier, expressed sympathy, Visconti-Venosta remained—particularly during the middle weeks of July—mystified and mistrustful of Russian policy, not least because of the Prusso-Russian agreement of 1868. "In contemplating the future," he told Paget, "it was impossible . . . not to foresee circumstances that would, if the war became general, place the Italian government under the obligation of reconsidering its position, unless that position were definitely fixed by arrangement with other Powers."[6] If the British would agree with the Italian proposals, this prospect might well be averted.

Paget agreed, and two hours later he put Visconti-Venosta's proposal on the wire to London. Granville, upon receiving it, conferred repeatedly, almost hourly, with Gladstone. On 17 July, Granville reported the results of his conversations to the Italians. The British were determined to do everything they could to preserve their neutrality. But what of Austria? The war of 1866 had already signified a considerable deterioration of Austria's security. That security would be even more weakened if France should suffer a defeat. Were the Austrians, therefore, not likely to go to the aid of the French? If so, what would be the position of Italy?[7] To this Visconti-Venosta replied (we are following throughout the records in the Ministero degli Affari Esteri) by emphasizing that the first thing he had already made clear to the Austrians was the need for neutrality. On the other hand, he knew that there were some figures in Vienna who believed that Austria could not allow injury to be brought to France—that France's continued strength was vital as a check to Prussia. Visconti-Venosta's statements captured the picture accurately; Paget found them compelling and was now convinced that the two countries saw things much the same way. The big question was, of course, Austria.[8]

It was with a view to ascertaining the attitude of the Austrians that Visconti-Venosta, even before the discussions had ended, composed a long dispatch to Vienna, inviting the senior officials of the Austrian government to reflect on the events now unfolding. The Italian government, he wrote, now had a single aim: to act with the others to prevent the interests of the neutral states from being drawn into or compromised by the war. The war must, at all events, be limited to the two belligerents. This was a view flowing partly from Visconti-Venosta's overall judgment, partly from his view of the situation at the moment. To localize the Franco-Prussian War, to keep it from becoming general as a consequence of the decisions that might be reached in Vienna and Petersburg—these were the considerations uppermost in his mind. To be sure, Vienna had expressed the deepest displeasure to the French over their handling of the great events of the crisis of July 1870. But Visconti-Venosta was not at all certain what the Austrians would do in view of the increasing pressure the French were said to be bringing to bear almost hourly for Austria's intervention on their side; worse still, what effects would be produced in the monarchy by early French victories over Prussia? Worried lest this mean that a new attitude could develop on the part of Austria, Visconti-Venosta decided as early as the night of 15 July to dispatch to Vienna Isacco Artom, Italy's minister to Baden, a man of impeccable character and intelligence, who had represented his country in Denmark and who had, during the July crisis, undertaken several delicate and sensitive missions for his chief. All available evidence suggests that this was a step taken on a personal level by Visconti-Venosta, that it was taken on the recommendation of his friends in the influential journalist circles (possibly with British support), but that it was taken in consultation with neither King Victor Emmanuel II nor the bulk of his cabinet.[9]

Artom arrived in Vienna on 16 July and immediately read out a letter Visconti-Venosta had written to Beust. The letter began by maintaining to the Austrians Italy's need for peace. From the very outset, Italy regarded a war between France and Prussia as something monstrously frightful and dangerous. In the midst of the grave problems precipitated by its outbreak, Visconti-Venosta was sure of one thing: so long as the war remained confined to France and Prussia, Italy could and should maintain its neutrality. Artom briefly reviewed the secret negotiations for the Franco-Austrian-Italian alliance of 1869, pointing out that the terms of the agreement, calling for Italy to dispatch two hundred thousand troops into Bohemia, had never been signed. But the French were apparently now making new demands upon Austria, and here the Italians were totally in the dark. What were these? Italy must know if the two powers were to work together. In addition to these observations on the main question he had been asked to clarify, Artom mentioned two or three other points of incidental interest flowing from his mission.[10]

For one thing, he pointed out that Italian military action would be "paralyzed" if the Roman question did not progress beyond a mere renewal of the September Convention. That pact was "onerous for our country and insufficient to satisfy us in time of war."[11] The Italians knew that Beust was in favor of allowing Italian troops to occupy the Eternal City but that for Napoleon, because clerical favoritism was one of the few pillars of support he had left, it was a poison pill and something to which he could never consent. By making Italian intervention on the French side dependent on concessions with respect to the Roman question that were manifestly not in the cards, Artom hoped to prevent Austria from committing itself to France.[12]

What is more, Artom noted that Visconti-Venosta was in the throes of composing an article for the influential Florentine journal *Opinione* in which he would express, in the strongest terms of which he was capable, his views on the question. Visconti-Venosta's piece appeared on 21 July and was immediately shown to the Austrians. It began by pointing out the disasters that would follow if the powers, other than Prussia and France, entered the war. The course of a great struggle was always uncertain; the injection of new interests and passions could only confound every expectation. However, there was some ground for believing that if the war could be ended quickly, it would remain confined to the present contestants. But—and here Visconti-Venosta came to the heart of the question—to shorten it, the nonbelligerent powers must undertake to form a league of neutrals. The beginning of wisdom, in the circumstances of late July 1870, was recognition of the fact that there was nothing worse the nonbelligerent powers could do than to fail to bind themselves to each other in order to prevent the war from becoming wider.[13]

Shortly after he finished writing the article, Visconti-Venosta learned from Artom that ominous events were transpiring in Vienna. The Austrians were fearful that Napoleon III was about to stir up trouble in the Danubian principalities with a view to inviting a possible Russian attack. There was in the areas around Bucharest a confused array of events—secret mobilizations, nocturnal undertakings, misunderstood or undetected signals, messages, warnings, sudden betrayals, and equally sudden reconciliations—all finding their culmination early in the morning of 17 July. Russian intervention in the principalities was the last thing the Austrians wanted, or the last thing those who wanted Austria to remain neutral did. For Russian action there was bound to arouse the fury of the Magyars, staunch antagonists of Petersburg since the events of 1849. Magyar hostility toward Russia could easily conduce to Magyar sympathy toward France and correspondingly increase the chances of Austrian intervention on the French side.[14]

While Visconti-Venosta and Artom were trying to pin down the Austrians, there took place in Florence an equally ominous incident that seemed to suggest that intervention, not neutrality, might wind up being the policy of Italy. A policy of neutrality was viewed with pronounced animosity by King Victor Emmanuel II, who was rapidly having second thoughts about the policy he had followed with respect to the proposed Austro-Italian-French alliance project of 1869 and was now wildly excited about coming in on the French side. An intensely ambitious and not overly scrupulous man, a glib, compulsive talker, and a shameless intriguer, Victor Emmanuel was, at bottom, strongly pro-French, and, had he been given his way, Italy would no doubt have gone it alone and entered the war on the French side.[15] Victor Emmanuel was aware that the bulk of his cabinet abhorred this idea, but this did not deter him. To the Austrian envoy in Florence, Victor Emmanuel made out that he was supporting a plan that had been worked out in Paris between Napoleon III and his own agents. It called for neutral mediation of the belligerents. But Austria and Italy alone would be the mediators, and the terms of the proposed settlement were such that Prussia was bound at once to reject them out of hand. Once Prussia had rejected this proposed settlement, the terms of the Triple Alliance would come into play. As for Rome, it was already settled—it would be evacuated immediately after the king gave Napoleon III his assurance that the September Convention would be respected.[16]

To Visconti-Venosta's mind, Victor Emmanuel's whole great chain of effort beginning in 1868 with the negotiations with France was misconceived, shortsighted, and deleterious in the highest degree to the development of Italy's relationships with the other Great Powers. Still, Victor Emmanuel was, as Visconti-Venosta knew, an experienced diplomat, and Paget pointed out to a colleague that the king "was no joke under these circumstances."[17] From the onset of the crisis, he had determined to bind Italy to France and succeeded on 16 July in rallying at least some of the ministers to his side. But a majority, led by the finance minister, Quintino Sella, opposed him. For the moment, Victor Emmanuel appeared to be stopped in his tracks. He wrote to Napoleon III: "I am obliged to indulge the susceptibilities of the ministry whose pacific goals cannot be doubted . . . the rapidity of events has prevented me from carrying out our old plans as I would have desired."[18]

Meanwhile, military events had taken a new turn. On 6 August, the Prussian forces had advanced across the Rhine and routed the enemy at the little village of Spicheren, in northeastern France. Many people were already becoming increasingly worried whether Italy would be best advised to pursue negotiations with the other powers or instead to proceed with an immediate statement of neutrality. The French defeat added to this feeling, causing many influential figures in Italy and elsewhere to envisage for the first time the possibility of a Prussian victory. The feeling was growing that the wartime objectives of the Prussians would expand and that the impending collapse of France would change the international picture for the worse. To cling to the pro-French policy of the king was, as many saw it, to play directly into the hands of the military party in Paris and to make it more difficult for the French moderates to advocate a reasonable accommodation with the Prussians.[19]

While King Victor Emmanuel was arguing with his ministers, Artom was in Vienna and reporting the results of a debate that took place in the crown council of 18 July over the course of Habsburg policy. The atmosphere of this discussion can best be characterized if one takes note of such evidence as exists of the relationship between Beust on the one hand and the two other principals who attended, Andrássy and the Emperor Francis Joseph, on the other.

Of the leading figures in the imperial court at Vienna, Andrássy was by far the strongest personality, a man of utmost integrity and character—a figure of considerable distinction and prominence in his native land of Hungary and in Austria, as well. At the time of the outbreak of war, he was the Hungarian minister-president; he was also a diplomat of wide experience and talent. His letters reveal him as an acutely sensitive and earnest person with a high degree of responsibility for the monarchy's interest. These interests, as he conceived them, could at bottom only be furthered by a firm stance favorable to Prussia, to whom the Hungarians owed their independence.[20]

Beust wasted no time in attempting to gain domination of the proceedings and poured out his sense of urgency by asking whether, especially with an eye to Russia, the current policy of neutrality made any sense, whether, that is, it should not be abandoned so that "we would not be left in the lurch by events."[21] Andrássy immediately took issue with this advice, and, during the course of the ensuing debate, he went so far as to reproach Beust for his pro-French sentiments that were driving the monarchy to perdition.[22] This accusation, coming from so formidable a figure as Andrássy, stung Beust to the quick and moved him to announce that "I am responsible for the conduct of foreign affairs and have executed my duties as I see them."[23] Andrássy was hardly surprised by this riposte. His relations with the chancellor had been strained and uncomfortable from the start. In this instance, that relationship was strained by everyone's awareness of Andrássy's aversion to Russia and his desire to give some assistance to Prussia. Beust, to counter this, had surrounded Andrássy with career officers who held him in check, lest he do something rash and ill informed and likely to embarrass the government. For this reason, the atmosphere at the chancery was tense and unhappy with a buzz of alarm and indignation whispering in the wings.

At the meeting of 18 July, Andrássy told the members of council of new French demands for assistance that were circulating in Vienna, that matters were much more serious than the government had supposed, and that the emperor would be best advised "to arm to the teeth or remain neutral."[24] Beust was filled with consternation at the realization that the French were being so intransigent. He expostulated: "When I see what is happening I ask myself whether I have become an imbecile."[25] But his position was made more awkward by the French foreign minister, the Duc de Gramont, who warned him that anything resembling a declaration of Austrian neutrality would be followed by a Franco-Italian alliance on Victor Emmanuel's terms. A declaration of neutrality was therefore ruled out by Beust. As he put it to the Marquis de Cazaux, the French chargé d'affaires: "Everyone knows that we cannot be Prussia's ally; therefore a declaration would mean that we are no longer neutral."[26] In his office, in fact, there was a sheaf of telegrams informing him of the French expectations. It was for Beust an intensely difficult moment. Andrássy was roaring and insisting that any hesitation could be misinterpreted by the other powers and cost Austria their good will and that unless neutrality were declared without delay, there was a great and real danger that the Russians would intervene and send troops into Galicia. "Austrian perfidy," which had so enraged the Russians during the time of the Crimean War, might well have been exaggerated, but, unless Austria clarified its position, there was no telling what would happen. Beust proposed to mobilize in readiness for intervention; this would show sympathy for the French. Andrássy did not object; he wanted to enlist Prussia as well as France for the coming struggle with Russia; to gain the sympathy of the former, he insisted on a declaration of neutrality, and one was issued on 20 July.[27]

In the meantime, Andrássy was running into trouble with those Hungarians who favored a firm and even an aggressive policy toward the Russians. The Hungarians feared, and many Austrians feared with them, that a Russian occupation of Galicia would render impossible the continued maintenance of an independent stance by the monarchy and that, with this, the position of Hungary would become complicated. That Andrássy should now even be forced to give this reassurance to the Hungarian Diet was clear evidence that he was no longer able to hold the line against the pressures for a defensive reaction, which the impending instability in Galicia was beginning to evoke among the leading Hungarian figures in the monarchy.[28]

Beust, for his part, was determined not to let the idea of some kind of help for France die quietly on the vine. This attitude was given strong impetus by the passionate feelings for closer relations with Russia that dominated the thinking of his underlings and subordinates. Beust still clung to his belief that the French had put themselves in the wrong by the belligerent and uncompromising way they had handled the July crisis; all the same, he sought to provide what assistance he could, writing to Metternich: "We shall consider the cause of France as our own, and will contribute to the success of her arms within the limits of the possible." He described Austria's declaration as a means of "completing our armaments without exposing ourselves to a sudden attack by Russia or Prussia."[29]

Beust was well aware of the dangerous effect the war was producing in the German states, and he was determined not to remain silent, hoping that some new turn of events would, before it was too late, enable him to bring his imperial master to a frame of mind more to his liking. He therefore determined to strike a deal with Russia. If he did not act, the last chink of hope, the last chance for an active and hopeful Habsburg foreign policy, would presumably disappear for all time. In the end, the hope was disappointed, and the Russian government, on 22 August 1870, acceded to an agreement with the governments of Great Britain, Italy, Turkey, Spain, and Denmark, thus forming a group of powers that would constitute itself as the League of Neutrals.[30] Notes to this effect were exchanged among the respective powers on 31 August and 1 September 1870. A deal between Austria and Russia was no longer in the cards. What had happened to prevent it from coming to fruition? Certainly it was not for lack of trying on the part of Beust. Note must be taken of this attempt and some explanation given as to why it failed.

The immediate background of the story may be summarized as follows. At a soirée given by Paget on 22 July, the latter found himself approached by Visconti-Venosta, who then proceeded to deliver a long and most important series of political confidences. The essence of these revelations was that the king, encouraged by pro-French figures in Florence, was about to triumph over his cabinet. Victor Emmanuel, Visconti-Venosta said, had recently summoned his most belligerent ministers (including some who were members of former cabinets) and had delivered a long harangue about the need to deliver Italy to France. After describing the political situation in some detail, Visconti-Venosta went ahead to claim (this actually was an exaggeration) that the only way to stop the king was for London to sponsor a multilateral treaty of neutrality, expressing the hope (also exaggerated) that the other powers would follow suit. The matter was urgent, for the British should not allow themselves to be deceived into thinking that the language used by the Italian foreign ministry represented the real sentiments of the king.[31]

Even prior to his talk with Paget, Visconti-Venosta had begun to feel a certain uneasiness over the royal intentions. He was, however, soon relieved by reports he received from London. The British disliked the idea of a multilateral treaty as the means by which their neutrality should be announced. They preferred separate but binding understandings with each of the nonbelligerent powers and insisted that the object on which Visconti-Venosta had set his heart could be achieved quite satisfactorily in this way.[32] Granville realized, of course, that Britain's position in Europe made it incumbent upon him to express great sympathy toward the Italian proposal. But there was, he made out, no small danger to which he was obliged to call attention: a treaty would deprive the British of the freedom of action on which they had always set great store. Visconti-Venosta did not react at once to this new proposal, but he was not insensitive to its stated objective. He, too, was now becoming increasingly worried over the possibility of a Franco-Italian alliance, which would be the prerequisite of Italy's entrance into the war, and his thoughts began increasingly to turn toward immediate agreement with London. He began, accordingly, to assiduously strengthen his relations with Paget. In the meantime, military events had taken a decisive turn. The Prussian victory at Wörth on 6 August shocked the senior officials in the Italian government. An emergency session of the cabinet was convened on 9 August.[33] On the matter of a Franco-Italian alliance, it decided to suspend all further talks. This news was welcomed in London. On 17 August, Granville fired off a dispatch to the Italian ambassador: "Her Majesty's Government . . . are prepared, and indeed think it would be very desirable to agree with the other neutral Powers and specifically with Italy, that neither party should depart from its neutrality without a previous communication of ideas and an announcement to one another to change its policy as regards its neutrality."[34] Italy's neutrality was ensured for the remainder of the war. The cabinet swiftly consented, and Visconti-Venosta's ordeal was over.

The Italian decision greatly influenced the Russians, who were made the object of a similar note and who followed suit with their own declaration on 22 August.[35] The Austrians were not so easily caught. Beust, long forewarned about the negotiations, accepted the Anglo-Italian formulation "in principle" but insisted that, should one power attempt to end the war under its own auspices, the others would immediately be relieved of the previous obligation to which they had been party. He wrote to his minister in London: "We give our consent to this agreement, but with the understanding, which appears imperative to us, that all our efforts should be directed to the immediate establishment of peace as a whole and to use our influence with a view to work for mediation."[36] In the meantime, he continued to work for some sort of alliance with France. This action was the source of immense pleasure to Paris. The new foreign minister, Henri de La Tour d'Auvergne, who had replaced Gramont on 10 August, wrote to Beust in the middle of that month that he was certain that "the neutral Powers who recently entered into the agreement can be controlled in such a way as to make the only possible basis of peace: the integrity of the territory of France and the maintenance of the present government."[37]

What Beust feared most was that Russia would, despite the agreement of 1868, now use its influence at Berlin and Paris to mediate between the two powers. This would only enhance Russia's prestige, its power, its influence. But the prospect of Russia presiding over a conference between Prussia and France roused in the mind and spirit of Beust a host of potential difficulties flowing from the dangers of the moment. Outstanding among these were (1) the deep commitment on the part of the Russians to the establishment of a new set of arrangements with respect to the Straits; (2) the fear that any Russian attempt to undo these arrangements could possibly at some point involve Russia in a war with Great Britain into which Austria, because it was par excellence a Balkan power, might well be drawn; (3) the suspicion that Russia and Prussia had not only been active in engineering Austria's difficulties in Galicia and other parts of the monarchy but would profit from them; (4) the keen awareness of the need for distracting Russia's military strength from that area; and finally (5) in light of these reactions, the firm desire to assist the French in some way even if short of military aid.[38]

Beust's fears as to the intentions of the Russians were not without foundation. The American representative at Petersburg, Eugene Schuyler, an intelligent and perceptive diplomat, had reported on 17 August that what sentiment existed for Prussia had been somewhat weakened. "The journals are full of stories of the nightmare that would result if Prussia extended her control of the North German Confederation to the states of Germany south of the River Main. The last victories of Prussia have filled the Russians with deep anxieties over two areas of vital importance to them: Poland and the Baltic provinces. There is a growing fear over the length of the war, a desire to end it quickly, and to do so by any means possible."[39] The success of German arms at Wörth and the collapse of the negotiations for a French-Italian alliance constituted the principal factors that impelled Beust into concerted efforts to improve relations with Russia. Strongly encouraged by his staff, Beust therefore, after much second-guessing, wrote to his minister in Petersburg, Basil Chotek, that Russia and Austria should adopt a common attitude toward the ongoing struggle in the west. It is clear from the text of Beust's message of 10 August that he envisaged a concrete agreement between the two cabinets.[40]

On 15 August, Chotek had a long interview with Tsar Alexander and his chancellor, Alexander Gorchakov. The former received him kindly, professed his desire to renew the good relations that had previously existed between the two courts, and expressed the hope that Francis Joseph would long remain on the throne. Twice during the course of the interview, the tsar took Chotek aside and rattled off the specific conditions he believed necessary for an improvement of relations between the two courts: cessation of Austrian armament; unqualified Austrian membership in the League of Neutrals as had been proposed by the British; jointly coordinated action in case of peace negotiations so as not to allow Prussia-Germany any freedom in imposing on France conditions that he deemed too harsh. In addition to this, the tsar called upon Austria to refrain from taking any measures that would affect the security of Russia in two trouble spots: Poland and the Near East. Chotek, in the interview, spoke sympathetically of Austria's desire to support a general congress in which all grievances of the powers of Europe would be addressed (here he was exceeding his instructions)—an unmistakable reference to the Black Sea clauses of the Treaty of Paris of 1856. The tsar and Gorchakov thereupon invited Chotek to return to Vienna and bring back to them a concrete response to their proposals. It may be that, considering the ultimate fate of the Chotek mission, the Russians were merely playing for time— making sure that Bismarck was aware of what was afoot, this in order to increase their bargaining power with him. But this, one should note, in no way served to diminish the wildly favorable impressions of his discussions with the Russians that featured in Chotek's report to Beust.[41]

The interview of 15 August constituted a change on the part of Russian policy. A new wind blew. At the onset of hostilities, Russia's major concerns had been to keep Austria neutral and to prevent any infringement of Danish neutrality. Now Russia was seemingly embarking on a new course, one designed to organize an intervention into the war on the part of the neutrals and to stop the progress of Prussian arms in their tracks. This policy seemed much more conservative, internationally minded, generally westernized, and distinctly less Russian than had been the case hitherto. Pulling out all the stops, the tsar seemed bent on preventing a drastic reduction of French power and saving France from the consequences of the reckless policy upon which Napoleon III had embarked during the crisis of July 1870.[42]

Five days later, Chotek, back in Vienna, reported to Beust the results of his meeting with Tsar Alexander II and Gorchakov. On 22 August, Beust called a conference of ministers to consider the direction of Austrian policy. He reviewed the policy of Austria from 1866 to the present and speculated about what could be done to prevent further Prussian success from damaging the monarchy. As to the proposed question about adhering to the League of Neutrals, there was little for Austria to do but accept; to do otherwise would have cast a shadow over Habsburg intentions. But in all else the discord and disagreement among the participants was considerable. Prominent among the questions that gave rise to these was that of the Pan-Slavs, who were becoming increasingly influential in higher Russian circles. These were people who saw Russia as the natural protecting power for the peoples of the Balkans and central European regions. It was, of course, inevitable that persons so

Emperor Alexander II, tsar of Russia. (von Pflugk-Harttung, *The Franco-German War*, 597.)

inclined would see the Turkish and particularly the Austro-Hungarian empires as obstacles to the realization of their dreams and so could not fail to advocate policies that would impinge upon the interests of these neighbors. Large sections of the Russian press gave strong support and expression to this group, and it would be necessary to ask the tsar to do something about it. In return, Austria would promise to restrain from supporting subversive elements in Poland.[43]

Some ministers, with Andrássy at their head, viewed such action with the liveliest of suspicions. Believing the prospect of any Russo-Austrian cooperation highly unlikely, they warned of the great danger of such a course for Austria itself. But in this they were opposed by Beust's underlings in the foreign ministry, all of whom were inclined toward a pro-Russian orientation of Austrian foreign policy. "The idea of an alliance with Russia," wrote one of them, "was so common even among those close to Beust that some of his most intimate advisers heaped reproach on him because he did not seize the idea."[44] Thus, even finance minister Meinhard Lónyay, no Russophile by any means, expostulated: "I think we should take a hold of the thread spun by Russia and strive to also pull in England so as to then, in the interest of peace and harmony, launch a Russian-English-Austro-Hungarian mediation, even if this requires military preparatory measures. Every day wasted on not doing just that is a lost day."[45] This proposal was passed on to the French minister in Vienna, who duly relayed it to Paris. It was, of course, music to the ears of the French. Metternich minuted: "Here is what Tour d'Auvergne would like to see without appearing to have provoked it. Diplomatic mediation undertaken by Russia and the neutrals. If refused by the Prussians, armament of the neutrals with a view to armed mediation. This proposition would be put forward by us."[46]

Whether Beust was moved by these objections was not fully apparent. In any case, he proceeded to go even further with the Russians than he had earlier. On the night of 25 August, he drew up in his office an actual draft of a possible Russo-Austrian treaty. The draft, predicated on the assumption that good relations with Russia could be renewed, proposed the following bases for cooperation in ending the war: (1) the possibility of an intervention in it by all neutral powers; (2) an outline of the terms upon which peace between France and Prussia-Germany would rest; (3) the position to be taken by the neutrals in the event one of the belligerents rejected the terms of peace proposed by them; (4) a possible mobilization of the Austrian army in Galicia in return for which Russia, if it chose to do so, could mobilize also; and (5) a personal letter from Emperor Francis Joseph to Tsar Alexander II professing loyalty and friendship.[47]

It was with these documents in his pocket that Chotek, on 27 August, returned to the great city of Petersburg and, in the late afternoon of the next day, had his appointment with the tsar and Gorchakov. The interview was not, to say the least, a wholly satisfactory encounter. Chotek outlined Beust's proposals for "closer cooperation between Austria and Russia and for the partial mobilization of the forces in both countries." The tsar was stunned and intensely angered by what he heard. His anger was further exacerbated when he realized that Austria's proposal would put Russia and Prussia on a collision course as a consequence of which they could wind up as enemies. The tsar made no effort to conceal his indignation over what he was hearing: "There is a lack of consideration on the part of Austria for Russian wishes; there is also malicious pressure, intentional deception, and imposition of conditions."[48] Not only that, the idea that Austria would continue military preparations was out of keeping with the declaration of neutrality on 20 July. If this were to continue, Russia would feel constrained to do likewise, and, in the words of Gorchakov, "the armies of two empires mobilized in central Europe without identical aims would pose a grave danger to the peace."[49]

The two Russian rulers pointed out, as well, that military actions called for a reappraisal of the situation. The indecisive but hard-fought actions on the Chalons road on 16 and 18 August had been seen as unfavorable to the prospects of France, and the Russian press was now striking a different note. And the idea of joint mediation? Out of the question. Prussia would never accept it. All in all, the Russians found the Austrian proposals to be defective in the extreme. They were, in short, nothing less than highly injurious to the aims of Russian policy. If this was the way the Austrian government chose to treat Russia's interests, then there need be no Austrian ambassador in Petersburg at all.[50]

Chotek was thunderstruck to learn these views and, his mission in tatters, made preparations to immediately depart the Russian capital. It is doubtful whether anyone could have succeeded in accomplishing, with respect to

Russian-Austrian relations at this time, what Beust had intended of Chotek. But matters were made considerably worse by the striking differences among the personalities concerned. To start with Chotek: although generally thought to be a man of considerable dignity of character, he had certain personal characteristics that made it difficult for him to fit easily into the confused pattern of responsibilities and relationships that marked the relations of Russia and Austria at this particular time. Not the man to doubt that any recommendation of his would be instantly accepted, he was generally both uncomfortable and impatient with governmental procedures. He had little idea of the painstaking precision that is necessary to make communication between governments effective and useful. His concept of diplomacy was a deeply personal one in which understanding came to rest upon the fire of a glance or the firmness of a handclasp. These were counterparts of a corresponding emotional makeup: vigorous, masterful, intensely loyal to a few, dramatic to the last vein.[51]

Also contributing to the failure of Chotek's efforts was the personality of the man to whom they were directed: Tsar Alexander II. Although possessing imagination, charm, and not inconsiderable facility of communication, he had some negative qualities as well: irresoluteness, lack of firmness and persistence of decision, the tendency to evasive ambivalence and susceptibility to contradictory reactions, as well as promiscuity in relations with the other sex. He had less sympathy than others at his court to Pan-Slav outlooks and less interest than they in an ambitious and essentially expansionary policy in the Balkans and at the Straits. But he was by no means totally devoid of these outlooks and aspirations. It should be noted that along with this interest in the Balkans and the region of the Straits there went a strong dislike and suspicion of Austria-Hungary. The resentment over Austria's failure to support Russia at the time of the Crimean War, coming as it did on the heels of Russia's intervention in Hungary in support of Habsburg power there in 1849, had affected his feelings and Russian policy ever since.[52]

And then there were Alexander's feelings for King William I of Prussia, a man whom the tsar liked and admired more than any other sovereign in Europe and whom he saw, unlike Napoleon III, as a force of stability, well inclined toward Russia. Partly because this relationship was familial—Alexander was William I's nephew—and partly because of cultural and dynastic ties, the affection was real and genuinely felt. This was shown in the predominance of German Baltic officers in high positions in Petersburg. Alexander II had no objection, as his son would have, to the speaking of German in his household and at court, though it must be added that he had no objection to the uses of foreign languages generally in high Russian society and was content that the internal correspondence of the Russian foreign office proceeded in French.

Finally, whatever reservations were entertained by the tsar with respect to Austria-Hungary, one thing is certain: those reservations were enthusiastically encouraged at every turn by the hand of a third personality: the Grand Duchess Helena. Of her, brief note must be taken at this point.

The daughter of a former Württemberg prince, the widow of the tsar's uncle, well connected in German and Russian circles, Grand Duchess Helena was a woman of passionate political temperament, great force of character, and exceptional intellectual vigor. Off and on, during the period to which this narrative is addressed, her circle was one of the leading literary and political meeting places in Petersburg. Memoirs and papers poured from her untiring pen. But her deepest commitment was to politics. Of all her enthusiasms, the greatest and the most consuming were her hatred for France and her admiration for Bismarck (whom she never met personally). Helena's interest in Prussia was an obvious extrapolation of her desire to see France brought down. She was, without question, the head of the pro-German faction at court. Her sympathies for Prussia were further stimulated by a visit she paid to Berlin in August 1870. The visit cannot be said to have been a wholly successful one. There was, for one thing, no one of senior rank at Berlin to introduce her to higher society. But she was not slow to take advantage of the political situation there. She returned to Petersburg full of exuberance for the Prussian cause. She continued to press behind the scenes with the Prussian representatives at Petersburg (particularly with Heinrich Reuss, the ambassador) for vigorous explorations of the possibilities of a Russo-Prussian front against all comers. Deeply devoted to the conservative monarchial institutions of both Prussia and Russia, she was prepared in the years 1870–71 to support a close relationship between Russia and the Prussian court as an arrangement conducive to the preservation of the institution of monarchy.[53]

Other factors, of course, played a role, as well—chief among them the

Prince Alexander Gorchakov, chancellor and foreign minister of Russia. (*Sbornik izdannyi v pamiat' dvadtsatipiatilietiia Upravleniia Ministerstvom inostrannykh diel Gosudarstvennago Kantslera Svietlieishago Kniazia Aleksandra Mikhailovicha Gorchakova, 1856–1881* [St. Petersburg: V tipografii Vtorago otdieleniia sobstvennoi E.I.V. Kantseliarii, 1881], frontispiece.)

tsar's agitated state, arising out of not only the proposal for an Austrian mobilization in Galicia but Beust's suggestion for common mediation of the two powers in the ongoing war. This filled the cup of Russian resentment to the brim. Prussia had now gained the upper hand on the battlefield and so was sure to refuse. It did not require much foresight to see that the real possibilities open to the Russian and Austrian statesmen for cooperating in any meaningful way over the Franco-Prussian War were extremely limited, no matter what Chotek had reported about his meetings with Alexander II and Gorchakov and no matter what rosy notions about such possibilities happened to dance in the heads of Beust and his subordinates at the Ballhausplatz.

As for Bismarck: he had, with great interest, followed the passionate diplomatic activity that, on 31 August and 1 September, came to fruition with the League of Neutrals. He does not seem initially to have been inordinately concerned about its formation, and, in the first stages of the war, there was no very good reason why he should. There was no secret about the direction and objective of the League. The British, despite refusing to discontinue their trade and commercial dealings with the French, had made it clear that they had no desire to enter the war, and the great majority of the Italian government felt the same way. The efforts of Visconti-Venosta and Granville to create a situation in which none of the signatories could depart from their neutrality without notifying the others did not strike him as cause for an abrupt change in Prussia's policy toward these powers. In a word, the League of Neutrals was something he anticipated. How effective the League would be was something no one could say, but the beginning of wisdom was to accept the fact that there was nothing Prussia could accomplish by hot and excited reactions to its formation.[54]

Quite different was his view of the situation that would arise if there were an attempt on the part of the neutrals to intervene in the war. This would at once upset what had been the foundation stone of his policy: to keep the conflict isolated. Concern over this prospect was given fresh impetus by three great events that took place at the beginning of September: (1) the defeat, on the first of that month, of the French army at Sedan; (2) the capture of

Napoleon III as a prisoner of war the next day; and (3) the establishment, on 4 September 1870, in Paris, of the Government of National Defense. The story of these events is best told in a separate chapter, but a word or two about them in connection with the League of Neutrals and the prospect of foreign intervention will not be out of place here.

It was easy for official circles throughout Europe, in the excited atmosphere of the time, to jump to the conclusion that a pronounced weakening of France was imminent and that plans should be made for dealing with this. This was the situation—in Great Britain, in Austria, and in Russia—that Bismarck faced in the first weeks of September 1870. There were sensational reports, first appearing in *The Times*, that members of the Orléans family, the junior branch of the French monarchy, were roaming Belgium and conspiring to place one of their members on the throne at Versailles. Bismarck was at pains to announce that such a development would affect Prussian policy not in the slightest: "The appearance of new royalty as a mere decoration change would have absolutely no effect on our conduct of the war. We would face the same dangers next year that an Orléanist France would again make. The band of robbers would remain the same even if their captain changes."[55] And again in a message to Prince Reuss at Petersburg: "It is not merely Napoleon III; it is France herself by her aggressiveness that puts us in danger—with or without Napoleon. Against France we have no other considerations except our individual and general interests."[56]

Still, Bismarck was by no means sure that these statements would have the desired effect on various personalities to whom they were addressed. His misgivings grew in the middle of August as a crop of reports reached Prussian headquarters concerning the prospect that one or more of the neutral powers was bent on intervening in the conflict. As early as 7 August, Reuss reported from Petersburg: "The language used by the British minister betrays a concern over any reduction in the power of France. According to him, a union of the neutrals should emerge as the peace negotiators. Prince Gorchakov, to be sure, said nothing that would suggest what was in the back of his mind."[57] The following day, Reuss telegraphed Bismarck with the news of the conversations that had taken place between Chotek on the one side and Gorchakov and the tsar on the other: "The idea of a neutral league preoccupied the participants but concerning this there was, I think, only a general discussion. The idea of a general congress is very much on Prince Gorchakov's mind."[58] Even more telling was the ambassador's telegram of 19 August: "The tsar asked me whether a change of monarchs in France would constitute a suitable end to the war. . . . He spoke to me for the first time about peace, about the need for moderation on the part of victors, advised that territorial acquisitions would be the germ of future wars, and argued against an indemnity or the raising of fortresses. Prince Gorchakov spoke along the same lines though without the same degree of precision."[59]

Bismarck's anxieties could only have been heightened by these ominous dispatches. From the standpoint of Prussian security, Russia was of outstanding importance, not only because of its geographical position but also because it had promised to restrain Austria. The Austrians were now approaching Petersburg with a view to mending fences and adopting a policy of collaboration. The days following Reuss's presentation of the situation in Petersburg were a period of uncertainty, nervousness, and barely concealed crisis in Russo-Prussian relations. The tsar, as Reuss had pointed out, was now in a state of great bewilderment and concern over the kind of peace that would emerge from the war. Despite his fondness for his uncle, William I, and his promise of 1868 to take steps to hold Austria in check, he seemed on the point of undertaking preparations for a possible intervention in the conflict. In this he was doubtless encouraged by other Russians at court, including, most outstanding, his Danish wife and some Pan-Slavs. The former, neglected and ill treated, was decidedly receptive to Pan-Slav tendencies. Also at work were the policy and personality of the Russian foreign minister, Gorchakov, himself a bumptious and devious figure. Held in contempt by many of those closest to Alexander II, widely disliked and distrusted by his ambassadors, Gorchakov displayed freewheeling and not always predictable propensities. There was, however, one propensity that was unmistakable: his dislike of Bismarck, upon whose shoulders Prussia had, between 1862 and 1866, risen violently and suddenly to the top of the ranks of the Great Powers. Gorchakov was intensely envious of Bismarck (of whose dislike for himself he was not unaware), had dreams of exploiting his feats, and seldom lost an opportunity to undermine his reputation in the eyes of the senior military and diplomatic figures at the Russian court. All this being the case, he was naturally eager to insert himself as prominently as possible into the process of

Prusso-Russian relations and to establish himself in the eyes of all European statesmen as the real architect of peace between the two belligerents.[60]

Bismarck was well aware, as early as August 1870, of the tsar's vacillations, of the seriousness of the challenges being raised to the previous Prusso-Russian relationship, and of the tenuousness of the ties he had so long cultivated between the two countries. At the same time, shaken as he was, Bismarck, in his dealings with Petersburg, pursued a policy of great prudence and reserve, not making official use of various disturbing phenomena, professing continued confidence in the relationship between the two sides, leaving it to the Russians to say so if they had misgivings over the conduct of the war. There was, however, one point Bismarck sought to drive home with great clarity to the tsar, and that was the damage that would come to the peace and tranquility of central Europe if Prussia were forced to conclude a peace that would be viewed as unsatisfactory in the eyes of German opinion. "It would," as he instructed Reuss to point out to Alexander, "break the ground for socialism and a republic."[61] A situation would thus be created in which Bismarck and William I would be in real danger of losing control.

The idea of using revolution and upheaval as a weapon was one Bismarck knew could not fail to have a powerful effect on the mind of the tsar. This would create a new rationale for supporting the German war effort. In using this argument, Bismarck showed how strongly the heady nationalism of the late nineteenth century had seriously affected foreign policy and conduced easily toward revolution. Here Poland, always Russia's blind spot, was a case in point. Should revolutionary agitation break out in central Europe as a result of a peace treaty that German opinion could not accept, there was no telling how far it would spread and what actions the governments threatened by its appearance would find themselves obliged to entertain. In Germany, the democratic and republican forces would gain considerably from an unsatisfactory peace, one made all the more unacceptable because of the victories the Germans were now experiencing on the battlefield.[62]

But, for the time being, Bismarck was not ready to change course. The failure of the Chotek mission spelled the end to any joint Austro-Russian intervention in the war. With the Austrians, moreover, Bismarck could afford to strike an attitude unlike that he adopted with respect to the French. The peace of 1866 was not punitive—realistic, to be sure, but certainly not harsh. Better relations with Austria were out of the question as long as Beust remained in power, but the survival of Austria as a Great Power was essential for German interests, not so much as an ally but as a dependent state, essential for preserving order in southeastern Europe and seeing to it that the nine million Catholic Austro-Germans were excluded from a new German Reich. Moreover, if Russia, in the prevailing circumstances, was not dependable as an associate—and Gorchakov and Alexander II too exemplified this tendency—then it was essential to begin work that would make Austria friendlier. It could no longer be left on the loose. Without some gesture of future improvement in the relations between the two courts, Germany ran the risk of isolation. Once that friendship and support were ensured to Germany, then it would be Russia that would face this danger. It would then be easier to deal with and the cultivation of friendly relations would be a more realistic possibility. This attitude we see reflected as early as 24 August 1870, when Bismarck instructed his ambassador in Vienna to directly approach Emperor Francis Joseph: "Aim: Confirm the truth that we support no oppositional elements [in the monarchy] and after the war envisage the possibility that not only the Vienna court, but eventually . . . the two of us and Russia would come together for the purpose of maintaining existing relationships and national order."[63]

Bismarck here was clearly holding out the possibility of improved relations with the two other monarchical powers in the future as a means of preventing their intervention while the war was being fought. Neutral intervention would at once introduce into the political structure of Europe questions so complicated and fragile as to result either in a wider war or in a war in which the Germans would be placed in a position of having to accept an imposed peace. Bismarck, in short, wanted the war to proceed along lines that were simple and direct and without undue complications. But he plainly realized, as August drew to an end, how difficult this would be. Each of the neutral powers faced serious domestic problems and saw in the present state of hostilities between France and Prussia a possible way to address them. Bismarck was thus left with his doubts and anxieties, and no clear way of escape was apparent to him. Of those who have studied and pondered the course of his diplomacy in the period 1870–71, none has examined it more scrupulously, judged it more dispassionately, or done more to help others understand it than Eberhard Kolb of the University of Cologne. It may be fitting, therefore, that this discussion of Bismarck's attitude toward the League of Neutrals conclude with Kolb's final words about this extraordinarily complex and dangerous problem.

> [To sum up], by the end of August it was certain that the localization of the war had been successful. But what was becoming increasingly apparent, even at this point, were the difficulties working against Bismarck's desired "localizing of the peace negotiations," i.e., the conclusion of a peace treaty with France in bilateral negotiations without an intervention by or the participation of the neutral powers. . . . But what was now disturbing him was the evident intention of these Powers to participate in some way in the shaping of the peace, and this Bismarck was determined to prevent. Only if a peace treaty could be concluded without the neutrals did it seem possible that he could realize the German war aims that had, during the course of August, become more and more crystallized.[64]

This was the situation that Bismarck faced—in Russia, in Austria, and in Great Britain—as August 1870 came to an end, and it is easy to understand that he must have seen in it a real danger not only to his policies of the moment, in the narrower sense, but also to the entire set of objectives he had created for Prussia-Germany and on which he (with good reason) saw the successful prosecution of the war as depending. Such a conclusion called for preventive action, and Bismarck was, as we shall have occasion to see, not slow to take it.

4

The End of Napoleon III

Mention has been made already of the climate of opinion that came over the two populations after the French declaration of war had been presented at Berlin on 19 July. In order to understand how the German war aims developed as they did, let us return to the second half of July 1870 and discuss, at the risk of slight repetition, what that reaction had been.

On the German side, it was a curious compound of uncomplicated patriotism and romantic joy at the prospect of participating in a great adventure. Somehow, it was widely believed, the conflict would solve all the problems that had piled up over the years. Most Germans believed that the fatherland was the victim of a brutal assault from a hereditary foe. A British correspondent, commenting on the situation, noted "a steady Teutonic determination,"[1] an impressive closing of the ranks. The French declaration of war released a heady steam of excitement that swept the whole of Germany. To those who fought it, it offered an exhilarating holiday from the dull routines of normal life and a promise of self-fulfillment. But such sentiments were by no means limited to the soldiers. It included, one must note, elevated persons of status at court, high officials of the governmental bureaucracy, members of the high command of the army, senior clerical figures, prominent businessmen, and, finally—and most important—leading editors, publicists, and writers.[2]

That it was the French against whom the Germans were fighting carried a particular significance, and that the French were led by Napoleon III only heightened already inflamed passions. Was not this Napoleon III, the nephew of the despised monster who had reduced the states of Germany to a status of the most ignominious servitude, a man whom no German could ever forget, a man dominated by an insatiable vanity and love of power, a man of inordinate touchiness, an endless vindictiveness, and an inability to forget an insult or slight, a man possessed of a thoroughgoing hatred of everything not French and a high degree of bloody-mindedness toward anyone who disagreed with him or questioned his aspirations to the mastery of Europe? Napoleon III was Napoleon I in later-day dress. He had proved himself a man with a most extraordinary talent for political tactics and intrigue, a consummate actor, a dissimulator of genius, a master, in particular, of the art of playing people and forces off against each other for his own benefit. The philosopher Rudolf Haym exemplified the sentiments of the time when he wrote in his letter of 2 August 1870 to his friend Max Drunker: "I can say that one could only mistake this world order if one did not understand that this incomprehensively evil, outrageous, and mendacious Napoleonic character must be brought down."[3]

If we picture to ourselves a man of this temperament, imagine the hatred of him that was firmly implanted in the German breast, and then bear in mind the situation in which, as we have just seen, Germans then found themselves placed, it will not be difficult to see why Germans everywhere reacted in the ways they did. Adding to the intensity of this feeling was the announcement by the French government of the punitive peace it would inflict upon its enemy in the event of a French victory. Particularly instructive and remarkable on this and other subjects are the dispatches of the British minister at Darmstadt, Sir Robert Morier. Writing to London on 17 July 1870, he reported: "I cannot hesitate to say that an almost unbelievable change has completely overtaken public opinion since I left here a few weeks earlier." And two days later: "It is no rhetorical flourish to state that M. de Gramont has, with respect to the idea of the promotion of German unity, done more in fourteen days than has Bismarck in the four years since the battle of Königgrätz."[4]

Alongside this eruption of patriotic fever against France were a corresponding fear of something more dreadful, namely a French incursion into Germany, and concerns about the security of German borders in the southwest. And the situation in the days immediately after the declaration of war saw excitement and concern over the prospect of such an incursion. It was not

Napoleon III, emperor of the French. (von Pflugk-Harttung, *The Franco-German War*, 5.)

difficult for local residents to envisage a French push into southern Germany and, once they were in control, the promotion of plans for the dissolution of the states of the North German Confederation. This was particularly the case in Baden, where a French invasion through Strasburg was thought imminent. The French had supposed that separatist feeling existed in this area, and local authorities in Baden began, in the second half of July, a campaign to evacuate the state. But their position at this time was tenuous and even feeble. Adolph Wagner, a professor at the University of Freiburg, wrote to his friend on 16 July 1870: "Here . . . we expect either very soon, perhaps today or in the next few days, coming from Breisach, a French army of occupation which will attack us, or, even worse, an infestation of nomadic garbage from Mulhausen."[5] The Bavarian representative in Karlsruhe spoke in the second half of July 1870 of "a time of panic-stricken [citizens] aghast at the prospect of being overrun, as public opinion thinks they will be, by roguish bands of African hordes."[6]

It should be noted that these fears quickly proved unfounded as the Germans won a first round of victories in the war. But the process of disaffection and anxiety that reached its peak in the second half of July never wholly abated, and those Germans in the southwest quickly formed the opinion that something had to be done about it. During this time, in particular, the reports, stimuli, suggestions, and pressures coming to senior political and military officials of the Prussian government in connection with this question assumed formidable proportions. The telegraph tapes and newspaper writings poured out a bewildering plethora of reports, information, and recommendations about the security of the German borders.

Here the names of two provinces that were destined to play a fateful role in the war first made their appearance: Alsace and Lorraine. From the very beginning of the war, the question of these two provinces bubbled up in the German consciousness as did nothing else. The question was always not whether but how and on what grounds Germany would acquire them in the event of a victory over France. To the Germans, Alsace and Lorraine represented a part of the medieval German empire that had been hacked away by the French at a time when Germany was a series of small and weak kingdoms beset with disorder. During the July crisis, the question received scant, if any, attention. But, once the French had declared war and fears concerning the borders gained currency, sentiment about Alsace and Lorraine began to stir. By mid-August and the first German victories, though no official statement had been made, there was virtual unanimity of opinion about the two provinces throughout the country. When the senior German statesmen would meet to shape the peace that was to justify all that the Germans had endured for centuries, it was expected that the result of their labors would be not merely a peace but something resembling a new world order. In the sweeping, total nature of the gains that would flow to the German people as a result of victory, in the inordinate increase in prestige that would accrue to William I and the German army as a result of it, in the vast amount of new power that it would represent, it was axiomatic that Alsace and Lorraine would again become what they had once been and should always be, that is, a part of Germany. As Adolph Wagner put it: "A German statesman who thought of winning back Alsace would until recently have appeared before the population as a dreamer. We Germans have for a long time been masters of resignation. Scarcely do we mention Alsace and Lorraine when the vainglorious French scream without any scruples about robbery of the left bank of the Rhine. . . . Our great newspapers raise the question of the upper left bank of the Rhine that we and the rest of Europe regard as something that is ours by God's will and the French hysterically react like a bunch of oversensitive women."[7]

Bismarck was thoroughly familiar with the cries for annexation that were now filling the air, but they did not determine his fundamental policy, which was strategic—to secure the borders of Germany. The hard-fought but decisive German victories over France in August gave rise to the question of what territory would accomplish this purpose. Bismarck himself raised this question in conversations with diplomats, through official circulars, and by organized press campaigns. Actually, as Gordon A. Craig has pointed out, he could have spared himself all this effort, given that local papers were screaming for annexation and men of considerable dignity and character, including Ferdinand Gregorovius, the historian of medieval Rome, were maintaining that a bloodthirsty France could be countered decisively only by Germany's permanent acquisition of her natural frontier, the Vosges.[8] But Bismarck evidently thought a press campaign necessary to establish an official Prussian position on the matter and to make it clear to foreign courts that annexation of French territory would be the price France would have to pay for its

71

defeat and the prize the Germans would take for their military success. This idea he conveyed to Prince Reuss, in Petersburg, using the term "realistic guarantees" for security against a hereditary foe of two centuries. Still, there was no mention of Alsace or Lorraine. This would first occur on 15 August 1870 in a dispatch Bismarck sent to Hermann von Thile, an undersecretary in the foreign office at Berlin, and then it was more in the nature of a velleity, a pious wish, rather than a concrete demand. Said Bismarck: "Alsace will be kept by us in peace if God wills it."[9]

There followed a pair of important articles in foreign newspapers. The Russians were told quite clearly in an article that appeared on 15 August in the semiofficial *Journal de Petersbourg* and the British the same day in the *Indépendance belge* "that in all our [news] papers . . . anger is boiling over the prospect of foreign intervention in the present conflict and that, against another rise of a foe who has been a robber for two centuries, the will of the people demands nothing less than the borders be made secure through territorial adjustments."[10] On 28 August, Bismarck instructed his press agent, Moritz Busch, to publish immediately an article in the semiofficial *Norddeutsche Allgemeine Zeitung*. Bismarck wished to show that the question of annexations now had been officially sanctioned by the highest authorities in the Prussian government. Even more important was the fact that the language in the article corresponded to what had been said privately in various diplomatic communications; the piece struck the members of the diplomatic community all over Europe with the force of a thunderbolt, and these diplomats now began, as we shall see shortly, to devise schemes that would give the Germans some of what they wanted, but not all.[11]

In any case, the August victories confirmed to Bismarck, as nothing else could, that peace with France was impossible without the annexation of Alsace—how much of Alsace he was not certain, and he seems for a while to have toyed with the idea of ceding to Switzerland its southernmost tip. But to all solutions short of outright annexation of the province Bismarck turned a decidedly deaf ear. This was particularly telling because the German headquarters, one might mention, were rocked in just those days, as was much of the rest of Europe, by the appearance in rapid succession in *The Times*, which until recently had been considered relatively close to the

Self-preservation—One must cut off the claws of the beast to have peace in the future. Bismarck cuts the claws "Alsace" and "Lorraine" off a bear representing France. Cartoon from *Kladderadatsch*, Berlin, 4 September 1870. (Bildarchiv Preußischer Kulturbesitz [BPK]. Used by permission of Art Resource, New York. ART428954.)

foreign office, of a series of articles calling for the neutralization of the province, the demolition of all existing fortresses, and a binding obligation to be
undertaken by the French to construct no new ones. Bismarck at once ruled
out these ideas with great definitiveness. Part of a circular written by his factotum, Heinrich Abeken, on 24 September 1870 put it thus: "A solution of
this kind could only lead to the creation and growth of feelings of humiliation
and subordination between our two peoples."[12] For one thing, it would not
give Germany the secure borders demanded by the new set of circumstances
created by the war. For another, the proposal would strike at the heart of
French sovereignty. The cynics of that day would have dismissed Bismarck's
statement as a smokescreen for his real ambitions. This frequently levied accusation, still sometimes repeated in the historical literature, is thoroughly
wide of the mark.[13] Bismarck had no desire to take any steps that would undermine the position of France as a Great Power, and his later battles with
Moltke over the course of the war confirm this point. As Eberhard Kolb has
written: "[Bismarck's attitude] was no doubt a reflection in large measure of
his experience as ambassador to Russia from 1856 to 1859. There he had seen
firsthand the wound inflicted upon Petersburg by the Black Sea clauses of the
Treaty of Paris which deprived Russia of the ability to defend her borders."[14]

Bismarck struck a similar note on 9 September 1870 in a letter to Reuss.
Touching even more emphatically on the nationalist feelings to which the war
with France had given rise, he wrote that "the collapse of Napoleon would
give those in Germany no guarantees against a new threat that we would face
in the next year or the year after that from the French. Our quarrel is not with
the French leadership; it is with the French people of whom their leaders are
but a product. Nothing good will result from a *Scheinfriede* [a hollow peace],
nothing good from the French point of view and for the German nation such
a peace would be completely unacceptable."[15]

To repeat: Bismarck did not start the war with ideas of annexation. Here—
as in the immediate origins of the war—he was improvising, rather than
meeting long-range goals or plans. As for his motives, three stand out: (1) the
willingness to at least go along with the idea that security—a more defensible
frontier militarily—was imperative, along with the view that over time the
French would learn to forget or get over the loss; (2) a bow to German public opinion, especially in southwest Germany, the target of so many French

invasions and since the 1830s the center of considerable Francophobia and militant liberal nationalism; (3) the desire to give the new "united" Germany a common prize (Alsace-Lorraine as *Reichsland*) to administer and defend. But all these add up not to a planned, calculated decision but rather to an improvisation by a clever rational gambler who could prove to be wrong. His decision to support annexation was not unlike his decision in 1882 and later to go after colonies, after a decade or more of resisting the idea: not a major change of heart, but something he decided to do because there were more reasons to do it than reasons not to. Later on, he saw that it had not been worth it after all, just as he did with the colonies.[16]

While diplomacy was proceeding, the French had commenced military operations against Prussia. But the Prussians were more than a match for them. In the middle of August, before the French could implement any of their battle plans, Prussian forces pushed through the Lorraine gap in the northeast of France and defeated, though not without heavy losses to themselves, the enemy at Mars-la-Tours, Gravelotte, and Saint-Privat, in the province of Lorraine, and then stationed themselves between Paris and the two great French armies under the respective commands of Marshals Bazaine and MacMahon. Bazaine was pushed backward and eastward and was tied down in the fortress at Metz. The French armies now fell into a state of almost incredible disarray. MacMahon's army, now joined by Napoleon III, attempted to relieve the pressure put upon Bazaine by the enemy, but, before it could do so, its southern flank was cut to pieces by the crack units of the Prussian IV corps, the Royal Saxon XII army corps, and the I Bavarian corps at Beaumont; the bulk of his troops were pinned against Sedan, the great fortress on the Belgian frontier that harkened back to the time of Louis XIV and to which the unrelenting fire from the redoubtable Krupp steel breech-loading guns manned by the Bavarian, Silesian, Hessian, and Saxon troops had laid waste.[17]

The decision by the French to split their armies rather than defend the line they had established on the Meuse River set them up for a "Zirkelschlacht," or circle battle, a form in which the Germans specialized. Moltke gleefully announced: "Now we have them in a mousetrap"; he then proceeded to snap

Napoleon III and his generals. (von Pflugk-Harttung, *The Franco-German War*, facing p. 48.)

it shut.[18] The French general commander, Felix Wimpffen, an otherwise highly competent officer who had been sent from Africa to rectify previous disasters, begged Napoleon III to advance from Sedan; while he did so, Prussian artillery devastated the entire French front. Moreover, once William knew that Napoleon III was inside the fortress at Sedan, he immediately ordered every available gun turned on it. This decision resulted in a not inconsiderable number of German casualties, but it proved decisive. A Württemberg officer, rejecting an appeal from a Bavarian to slow down, replied: "We've dragged these dammed cannon all over France without taking a shot at anything; now we're going to fire and no one's going to stop us."[19] Forming a semicircle, the German artillery pounded away and chewed up the entire French armies. Observing the carnage in the company of Bismarck and Moltke, the American civil war general Philip Sheridan puzzled as to Napoleon III's fate: would he die or flee? Bismarck expressed no uncertainty: "The old fox is too cunning to be caught in such a trap. He has doubtless slipped off to Paris."[20]

Not quite. Having packed off the prince imperial to Belgium at the end of August, Napoleon III frantically conferred with his commanders. Wimpffen, who was awarded supreme command over the French generals by a new government that had been stitched together in Paris, demanded that the emperor try to escape from Sedan, take charge of the last army, and attempt a breakaway, but the numbers told against such a strategy. One general, shaking his head in disbelief and fighting back the tears, announced: "I have only three intact brigades, little ammunition, and no artillery."[21] Under circumstances such as these, who could engage the Prussians in the rear or anywhere? Napoleon thereupon raised the white flag, and he drew up a letter that an aide took to William I, who, in the company of Moltke and Bismarck, at once read it out: "Having failed to die amongst my troops there is nothing left for me to do but place my sword in the hands of Your Majesty."[22] Moltke, unaffected by these words, which were otherwise universally applauded by those around the Prussian king, urged that he grant Napoleon a ceasefire and stole away at once to prepare for battle the following day. Bismarck was not so indifferent and at once drew up a reply: "Monsieur, mon Frère: Regretting the circumstances in which you find yourself I accept the sword of Your Majesty and appoint General Moltke . . . to negotiate the capitulation of the army that has fought so bravely under your command." Presented with a flask of cognac by his nephew, Bismarck promptly accepted it, drank it down in one swallow, and in English proclaimed: "Here's to the unification of Germany."[23]

It now fell to Wimpffen to approach the Prussians with a view to negotiating an armistice, and one need scarcely comment on how thankless a task this was. Bismarck and, even more, Moltke wore all their anti-French prejudices on the outside and, like steamrollers, demolished one by one Wimpffen's pleas for an "honorable capitulation," that is, for arrangements that would allow the French army to depart from Sedan with arms, baggage, and full military honors. With the French emperor a prisoner of war, Moltke quickly formed the opinion that there was no prospect for stability until the entire army at Sedan was disarmed and a treaty of peace signed. But Wimpffen refused to give up, now inundating Moltke and Bismarck with a flurry of desperate appeals arguing that generosity was the best—indeed, the only—way for the French and the Germans to establish the basis for a stable postwar relationship and warning that a harsh peace would only set afoot such great feelings of bitterness and resentment among the French people that they would never—no matter what form of government happened to conceive itself—be able to overcome them. Bismarck would have none of it. "One should not," he at once shot back, "rely on gratitude and especially not on that of a people. If France had solid institutions, she might deserve gratitude, but such institutions, she has not. One can rely on nothing in your country." On the contrary—and now a note of vitriolic emotion began to creep into Bismarck's principled statecraft—"the French have presented themselves as disturbers of the European peace for eighty years, they have threatened Germany for nearly eight hundred." The tables now had turned. The German army would march on Paris. "The fortune of battle has delivered to us the best soldiers, the best officers in the French army; to voluntarily set them free would be to risk seeing them march against us again, and this would be madness."[24]

Thereupon General Felix Castelnau, a member of the emperor's staff who had accompanied Wimpffen to the Prussian lines, took up the running. The emperor, he implored Moltke and Bismarck, had laid down his sword in the hope that William I would show mercy and grant honorable terms in return for the prospect of the end of the bloodshed. Moltke was unaffected by this remark, but it struck Bismarck with the force of a thunderclap. Did Napoleon surrender his sword as head of state of the French nation? Or merely as the commander of the French army? If the former, everything at once would change; what was occurring would be not the surrender of an army but that of a power. An electrifying silence filled the air, until Castelnau replied that Napoleon's surrender was a personal gesture. Moltke stormed back: "Nothing has changed."[25] He then declared that his terms remained as he had stated. The conversation was over—and quickly forgotten—but, with hindsight, the incident may be seen as the first in a series of sallies between Bismarck and Moltke that, as Michael Howard has written, "in significance and intensity was to come almost to rival the war itself."[26]

Wimpffen returned to Sedan and briefed his colleagues, who now saw quite clearly the size of their disaster and immediately signed a note agreeing to the Prussian terms. Together with Wimpffen, they made for the Prussian headquarters. Napoleon III remained behind, convinced there might still be some way to restore his dynasty. Napoleon thought he saw a way out. If by some stroke he could wrest control of the situation by a direct appeal to William I over the heads of his advisers, his troubles would dissolve. He could march into Paris, install himself in power, and make a generous peace with the Prussians. With this goal in mind, he saddled up on 2 September and rode toward Donchery, where William I was staying. Bismarck was too quick for him. He intercepted Napoleon III, told him that the king was not available, and took him to a cottage about halfway between Sedan and Donchery. There, stone faced, Bismarck politely, though somewhat impatiently, listened to his schemes; upon learning that Napoleon III viewed himself as a prisoner of war, not as a head of state, Bismarck said he could be of no help to him. A full capitulation had not been signed, and, until it had been, Napoleon's request was impossible. It was left to Moltke, whom Napoleon saw an hour later, to complete the destruction of the latter's hopes for German sympathy, let alone German support. Recapitulating first Napoleon's idea, freshly broached, that French troops could be transferred to the Belgian frontier and sweeping aside his argument that such a move would pave the way for peace, Moltke made it clear that there could be no question of anything of the sort. And then, turning to Napoleon's political situation, he announced:

"It is high time you realized how desperate your situation is. You have set great store on the army of Bazaine. It has not gone to the aid of the Empress. It is pinned down. It is high time you signed the capitulation and reminisce about the adventures of your misfortunes." Napoleon replied: "Ja dann ist alles verloren."[27]

The capitulation was immediately signed. The terms that Moltke presented to the French at the Château de Bellevue, an industrialist's mansion not far from Frénois, were there accepted unconditionally. They were harsh. The army's soldiers were to be taken prisoner of war. Its entire supply of arms and matériel were to be taken, as well, including the great fortress of Sedan. The only concession was given to the officers, who, in return for swearing their intention "not to take up arms against Germany nor to act in any way prejudicial to the interests of Germany until the close of the present war,"[28] were set free. All told, the Germans took eighty-three thousand prisoners, adding to the twenty-one thousand they already had. In addition, their victory landed them a thousand wagons, six thousand horses, and 419 guns. Their own losses were slight: nine thousand officers and regular troops. More important still, the front-line army of the French army was still pinned down at Metz, the second-line army obliterated.[29]

The capitulation concluded, Bismarck saw no reason to stand in the way of Napoleon's request for an interview with William I, and this took place in the late afternoon of 2 September. Napoleon was a physical and emotional wreck, plainly on the verge of collapse. Visibly nervous, his eyes glazed and dull, tears flowing down both sides of his face, he entered the room with four adjuncts behind him. William's delight was aroused not only by this sight but also by the satisfaction that Prussia had now attained revenge for Tilsit, the French-dictated settlement of 1807 that nearly cut the country in two. There was little for either sovereign to say, Napoleon confining himself to congratulating the king on his performance in battle and asking only that he be allowed to pass into captivity through Belgium, thus avoiding any contact with French soil. To this suggestion, Bismarck gave his consent. The capture of Napoleon could well turn into an advantage, and "it would not do any harm if he took another direction . . . if he failed to keep his word this would not injure us."[30]

Napoleon III, escorted by Bismarck, on the day after the battle of Sedan. (von Pflugk-Harttung, *The Franco-German War*, facing p. 255.)

The capitulation of Sedan, 2 September 1870. Based on a painting by Anton von Werner. (von Pflugk-Harttung, *The Franco-German War*, facing p. 260.)

All in all, Bismarck had not done badly. The decisive battle of the war had been fought; there was now no question that the Prussians and, indeed, all the Germans who fought with them would emerge victorious; Napoleon III's plans to gain regain power through the favor of William I had been completely dashed. As he rode through the fields at the end of the day's fighting, however, Bismarck felt not elated but depressed, and his mood was not lightened when he discovered a few hours later that Moltke had ordered an immediate advance on Paris. This order filled Bismarck with unease. He wrote to his son: "My wish would be to allow these people to stew in their own juice, and to install ourselves in the conquered provinces before advancing further. If we advance too soon that would prevent them from falling out among themselves."[31] But he dared not estrange Moltke with the same vigor, sarcasm, and emotion he had used to defeat Moltke's plans, in the Austrian war of 1866, for crossing the Danube and carrying the war to Vienna and for which, he was soon to learn (if he did not know already), the soldiers had not forgiven him. Nor was this all. There was the question of logistics. The German supply lines were long, and on either flank of the line French communications remained sound. Finally, many Frenchmen did not regard themselves as defeated; they were at this very moment in the throes of building a new army along the Loire. It was an unnerving end to a day of triumph, and it is not unlikely that, as he wiped his brow of the sweat produced by the hot September sun, he ruminated over what lay ahead and reflected unhappily that in politics success often brings as many problems as failure.

It would be difficult to overstate the effect on German opinion of the victory over the French at Sedan on 1 September 1870. The sheer magnitude of the success fanned the passions of all Germans to a white heat. There were elaborate and excited jubilations among the public; placards were nailed to notice boards in the major cities to huge enthusiasm. Traces of this sentiment were sometimes to be found in Prussia even before the stunning September achievement. As early as 20 June 1870, the historian and publicist Julian Schmidt wrote: "There is present here an atmosphere we have never before experienced in Prussia, only the records of our fathers from the years 1813 and 1814 come anywhere near to matching it."[32] In a letter to his friend Oskar von Bülow, the jurist Rudolf von Jhering laid down: "How I thank God that this is a time I can now live to see the rebirth of the German nation; sinned against in the course of a thousand years, within the course of a few weeks, she has been created; she arises now as one nation, a Hercules in the cradle."[33]

Thus was inaugurated an outpouring of public festivities, demonstrations, and general political and social frenzy such as Prussia and, indeed, Germany generally had not seen the likes of since 1813 and would not see again until 1914. One letter, speech, proclamation, and demonstration celebrating the victory followed another. There seemed not to be a moment of respite. Among the huge and wildly enthusiastic crowds, news was passed that greater victories lay ahead and that, indeed, all of France would be made to pay a devastating price for the folly of having deliberately provoked war with Prussia. The outbursts made a profound impression everywhere in Europe—an impression as dramatic, in truth, as the circumstances warranted. Although unaware of what was occurring behind the scenes, the European chancelleries and newspaper offices attributed to the demonstrations that were taking place all over Germany a significance remarkably similar to that which was being assigned to them by the Germans themselves, and they saw them as the symbol of a real turning point in the war.[34]

It is clear from all the available evidence that the outpourings of public sentiment against France, not to mention the pride produced by the successes of the German military, made a profound impression upon the diplomats of Europe. Even more important than the force of the substantive arguments themselves seems to have been the fact that diplomats like Morier and others came away from them persuaded that they reflected the passionate feelings of great and influential portions of all of German society—feelings of such intensity that they deserved deference regardless of how well or ill founded they were. Here was, as Morier observed in his communications to Granville, a new note in the psychology of the German people. Seldom if ever before had he confessed to reckoning with such a thing as German opinion. The opinion of the king of Prussia himself had normally been what counted. However that may have been, the effect of the letters, public utterances, and journalistic pronouncements was not only profound but, for the moment, politically decisive.[35] Without knowledge of this background factor, one cannot fully understand Bismarck's behavior over the next four and a half months.

The scene now shifted to Paris, where news of the disaster at Sedan shocked and disgusted the city. Its effect was to set in motion an uprising, sometimes referred to as the revolution of 4 September, that marked the downfall of the Second Empire. To attempt to describe this event would surpass the limits and purposes of this study. But there are certain features of it that are worth noting here.

First of all, it was not a contrived uprising. No one planned it. No one organized it. Even the republicans, who had long dreamed of such a day and had viewed themselves as professionals in the art of revolutions, were for the most part taken by surprise. What happened on the afternoon of 4 September 1870 was simply the sudden, crashing breakdown of an old dynastic-imperial system caught between the stresses of a modern major war, for which it was unprepared, and the inertia of an imperial court that had lost its orderliness of procedure, its feel for events, its contact with the people, and even the respect of the ruling bureaucracy. So long as the structure of imperialist power held together, the latent antagonisms among the diverging elements opposing it were in part concealed and disguised by their common hope for change; once the empire was gone, there was nothing to keep the manifold antagonisms from coming out into the open, greatly accentuated by the unexpected competition for the succession into which the various elements now found themselves thrust.[36]

A great many Frenchmen had dreamed—like the more radical elements of the population of Paris—of a revolution in one form or another and had chafed under what seemed to them to be the interminable delay in its arrival, but, from the standpoint of the ideals to which most of these people aspired, the revolution of 4 September may be said to have come, if not belatedly, then at a most inopportune time. For one thing, the country was still endeavoring to conduct a major war, involving extensive mobilization of manpower and a great strain on the entire economic and administrative system. This was an involvement that, as the leaders of the new government were soon to learn to their sorrow, would not easily be liquidated and that could not fail to add to the burden of any new regime assuming power at that time.[37]

But, beyond that, there was not adequate unity among the various political groups available to share in or compete for the inheritance of the emperor's power. The republicans were a diverse lot; some entertained the notion that peace would follow the overthrow of Napoleon III, while others pined for a revolutionary war against Germany. There was not, among them, even that modicum of consensus on the terms of political competition that would have been necessary to make possible any orderly transition to some stable form of government. The French political society that simmered under the crust of imperial power and had yearned for its disappearance or moderation was actually riven itself by tragic and scarcely reconcilable divisions. The events of the abortive revolution of 1848 and, more recently, the stress of the war against Prussia had carried some French socialists to a point where their hatred and distrust of "bourgeois" parties was extreme. Thus, declared an early government communiqué, "there can be only *guerre à outrance*; anyone who dares advocate anything else is a traitor to the nation," and the first batch of reports from the smaller cities and mountain villages solemnly pledged to repel the invasion by every means possible.[38] The less extreme elements, on the other hand, tended to view the more hardline radicals as irresponsible demagogues. The situation was further complicated by conservative tendencies found in many parts of the country—tendencies inflamed by the unhappiness of the time and now greatly stimulated by the disappearance of the dynastic center that had long been at least a symbol—indeed, the only symbol—of political unity.

But there were those in Paris who were determined to bring the situation under control. At noon on 4 September, the members of the old *Corps législatif*, the body that constituted the legislative branch of government under the empire, met to consider a number of proposals for handling the emergency situation that now confronted Paris and the nation. But their deliberations were made impossible by a large throng that first crowded around the palace and then burst through, paralyzing the body and bringing its deliberations to an abrupt halt. It was in this atmosphere that the parties of the left broke through the pandemonium. Breathing the fire of 1848, they pushed their way through the throngs and rushed to the Hôtel de Ville to proclaim, once more in the name of France, a republic. It was decided that a Government of National Defense would be set up, choosing as its members deputies who had been elected by the Department of the Seine—a decision that, as

Michael Howard has written, placed, as so often before, "the country firmly in the hands of the moderate left."[39] It was these delegates who, after all, commanded, albeit shakily, the confidence of the city. But there was, with respect to this new government, a dangerous duality of authority. The government could function as the repository of state power only in the city of Paris, and even within the government itself there was uncertainty—no ordered relationship, no intimacy, no consensus.[40]

This situation had two major implications from the standpoint of Prussia. First, it meant that the new regime's chances for political stability were small indeed. Plainly, such a state of affairs could not endure for long. The fall of the Second Empire had been only a prelude to a struggle for real power. Particularly ominous was the fact that, among large sections of the French public, attachment to the principles of the provisional government was weak or nonexistent. The common people had little conception of what the new government stood for. Many in the provinces were not sure that left-wing republicans ought to have any share at all in the political life of the state. Only in the limited urbane circles of Paris, soon to be left isolated from the rest of the country, was there any real conception of political stability.[41]

Second, this situation meant that the prospects for France's continued participation in the war were unclear. The attempt to continue the war would have taxed the resources of even a unified and firmly entrenched regime. The idea that such a war effort could be carried out by a government lacking real authority over the troops, acting through officials who had no contact whatsoever with the rank and file—this in the face of the fact that large masses of soldiers were war-weary and largely indifferent to the issues of the war, and in the face of the further fact that a number of the members of the provisional government were already committed to the view that the war was an imperialist one, serving no purpose other than to glorify Napoleon III and his court—was among the complications that inflamed the situation at the beginning of September 1870.[42]

It is now time to introduce the leading figures of the new provisional Government of National Defense that was established on 4 September 1870, and one might as well start with its president, the figure who was, by unanimous vote of his colleagues, installed as its governor of Paris, who served as commander of the forces defending the capital but quickly switched sides on the news of defeat, and who, from 4 September 1870 to 22 January 1871, was the de facto head of state: Louis Jules Trochu.[43] It is difficult to state briefly and succinctly the outstanding features of the personality of this extraordinary child of the Franco-Prussian War. But some of these characteristics should be mentioned. To begin with, Trochu was a general of long and distinguished experience that reached back to Algeria in the 1830s and the Crimean War twenty years after that. Trochu had published *L'armée française en 1867*, a devastating polemic that addressed the state of the armed forces at the time. The book was a sensation, running through sixteen editions in three weeks and creating as much a stir in political circles as it did in military ones. From that time on, Trochu never lost interest in the reform of the army, in the Prussian army, and in the military difficulties that would attend any Franco-Prussian confrontation. For these and other reasons, it was only natural that Trochu would enjoy strong support among the politicians who came to power in Paris on 4 September 1870.

Certain of Trochu's papers are reproduced in extenso in his *Oeuvres posthumes* and in the extensive series *Enquête parlementaire sur les actes du Gouvernement de la Défense Nationale*, published in 1873 by the committee of the French legislature that investigated the conduct of his government during the war. One gains from these materials a clear and detailed picture of Trochu, the military governor. It is a picture of a serious, honorable, dedicated, and highly competent officer—a man of distinguished bearing, tenacious, yet tactful, excellently qualified for the highest tasks of military staff work. It appeared, at least at first, that France could consider itself fortunate to have at hand at this crucial time an official of such qualities. Industrious, studious, a man of facts and figures, accustomed to doing his homework and familiarizing himself thoroughly with the actual facts of any problem by which he was faced, Trochu not only was a distinguished general in the military sense but showed—again at least initially—a marked talent for organization and administration. His work in a wide variety of fields brought him into close contact with many elements of the financial and diplomatic worlds and the municipal state bureaucracy. To be sure, the history of the later French attempts to outdo the Prussians and to allow an army of more than one hundred thousand men to break out of Paris show him to have been dreadfully enmeshed in the entanglements of that incredible confusion. But that episode lay in the future. For the period immediately after the September revolution, we have before us only this impressive and informed figure: dignified, industrious, highly persistent, everywhere respected—the waxwork model of a superior military officer. Behind that—only a question mark.

Some idea of the austere aloofness and the impressiveness of General Trochu can be gained from the vivid description of him offered by an anonymous staffer at the time he took power in Paris. The most notable things about him were his bald head, thick moustache, and long goatee. There was always a look of concentrated attention in his eyes, but from time to time they blinked with a nervous tic, and he was always wont to pluck his moustache with an ungloved hand. With sharp, blinking eyes he looked out upon the world; his practice of smoking cigars and drinking brandy after long days of exacting work gave his cheeks a veined and purple look. As he passed through crowds, onlookers would raise their hats, and he would return the salutation politely, like a man of very high rank, some Prince of the Church, who, knowing that he might excite envy, was at pains to disarm it by the perfection of his manners.

No mention of Trochu and his activities in the provisional government would be complete without a word about the figure who sought to guide his steps from the time he assumed power and who served as the minister of the interior (and, later, of war) in the cabinet over which he presided: Léon Gambetta.[44] The personality of Gambetta (1839–82) and his role in French politics during this period are so well known that one shrinks from once again recounting them, but certain features will stand a word or two of comment. An orator and publicist of the highest capacity, ambitious and young—he was thirty when he snatched from the hands of his languid colleagues the vital post of minister of the interior—Gambetta was a firebrand, a romantic, and withal a man of great physical vigor. He seemed a character straight out of a Jack London novel. Magnetic, vibrant, somewhat lonely, given to fierce loyalties and equally fierce suspicions, Gambetta dominates the history of the five months of the provisional government, romanticizing—not without a touch of genius—itself and everything with which it came into conflict,

General Louis Jules Trochu, governor of Paris, president, Government of National Defense.
(von Pflugk-Harttung, *The Franco-German War*, 267.)

communicating a curious unreality to the whole story, lending to it, for the historian, a tinge of fiction instead of history. He was charismatic, a man with a sense of mission, destined, or so he believed, to lead his country in the moment of supreme danger. His youth, at the time he assumed his position, only strengthened this attitude. According to a contemporary: "There was authority even in his laughter. Before him the will bowed even if the intelligence was not conquered, and it seemed as natural for others to obey as for him to command."[45]

In 1870, Gambetta was a man who was, as the saying goes, feeling his oats. Born in the southwestern city of Cahors, famous for its good wines, Gambetta was very much the product of his environment. The color and beauty of the south of France produced an impression that was never to leave him. Having lost his left eye in an accident early in his life, he came to Paris in 1857 to study law. Here, being both a republican and a devout Christian, he became a political and religious evangelist, throwing himself into republican causes. Among other things, he took part in the defense of the journalist Louis Charles Delescluze, a gifted and energetic figure, who was prosecuted successfully—albeit mercilessly and ruthlessly—by Napoleon III's government for supporting an opponent of the coup d'état of 2 December 1851, by means of which Napoleon had destroyed the constitution and established himself as dictator. It was during that trial that Gambetta took advantage of a number of qualities that fitted him well for the role he now assumed—abundant energy, considerable forensic ability, some acquaintance with the labor movement in France, and a lively interest in the French revolutionary tradition. His picture of France in 1870 had been gained from deep and intense experiences as an opponent of the imperial government, as well as from his strong sense of excitement about the new republic that had just been stitched together, and these impressions combined to produce in him a state of metaphysical exaltation conducive more to enthusiasm than to discrimination as he approached his tasks.

As well, Gambetta possessed other certain personal characteristics that made it difficult for him to fit easily into the confused pattern of relationships and responsibilities that marked the Government of National Defense at this time. He suffered, for one thing, from an inability to find any middle ground between the extremes of passionate loyalty to and dark suspicion of his counterparts. He was an actor, a sentimentalist, but with it all a man of great force of character, exceptional intellectual and physical vigor, and—above all—unquestionable idealism. He threw himself into problems with that boundless self-confidence that was always characteristic of him but that was often belied by his tendency to underestimate their magnitude, by his tendency to inattention of detail, and by that inclination toward self-indulgence that many of his colleagues always mocked. It was from this background that Gambetta derived his almost religious fervor and his faith in the republican tradition, but it was also from this background that he derived that lack of roundness, of tolerance, and of patience with the sad necessities of his country's political existence that was to make his career as a figure in the provisional government so stormy, so episodic, and, in the end, so tragic.

In leaving for the moment the subject of Léon Gambetta, it might be well to glance also at the activities during this period of another personality that will be frequently mentioned in connection with him, a man who was to play a leading role in the negotiations between the provisional government and the enemy. This was none other than Jules Favre, who held the offices both of vice president and of minister for foreign affairs.[46] For the four decades from 1848 until his death, in 1890, Favre was a prominent and, in many ways, a unique figure on the French political scene. Born in 1809, brilliantly educated in the classics and humanities generally, elected in 1848 from his native district of Lyon to a seat in the constituent assembly of the Second Republic, Favre was to remain a parliamentary deputy for many years—until he became a senior figure in the Paris government that overthrew the Second Empire. Favre was in all respects an excellent tactician and parliamentarian; and it was in dealing with parliamentary issues, rather than in the rough-and-tumble world of party politics, that he was most at home. He had, like Gambetta, an outstanding ability as a parliamentary speaker, even inaugurating, in this capacity, a new style of oratory, often florid, sometimes burdened with classical quotations, but still addressed to the subject matter at hand. Very tall, slightly stooped, with long white hair and an even longer free-flowing beard, he was always an impressive and distinguished figure at his post.

Favre had no doubt that measure of self-esteem—or even of ambition, if

Léon Gambetta, minister of interior, Government of National Defense. (von Pflugk-Harttung, *The Franco-German War*, 606.)

not of will—without which no one rises (or perhaps should even rise) to emi-
nence under a democratic system, but this was not the ruthless ambition of
the power-hungry parvenu. Perceptive, nimble, possessed of a sensitive mind
and a keen imagination, he yet remained, throughout his career, the lawyer
and the parliamentarian rather unsuited to the world of high politics. He
was, on the whole, "independent" in his political thinking. His undeviating
attention to the principle of republican-democratic rule kept him from as-
sociation with parties of the right; his innate conservatism held him similarly
aloof from those of the radical left. He found his most suitable (if not always
comfortable) place on the moderate flank of the liberal "centre gauche." He
seems to have enjoyed universal respect, even on the part of his most deeply
committed political opponents, but he was now called upon to assume high
executive office at a time of great external stress and danger, only to find
himself rejected, sometimes quite unjustly, in the intervening doldrums of
political squabbling and maneuvering.

Favre's gifts as a parliamentarian and speaker need no emphasis here, but
one of his great weaknesses (or what I view as weaknesses) ought to be noted
in this connection. This was a tendency to exaggerate and overdramatize any
incipient dangers when he saw, or fancied that he saw, France being ex-
posed, badly treated, to appear more alarmed and concerned than the situation demanded, rather than use the occasion to haggle and negotiate. He
hoped by these means to give those he saw as authors of these threats the
impression that France could be roused to major violent, defensive action
and to encourage them to conclude that they had thus started more than they
had bargained for and had best quickly back down. Usually courteous and
conciliatory in official contacts, he was nonetheless emotional, highly strung,
and given to compulsive volubility. When he took over the post of foreign
minister, he was relatively new to the problems of diplomacy, and this often
made him appear inexperienced, naïve, and erratic. He liked to play the he-
roic party, believing that he would nip in the bud tendencies that, if allowed
to develop, could become truly threatening to France's interests. Sometimes
this worked; sometimes it redounded to France's detriment.

Such were the three outstanding figures in the Government of National
Defense. But there was one other among the personalities prominent in Paris
at the time when it was formed who deserves mention. He was not a member

Jules Favre, minister of foreign affairs, Government of National Defense. (von Pflugk-Harttung, *The Franco-German War*, 603.)

of the new government. He appears only briefly and incidentally in the sequence of events to which this chapter refers. Yet his figure is so much a part of the setting and his reactions so intimately revealing of the difficulties the French now faced that no such survey seems complete without him. The reference is to that tireless diplomat whose experiences spanned four decades of French political life: Louis Adolphe Thiers.[47]

Thiers needs no introduction to the student of this period. Born in 1797 to neither wealth nor title, the son, in fact, of a man who held the deceptively modest position of a locksmith who lived at Marseilles but had traveled in the Levant, Thiers nevertheless had the good fortune to be educated at two of France's finest institutions: the Lycée de Marseilles and then the law school of Aix-en-Provence. Entering the bar immediately upon graduating from the school at Aix, he soon embarked on a journalistic career that included a year of service at the *Constitutionnel*, a liberal organ. As well as a publicist and journalist of the highest capacity, Thiers was also a famous (if not always an accurate and reliable) historian. His *Histoire de la Révolution française*—consisting of ten fat volumes written between 1823 and 1827—was widely read in Paris and elsewhere, and its influence, if the history of Carlyle be excepted, probably outweighed that of all the other histories of the revolution during that time.

Despite these academic predilections, Thiers was gradually drawn to the world of politics. In his early views of internal affairs Thiers was a moderate conservative and in foreign affairs a nationalist. His affinity for King Louis-Philippe led him, on 22 February 1839, to be called to the prime ministership of his country, where he found himself faced with a series of terrible and complex problems. Outstanding among these was a nasty crisis in the Near East into which had been drawn all the Great Powers of Europe, save France. They were pitted against Mehmet Ali, the reformist pasha of Egypt, who had managed to detach himself from the control of his master, the sultan of Turkey. Thiers's sentiments, for a number of reasons that need not be gone into here, ran strongly toward Mehmet Ali and against the other Great Powers of Europe. A war scare with Prussia arose, and hostilities with that country were averted only when, in October 1840, Thiers was dismissed by Louis-Philippe.

The following years were again taken up with writing. But in 1848 Thiers

Louis Adolphe Thiers, skilled French negotiator. (von Pflugk-Harttung, *The Franco-German War*, 605.)

returned to the political scene and supported Louis Napoleon Bonaparte in the presidential election of December of that year—a stroke that did not commend him handsomely to the victor, with whose policies, especially after they, in 1852, became imperial sovereign, he grew increasingly disenchanted. In the crisis of July 1870, he offered up his services to Napoleon III in the hope of averting war between France and Prussia. But his offer, though sincere and genuine, was received with suspicion and then rejected by Napoleon III's government. He continued to comment widely on the crisis, and his views were by no means devoid of merit. No historian who has studied this period can read without deep admiration and sympathy the words with which Thiers, in July 1870, endeavored to explain to his countrymen how it was possible that an intense interest in averting war with Prussia did not necessarily mean sympathy with Bismarck or a desire to see him succeed in the promotion of his European aspirations. Though of course saddened by the debacle of Sedan, Thiers was not sorry to see the revolution of 4 September 1870. His policies had, he believed, been vindicated.

A small and bespectacled man, with a shrewd, trouble-lined face and quick penetrating eyes, careful and conventional, but not elegant in dress and walking with a slight stoop, Thiers was consistently underrated by the more high-powered figures in the courts of Europe. In the days immediately after the September revolution, he was often criticized by his contemporaries for colorlessness and timidity, but, as the months passed, he gradually won their almost universal respect. All who knew him seem to have been impressed by his deep experience, his calm judgment, and the reliability of his word. No one ever questioned his honesty or integrity. Even Bismarck, not predisposed to uncritical enthusiasm for any foreign statesman, came gradually to respect him. He stands, on close examination, as one of the most interesting and impressive figures in the history of French diplomacy.

Thiers's immediate concern was to reconcile the differences among his colleagues in a way that would win them the confidence of the powers in the government they had formed. With a view to doing so, he developed what he considered a hatred for "indoor knowledge." He was constantly on the move, dashing from one place to another, seeing an extraordinary number of people. He unquestionably saw more foreign diplomats during the month of September 1870 than any official member of the provisional government, and, while this experience did not always lead to accurate judgment on his part, at least it enabled him to avoid a number of erroneous impressions that influenced the thinking of his governmental counterparts.

So much for Thiers and the men who made up the provisional government. In dealing with them and their persons, I have tried to be less dogmatic about them than they often tended to be about one other, to remember that they were often harried, pressed, groaning under the limitations of physical and nervous strength, weighed down by the multitudinous pressures of high position. All of them will not always appear at their best, but it is pleasant to record that, though they were acting in bewildering and trying circumstances, there were none who sought personal gain from the situation, none who forgot for an instant the interests of his country, and none who did other than to follow, with courage and conviction, the voice of honest conscience.

5

Ferrières

As for Bismarck, his immediate problem in the first days of September 1870 was what it was to be throughout the coming four months: namely with which French government should he negotiate? Still relatively uninvolved in matters affecting Moltke and his officers, he was understandably concerned that the government of the North German Confederation now analyze correctly the problems it faced with respect to post-Sedan France and that it devise policies designed to hold to a minimum the prospect of foreign intervention resulting from the military and political situation to which this stage of the war had led. For this reason, not only did he fill his private letters with the record of his various anxieties, but he plagued whomsoever might be prepared to listen to them, primarily the king, with protests, urgings, and appeals of all sorts on matters of policies. The number of documents that poured forth from his pen was, one can say, so great as to preclude an extensive analysis of them in such a volume as this. But, since the thoughts they set forth were ones that would, during the months to come, enter prominently into various statements he would make, it might be well to summarize them here.[1]

Bismarck continued, throughout the immediate period that followed Sedan, to be an advocate—and the only advocate, one supposes, in the top echelons of his governmental service—for a prompt and clearly formulated armistice, which would be the first step on the path toward making peace. But his efforts in this regard were hampered grievously by the ominous new developments on the French side of the line. The ministers of the new government, with the possible exception of Thiers, were convinced that the war had been unleashed by Napoleon III and his chauvinistic underlings—by

them and no one else. It was they who had launched what in the eyes of the
new Paris government was an imperialist war, but these people now had van-
ished from the seat of power. Among the senior figures of the new republic,
the underlying thinking was this: there should be a just peace. By this they
meant a peace without annexations or indemnities; the peace should involve
not only the abandonment by the government of the North German Confederation and its allies of whatever plans and aspirations for any territorial
aggrandizement they might have entertained as one of the fruits of victory in
the war but also a prompt return of all prisoners that they had taken. And this
view was to shape French policy in the three months that followed. Not until
every conceivable possibility for support had been probed and failed could
the French leaders be brought to face the bitter fact that it was they, as much
as Napoleon III, who had lost the war and that losing it would come with a
price. Paris simply could not bring itself to realize this. On the contrary, Favre
and his colleagues believed with a zeal approaching religious intensity that
the Prussians would now rule out any territorial annexations. The assumption on which such thinking was based was utterly erroneous. No one who
knew anything about the Prussian government could imagine for a moment
that the revolution of 4 September would modify in any significant way its
attitudes toward the conflict. This would become apparent to all in the weeks
that followed.[2]

In an interview of 5–6 September with the representatives of Great Britain,
Italy, and Austria-Hungary, Favre made this view unmistakably clear, telling
the ambassadors that, with regard to territorial concessions by the new government, there could be no question of anything of the sort and that, if the
Prussians were to insist on this, there would be *"guerre à outrance."*[3] This
was part and parcel of Favre's policy to persuade the neutral powers to mediate an end to the war, and, with a view to this effort, in the days after Sedan,
he came in closer contact with the members of the diplomatic missions just
mentioned, particularly with that of the British ambassador, Lord Richard
Lyons. On the evening of 6 September, he took a further step. Succumbing

for the first, though not for the last, time to his emotions, he came out with a sensational circular that ended with the words: "We will not yield an inch of our territory or a stone of our fortresses!"[4]

What moved him to do this and at this particular time? It was unquestionably his encounter with the three ambassadors just noted and what he considered to be the salutary results that flowed from it. The meeting further convinced him that there was a real possibility of dealing successfully with the Prussian authorities at least on certain matters (e.g., the preservation of the territorial integrity of France) and of exerting upon them—through the neutral powers of Europe—the impression that these powers were prepared to give France aid of various sorts. The contents of Favre's circular, which was dispatched to the chancelleries of the powers, are worth reviewing at this point, both because of the circular's lasting influence on Bismarck, William I, and the Prussian generals (with Moltke, of course, at their head) and as a reflection of the political atmosphere of the time.[5]

The circular began with a bitter and plaintive acknowledgment of the difficulties in which the French, because of the mistakes of the previous government, now found themselves. But were these difficulties really so great? Were they—all of them—really insurmountable? By no means. The new government, infused with the spirit of young republicanism, was up to the challenge it faced. It was not, Favre wrote, abstract principles that should guide the new government "but rather that which is dear to the heart of everyone, namely the good of the fatherland."[6] France had its own individuality. It was not to be compared to other countries. The French republican idea was sui generis. As if to underline this, Favre chose to close his circular with a paragraph of devastating words addressed to the subject of Franco-Prussian relations:

> The King of Prussia has declared war not on France but on the dynasty which has gone. France has survived. Does the King of Prussia want to continue this war which will be no less fatal to him than to us? Free of him, we can assume our responsibilities. But if he wishes to defy us, we will accept the challenge. Before God, who has blessed us, and before posterity who will judge us, we only want peace, but if we are forced to continue this terrible war, which we have condemned, we will, knowing the righteousness of our cause, fulfill our duty to the very end.[7]

This circular was nothing short of remarkable because it was written precisely at the time when Favre was seeking to negotiate with Bismarck. To be sure, he evidently thought it important to avoid the impression that either he or the members of the provisional government were unduly influenced by the defeat at Sedan. Still, it is quite impossible to take the reasoning of Favre's circular at its face value because of the unsubstantiality of the factual premises upon which it was based. The image of reality put forward there as a foundation for a peace was almost wholly unreal. As noted earlier, it made absolutely no difference to Bismarck which French government had launched the war. The war had been launched by the French nation with almost universal enthusiasm, and the new French government must urgently come to grips with this unpleasant fact.[8]

But that was not all. The form and the terms of the circular were plainly meant to be offensive to the Prussian government. And the Prussian high command was not to be trifled with in this manner. Already deeply engaged in preparations for a prolonged siege of Paris, Moltke could not tolerate the uncertainty in which diplomatic negotiations would have left the Prussian front. As for Bismarck, the rapid degeneration of the French revolution into a new form of authoritarianism, animated by a violent preconceived hostility toward Prussia and its allies, was a phenomenon for which he was not immediately prepared. In any case, he now sought to disabuse the French of any illusions that they could have a peace such as that contemplated by Favre's circular. His initial reaction was one of alarm and indignation, coupled with the not inconsiderable doubt that the new masters of the French capital would succeed in holding power for any length of time. On 11 September 1870, he expressed himself in an announcement that appeared on his instruction in the Rheims newspapers: "The German Government could enter into relations with the Emperor Napoleon, whose Government is the only one it has recognized hitherto or with the Regency he appointed; it would also be able to treat with Marshall Bazaine, who has his command from the Emperor. But it is impossible to say what justification the German Government would have in treating with a power which *up to now* represents only a part of the Left wing of the former French assembly."[9]

These were not empty words. The written record reveals that Bismarck had indeed discussed with the king and with his advisers the situation that had arisen in Paris as a consequence of the events of 4 September, the effect of that new situation upon the conduct of the war, and the attitude to be adopted by Prussia toward it. A French observer at the Prussian headquarters put it thus: "One can understand the consciences of the people who have apparently just taken power in France. But abroad, where a coldblooded judgment must be rendered, it is hard to see that Prussia, having just won such an overwhelming victory, could conclude a peace that did not require cessions of territory. Favre's declaration comes at a bad time. Such a fiery expression as this will complicate appreciably the process of peacemaking."[10] Yet, Bismarck was careful not to burn his bridges behind him; for this reason he deliberately inserted the qualifying words *"up to now"* in the hope that the members of the provisional government would see that he might *not* break off altogether and treat only with intermediaries of the deposed regime.

Still, Favre's circular, even if it emanated from a government about whose durability Bismarck remained profoundly uncertain, could not go unanswered. In two communications, one on 12 September, the other on 16 September, the French ministers were warned in searing terms that German security required territorial cessions along the Franco-German border and that no peace could be concluded until the fortresses of Metz and Strasbourg were firmly in Prussian hands. But this statement did not deter Favre. Despite the problems created by his circular of 6 September, he continued to work intently and behind the scenes to establish formal contact with the Prussian side. Through the instrumentality of the British embassy and without the knowledge of his colleagues, he opened a channel of communication that was eventually to lead to an interview with the North German minister president. Both Lyons and Granville were pleased by Favre's *démarche*, and it was understandable that this should be so.[11] The British were haunted, particularly at this time, by the fear that the Russians might use the conflict between France and Prussia as a means to upset the status quo in the Near East. Their anxieties were given fresh stimulus in the middle of September when Sir Andrew Buchanan, their representative at Petersburg, reported that the tsar and his ministers were planning an announcement the effect of which would be to annul those provisions of the Treaty of Paris of 1856 that concerned the neutralization of the Black Sea. In any case, the British energetically and enthusiastically took up Favre's offer and, through Bernstorff, the North German minister, pressed it on Bismarck.[12]

The British proposal, not unexpectedly, met with an intensely interested reception on Bismarck's side. But his main problem for the moment was to clarify questions that were hanging fire before he could enter into diplomatic intercourse with the foreign secretary of the provisional government. On 16 September, while all the figures at the Prussian headquarters were still buzzing with excitement over Favre's defiant circular ten days earlier, Bismarck reached for his pen and the next day put on the wires to the foreign office a series of points that, on his instruction, were to appear in the press. These may stand as a statement of Bismarck's thought on the eve of the crucial negotiations with Favre into which he was about to enter and must therefore be quoted at length:

> 1) The British are eager to know if I will agree to meet Jules Favre when he arrives; this I confirm; 2) Who governs in France is a matter of indifference to us; we would accept a French Republic if the French want it; 3) We must assume that authority in the occupied portions of France belongs to the Emperor because no other government has indicated otherwise; 4) Whether Bazaine [commander of the Army of the Rhine] owes his allegiance to the Emperor or to the Paris government is unclear because he has made no declaration to either effect; 5) Academic question: should the southern part of Alsace be turned over to the Swiss?[13]

The month of September 1870 represented substantially the highpoint of Prussian success on the battlefield. Yet, Bismarck, never one to let military affairs distort his view of the broader picture, quickly turned his attention to the prospect of making a satisfactory peace with France. On the French side, too, desire to make peace followed quickly on the heels of Sedan. The bareboned structure of the diplomatic documents does not reveal more than the smallest part of the intensity of this desire. Yet, unless the reader is aware of this intensity and of the human stresses and emotions it engendered, the documents themselves lose much of their meaning. We can, in my view, better understand this human dimension if we glance briefly at what was happening in the lives of the major participants at the French end of the struggle as reflected principally in the experiences of one such actor.

When Jules Favre, vice president and foreign minister for the Government of National Defense, crossed the Seine on the night of 18 September, in the muggy, oppressive heat that is so characteristic of France in the late summer, he must have been greatly excited by the consciousness of his own importance. He was presumably the bearer of a message of great importance concerning the state of the new government in light of the overthrow of Napoleon III. He also presumably had in his pocket or somewhere on his person a highly confidential draft for a peace between France and Prussia—so confidential that he had seen fit not to reveal its contents to his own colleagues. Never mind his circular of 6 September. Never mind what Bismarck had said by way of reply to that circular a week later. Never mind that Bismarck had called into question the legitimacy of the government Favre purported to represent. Favre's imagination brushed aside all such obstacles, and political imaginations in those days of romantic nationalism were nothing if not feverish. One can imagine with what hope Favre set out on his journey and with what glowing satisfaction he—a talented, if frustrated, man with a great passion for oratory and drama—must have said to himself as he approached the site of his rendezvous: "Ah, I will bring back peace to my country."[14]

The meetings between Bismarck and Favre occurred at the great Rothschild castle of Ferrières, about thirty miles east of the beleaguered French capital. The palace was by no means an unfit setting for negotiations as important as these. With more than two hundred rooms, a magnificent chandelier overhanging an equally magnificent ballroom, a great dining table with more than one hundred chairs, a lake modeled upon that of Versailles, Ferrières was indeed an imposing edifice. No actual written record of the meeting has survived, but a number of secondhand accounts, together with what we already know of Favre's state of mind and aspirations of the moment, permit us to arrive at the following as a reasonably accurate summary of what, generally speaking, was said.[15]

The two met in the white house of the mansion, a small castle near the street, on the evening of 19 September and again on the afternoon of 20 September. Favre wasted no time in getting down to brass tacks, and

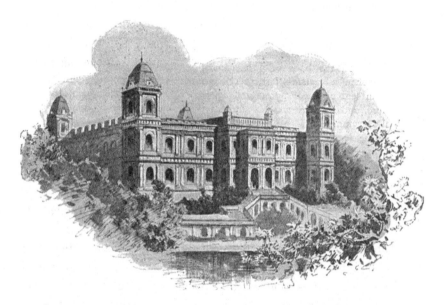

Castle Ferrières, scene of Bismarck–Favre negotiations. (von Pflugk-Harttung, *The Franco-German War*, 607.)

he now presented to Bismarck his view of what a peace between France and Prussia should look like. It must at least embody three points. The first was an armistice on the basis of the status quo. The Prussians had gone to war with the Second Empire; they had destroyed it. Surely they had no quarrel with the Phoenix of Republican France. His second point was that, in order to give legitimacy to the new government, elections must now at once be held. This would be in Prussia's interest; it was, in fact, Bismarck's desire that such elections take place as soon as possible. Third, Favre emphasized his desire for a peace between France and Prussia on the basis of a mediation by the other powers, where other outstanding questions could be settled in a way "that would lead to an honorable peace."[16] Precisely what questions Favre had in mind he did not say, but it was by no means unlikely that, knowing of the Russian dissatisfaction with the Treaty of Paris of 1856, he hoped that a congress would address this issue. As he put it in a note to the French minister to Russia: "In such a situation, the great honor of Russia will be engaged."[17]

So much for Favre's statement of the French position. There are one or two points of it that bear particular notice. The first of these was the belief, unfounded in the extreme, that the Prussian officials, having expended such an enormous amount of time and energy on their war effort and having, at Sedan, seen the extent of their success, would now quietly and unhesitatingly lay down their arms or that the Prussian generals or the German people, for that matter, would allow them to do so. Second, it is apparent from the last of Favre's points that the French had by no means given up their determination to bring in the neutrals—the last thing Bismarck wanted. And, finally, one must ponder the significance of the fact that, in this entire presentation, no attention whatsoever was given to the statements made in Bismarck's circulars of 12 and 16 September. The foreign minister, having come to Ferrières without the knowledge of his colleagues, was apparently fearful of saying or doing anything that might compromise his position.[18]

How were these oversights to be explained? The answer lies surely in the amateurism, the ignorance, and the emotional erraticism of the figures agitating for peace on the French side. Favre's proposals embodied the views of such people. Only people of such limitations could have indulged themselves in the illusion that Bismarck could be induced to forget all the redundant evidences of German opinion concerning border security, to accept the possibility of dangerous estrangement from the king should he do so, and, not least, to bring down upon his head the concerted wrath of the Prussian generals— and all this just for the sake of helping the creaky republican government save for France territory to which it believed the nation was entitled by history.[19]

At this point, Bismarck took leave of Favre to seek a meeting with the king, during the course of which he explained the French intransigence and his reply to it. Favre, Bismarck was convinced, wanted a peace that no German could rationally accept. It was a peace of phantasmagoria. It assumed that the war that had been fought was a war between Napoleon III and the Prussians, that the replacement of the former by the provisional government had settled every question under the sun, and that there could now follow a reconciliation of the two sides as a result of which all problems were now soluble. The one great source of evil—the imperial dynasty—had been crushed; the forces of good could now sweep forward unimpeded; and all worthy ambitions could be satisfied—this is precisely Favre's picture of the situation, and it was this picture that Bismarck painted for William I. Bismarck was able, without any difficulty at all, of course, to win the backing of the king. That backing having been secured, he arranged to meet Favre in the afternoon of the next day for further discussion.[20]

At this meeting, Bismarck made a set of proposals that, from the standpoint of clarity, left absolutely nothing to be desired. They were these: an armistice of fourteen days and the election of a national assembly, but nothing that would allow the French to develop the use of their arms or any other radical and far-reaching means of destruction along lines of which the Prussians were unaware and against which they might be helpless if taken by surprise. The military and German security demanded no less. As well, the fortresses of Toul and Strasbourg must be turned over to Prussia and, if Paris was to be replenished with respect to stores and supplies, all forts surrounding the city must be placed unconditionally in Prussian hands. In addition, to forestall the revenge on which Bismarck calculated the French would be forever bent, they must surrender "the key to our house"[21]—Alsace, as Favre put it, and about half of the province of Lorraine, including the fortresses of Metz and Château-Salins.[22]

Toward the end of the interview, the French minister, who had been containing himself with increasing difficulty as the session progressed, finally lost patience. Rising from his seat, he unburdened himself of a veritable tirade of accusation and abuse against Bismarck and his associates, charging them with being bandits who were bent on despoiling the sacred soil of the French nation. Others in the room were shocked and attempted to restrain their violent guest. But Bismarck was content to leave him alone. Favre thereupon tore away, made for the door, and rounded on his Prussian host by screaming: "You mean to destroy France. I made a mistake coming here . . . it is to be an endless struggle between two peoples who ought to stretch out their hands to each other. I had hoped for another solution."[23] With this, he stormed back to Paris.

Bismarck later that evening set down his impression of the meeting in a long memorandum to the foreign ministry in Berlin. He was, he wrote, at a loss to explain Favre's attitude and behavior. Surely, he reasoned, Favre had read and studied his circulars of 12 and 16 September. Moreover, not only had he agreed to see him, but he had spent the bulk of his time during two interviews trying to make him understand the nature of the phenomena with which he, at the Prussian headquarters, was daily confronted and which the provisional government and its representatives had to learn to understand if there were to be any chance of coping successfully with the problem of fruitful negotiations. So far as Bismarck was concerned, it had, to all intents and purposes, been like talking to a stone. Bismarck's reaction to the collapse of the Ferrières negotiations was certainly natural, indeed, unavoidable. And it did raise the question—and it was a question that was to plague Bismarck over the course of the ensuing months—whether a government so conceived was capable of conducting a mature, consistent, and discriminating foreign policy.[24]

The final Prussian terms to which the French minister was asked to set his signature on 20 September 1870 have frequently been represented as outrageously onerous. Considering that these terms came after three months of warfare for the outbreak of which the French shared at least a considerable measure of responsibility and that France was, from the Prussian view, in effect a defeated power; considering also that the French had made it clear that they would accept no terms other than those that amounted to a *status quo ante bellum* (in other words, the war might as well never have been fought), it is difficult to find justification for so extreme a view. The French, in the meantime, were growing increasingly desperate. (In fact, at this very time, calls were filling the air for a mass expulsion of the enemy; it was suggested that Paris's notorious *filles* could be let loose on the Prussians in a venereal version of germ warfare.)[25] These unnerving gestures, of which Bismarck was not unaware, made it essential to take every possible precaution. The requirement that the French government should turn over to the Prussians the great fortress of Metz was indeed a cruel cut to Favre, but it was not an unreasonable demand to be imposed on a defeated country at a crucial moment during which the French were to arrange for elections. To this it must be added that Favre entered into these negotiations with a faith that can, in the most charitable description, only be called naïve. In his two interviews with Bismarck, he distorted the facts (military and political) so fantastically as to indicate either great ignorance or a desire to make mischief. His view of the terms for an armistice, in particular, afforded no rationale for the mounting of a special aid program for Paris itself and roused in the minds of the leading senior figures on the Prussian side, civilian as well as military, only the harshest and most unconditional of attitudes. A negotiated settlement with the French was, in their opinion, sheer fantasy, a pipedream. Verdy, Moltke's chief of intelligence, noted on 20 September: "The demands we shall have to make on France are so heavy that the French people will not give up so easily, no matter what government is at the helm."[26] Roon, the minister of war, was of the same opinion: "We can, for the sake of our people and our security, conclude no peace that does not dismember France, and the French government, whatever it may be, can for its people's sake make no peace that does not preserve France's inheritance intact. There necessarily follows the continuation of the war till the exhaustion of our forces."[27] Blumenthal, a prominent general, was of the opinion that "they should treat the French as a conquered army and demoralize them to the utmost of our ability. We ought to crush them so they will not be able to breathe for a hundred years."[28]

Bismarck did not share these views, but he could ignore them only at great peril to his position as a principal adviser to the crown. The accent, he believed, must be put on Prussian security while the French prepared for elections that would give a government—the government—the legitimacy without which Bismarck rightly believed it could not legally claim to represent France. As Eberhard Kolb has pointed out, the terms imposed by the allies upon Germany in 1918 were infinitely harsher than those Bismarck unsuccessfully sought to impose on the French in 1870. That the Germans accepted these terms flowed from the fact that they knew that they were a defeated power. In 1870, this was not so. The French had been defeated, but they could not—it must be said once more—be brought to face this fact.[29]

In the meantime, Favre returned to Paris. Upon his return, there was a great explosion of opinion, the result of which was decidedly depressing to Bismarck.[30] This explosion was the result of an article that appeared on 20 September in the sensationalist newspaper *Electeur Libre* and that recounted in detail the conditions for an armistice that Bismarck had set down the day earlier. How the editors of this paper managed to acquire such information and in such a short span of time is not exactly known, but, since the piece reflected in overwhelming degree the position of the more sensationalist members of the provisional government, it is not improbable that it emanated from their lips or hands.[31] The origins did not matter; the consequences could not be escaped. Uproar followed. Demonstrations broke out in the streets in an orgy of heavy drinking, sexual adventures, and wanton violence. The cup of Parisian anger, so amply filled by memories of Napoleon III and Sedan, now seemed dangerously close to spilling over. Aside from the natural annoyance that sprang from Favre's having kept them in the dark, his colleagues were quick to dismiss the entire Ferrières business out of hand. It is doubtful they spent so much as a few minutes' discussion on the whole matter.[32] Nor did they worry themselves over the fact that the siege of the city was about to begin. Trochu and Gambetta, in particular, believed that the siege, if it ever occurred at all, would be over in a week, broken by a phalanx of republican armies.[33] But what armies? No matter; armies, if they did not now exist, could at once be raised. Paris was divinely sanctioned. There was no cause for alarm. In fact, there was a certain thrill and adventure in all of it. As Henry Markheim, a young Oxford graduate teaching English in the city, put it: "Paris is in the feverish state of a man about to fight a duel: we puff at our cigars, flourish riding whips, look at ourselves in the glass, and ask for seconds."[34]

In the meantime, Bismarck's view of the situation in Paris continued to blacken. Members of the provisional government were influenced, as he had occasion to point out to the king, not only by their desires of what would happen but by their estimates of what should happen. Bismarck, on the other hand, was determined to give no political concessions without a military equivalent. This was the note he struck in conversations with two formidable figures who had traveled to France to observe the situation on the battlefield: General Thomas Burnside, the hero of Fredericksburg, the site of a crucial battle in the American Civil War, and his friend and colleague the renowned British journalist Colonel Archibald Forbes. Both were men of superior character and intelligence; both wished to do what they could to bring the conflict to an end. On 6 October, they met with Bismarck at Versailles, the symbol of French greatness that the Prussians had, on 20 September, taken without so much as the firing of a shot. Possession of such a prize only added to the military's mood of hubris and exaltation. But Bismarck was more cautious, mindful always that his principal goal was to bring the war to a speedy end. The deadlock at Ferrières had given Bismarck the opportunity to ponder the situation with the provisional government. After some thinking, he decided to approach its members with another set of concrete proposals: an immediate, unconditional armistice of forty-eight hours, during which time the provisional government could issue a declaration calling for elections to a new constituent assembly and, prior to that, a semi-armistice of four weeks (except in Alsace and Lorraine), which the French could use with a view toward preparing for elections. This semi-armistice would be short enough to negate all talk of military equivalents to which Favre had so strenuously objected during the Ferrières visit. Such were the terms that underlay a preliminary paper that Bismarck presented to Burnside and Forbes on 6 October, inviting their attention to the difficulties Paris faced in the wake of the siege. This matter was the subject of several discussions over the course of the next few hours. In the end, it was decided that the two men would make an unofficial journey to Paris, the purpose of which would be to present Bismarck's new offer and to discuss with the French authorities the difficult and delicate problems of strategy with which they were faced.[35]

The visit of Burnside and Forbes duly took place on 8 October. On 10 October, the French reply was delivered to them. It could not have been more disappointing. The French flatly rejected Bismarck's proposal for a semi-armistice. An unconditional armistice lasting at least four weeks was the only arrangement they would consider. Not only that, but Paris must, during that time, be replenished with horses, food, and water. To such conditions, Bismarck, let alone Moltke, could, of course, never agree. Again, Bismarck's disappointment was profound. He had, he believed, really offered the new government a chance for a settlement. He had taken pains to meet Favre on two occasions at Ferrières and to use two interlocutors of the highest caliber as a means of effecting a new, if unofficial, channel of negotiations. His policy had failed singularly. For his effort to rescue something of the wreckage of the Ferrières negotiations the French had nothing but contempt. They simply did not believe it had really been put forward. They found it absurd to suppose that anything substantial was going to be changed by the idea of arranging a two-day armistice and by announcing that national elections would soon be held. All in all, Bismarck believed that the French, considering that the war had been an unnecessary and seriously bungled venture beyond their financial means, could well have accepted his proposals with good grace.[36]

But it was not to be. It was too soon for the new government to take kindly to the acknowledgment of overwhelming defeat. In fact, Paris was in no mood to pass the buck, and, as far as the great majority of its citizens were concerned, the buck stopped with Napoleon III. In the words of *Daily News* correspondent Henry Labouchère, a devout champion of the republic: "It is amusing to observe how everyone has entered into the conspiracy to persuade the world that the French nation never desired war—to hear them, one would suppose that the Rhine had never been called the natural frontier of France and that the war had been entered into by Badinguet as they style the late emperor, against the wishes of the army, the peasantry, and the bourgeoisie. Poor old Badinguet has enough to answer for already, but every sensible Frenchman has persuaded himself that he and he alone is responsible for war."[37] Republicans (or the most extreme of them), Labouchère speculated, never take kindly to defeat in war. Woe to the republican statesman who negotiates or signs a peace settlement that is anything less than a blatant triumph from the republican perspective. He is held personally responsible for the reverse, and his action is never fully forgiven.

For the Prussians, too, emotion was involved. The Austro-Prussian War had been a duel for power in which national feelings were only incidentally, if at all, aroused, and Bismarck may well have regarded the present conflict in the same light. Not so his countrymen. As Michael Howard has written: "For them it was a chance to pay off two centuries of old scores, besides redressing an uneasy feeling of inferiority buried in a thousand years of history. . . . If the Germans were still unappeased by victory, the French were still unconvinced of defeat."[38]

Hopeless as their military prospects were from any objective angle, the French leaders were still convinced that they could summon the population of an already war-weary land to drive the invaders from their soil. They were convinced even more strongly that they would eventually be supported by a general European intervention. They attributed Bismarck's stiff position at Ferrières to the fact that no real knowledge of their military position had become available to foreign governments. They therefore arrived at two major decisions of policy. First, since they were determined to fight, there was no sense in continuing to negotiate with the Prussians until such a time as international pressure could be brought to bear on them and upon Bismarck most of all to end the bloodshed. This meant that even if, for some reason, negotiations had to be resumed, the purpose of their diplomacy, from this point on, would be to stall for time. Second, with a view to scuttling any prospect for negotiations whatsoever, they determined to step up their campaign of inflammatory and propagandistic statements about the enemy. But this policy could work for only so long. As autumn progressed and the situation of the provisional government became more complicated and precarious, there came warnings from officials in the provinces that the assumptions upon which Paris's policy was based were becoming increasingly questionable. This was especially true of the masses in the provinces whose prefects sought to explain their problems to the capital. For example, Nantes's prefect proclaimed that the citizens would be better off as Prussians than as Frenchmen and on 22 September implored the senior figures of the government in Paris: "Make peace if you can. A plebiscite would ratify it."[39] As with Nantes, so with Mende: "The torpor of the Lozère country is really impossible to shake"; our people are "completely brutalized by the all powerful clergy of the country."[40]

The findings of these reports were not lost on so senior a figure as Gambetta. He noted in early October: "We must use all our resources . . . overcome foolish panics [and] multiply the partisans of war."[41] Such sentiments could be countered, it was felt in republican circles, only by a broadening of executive authority to the point that it could crush all opposition. "In keeping Imperial officials," groused one prefect, "we are losing France. . . . France can be saved by the Republic if the Republicans alone have the leadership. If you do not act thus, the Republicans will rise and insist that we shall have civil war."[42]

These descriptions are apt reminders of the condition of France in the autumn of 1870. One cannot understand this situation unless one understands the immense and hopeless bitterness by which various French political factions were divided from one another. Between the nobility, the monarchists, and the generals on the one hand and the republicans on the other, there was a gulf so profound, a hatred so deep, that one can describe the situation only as one of latent civil war. French society had literally come apart in the most serious of ways. Among the various elements, there was simply no bond of confidence whatsoever. Even the fact that they were all French appears to have meant nothing, except insofar as it made the treachery and duplicity of the other fellow even more heinous in the eyes of his opponents than would otherwise be the case. It is a disturbing experience to read the writings of the various French actors who were politically active at that time. Such a thing as charity or sympathy or human understanding in the judgment of others simply does not enter into the picture. Political opponents are invariably portrayed as fiends in human guise, devoid of redeeming characteristics. The writer is left as the sole repository of decent instinct, clear vision, and love of humankind. It is, in any case, to the credit of Bismarck that he was better informed at this juncture by his own instincts and convictions than by the expostulations of those who represented a country so torn, so confused, so full of desperation and impatience.[43]

There remains, if we are to complete the story of the events during the month of September, one important matter (already glanced at) to be recounted more fully. This concerns the question of relations between the Government of National Defense and the other powers of Europe. Here a word or two of background will not be out of place. The insistence on maintaining a diplomatic establishment in a foreign country is, of course, at variance with all diplomatic tradition and theory unless it is accompanied by actual recognition of the local sovereign authority. However one looks at it, the official representative in a foreign country is the guest of the local government. His privileges and facilities of residence flow only from its sufferance and favor and are dependent on its protection. Strictly speaking, if the governments represented by the diplomatic corps were not inclined to recognize the new Paris regime, they had no business asking its authorities (which by implication they did) to grant their official establishments the facilities and protection necessary to their continued functioning in that capacity. The anomaly of this situation was rendered even greater by the widely held view (among the supporters of Napoleon III) that the effect of maintaining diplomatic establishments in France was, in practice, to give ammunition to the provisional government and its sympathizers.[44]

But, in the days immediately following the revolution of 4 September, the situation was still too confused to admit of this logic. There still had been no formal notification to the foreign embassies of the establishment of a new regime. The new French authorities had yet to demonstrate, even to themselves, their ability to maintain power for any length of time. This made it difficult for the foreign representatives to arrive at any firm decisions. They continued to pursue, as best they could, the manifold activities, many of them wartime functions, in which they had been engaged: observing the course of events, conducting intelligence work, dispensing aid and advice to the new French leaders. They continued to regard themselves as spokesmen for their respective countries and, absent contrary instructions from their capitals,

routinely addressed themselves to the members of the provisional government to whom they were not yet formally accredited. But this was an anoma-
lous situation, pregnant with danger and embarrassment for all concerned. It
could not be expected to last for any length of time. The prospect of a siege
of Paris presented particular problems for the diplomatic corps, though it
does not seem much to have unnerved Trochu.[45] Conditions in the city were
unsettled, though not chaotic, with a small amount of incidental bloodshed,
but the disorder and violence were not as yet directed against foreigners. The
members of the diplomatic corps had to use their best discretion as to what
to do in these unsettled circumstances. Their main problem, for the moment,
was whether to continue their official establishments in the French capital at
all since the government to which they were accredited had disappeared or
whether to formally establish communication with the new group that had
assumed power.

The safety of their embassies appeared to this body to be endangered at
least to such a degree that they decided, on 10 September, to repair to the
western city of Tours, beyond the war zone. The provisional government, in
turn, felt itself obliged, on 12 September, to send a small delegation to represent its members to the diplomatic corps at this city. On a broader national
scale, a second center of government was thus established and bore the name
"the Delegation."

Difficulties arose almost immediately. The Delegation was supposed to
represent a channel of communication between Paris and the provinces. Its
powers, though extensive on paper, were in fact weak and almost nonexistent.
Paris insisted on calling the shots. In the words of one observer: "Such was
the habit of centralization that instinctively no one could admit any superiority except that of Paris, and in spite of the full powers accorded to the Delegation, the Government of the capital went on sending out orders until the last
moment."[46] Another, no less prescient, recorded: "Around me there is only
inertia and hesitation . . . anarchy; no consistent or energetic direction, no
strategic plan." According to still another: "The provinces need to be roused
and no one is doing it."[47]

The hesitations by which members of the Delegation were seized in their
dealings with the countryside as September turned into October were brought
on not only by weariness and pressure of duty (though these too played their

parts) but also by the evidence they saw of growing opposition to the Paris authorities, especially the impression they gained in the last days of September of outright opposition to it in the parts of the country over which they purported to exercise control. Controversy centered around the question whether elections, scheduled by Paris for 2 October, should be held. The atmosphere surrounding this controversy can best be realized if one takes note of such evidence as exists in reports of the prefects on the matter. According to one: "You know our peasants; you will have Bonapartist municipalities together with a Bonapartist national assembly. This will be our undoing." Another laid down: "Elections will deliver France up to an Orléanist-Legitimist coalition."[48]

Gambetta professed himself indifferent to these complaints and expressed nothing but contempt for those who voiced them. There followed mass resignations of the prefects all over the country, many of whom offered themselves as candidates in the election. Hot on the heels of this upheaval came the shock of Ferrières. These twin disasters ruled out whatever possibilities for peace remained. Republican aversion to appealing to the population now found company in the voices of a number of soldiers for whom politics was an unwelcome distraction from the great task of defending the country. As Gambetta put it later: "We could not have elections without an armistice, and the effect of an armistice would be to render impossible our efforts at national defense." On 24 September, the government announced that elections, both national and local, would be indefinitely postponed.[49]

The effect produced at Tours by this decision was nothing short of sensational. Some members of the Delegation worried about the impression this decision would have on the powers of Europe. Others, further to the left, feared that it would give monarchists the time they needed to organize. Still others predicted that it would prompt the south to break away. All believed that Paris had lost contact with reality. The Delegation therefore determined to countermand the pronouncement of Paris with one of its own, a communication to the country on 29 September that it was assuming all responsibility for governing France and that elections would be held after all.[50]

This was too much for Gambetta. On 7 October, he decided to act. Nervously mounting a balloon powered by hot air, alongside a cargo of 1,600 kilograms of mail and sixteen carrier pigeons, he took off for Tours. The balloon made its way over the Prussian lines at less than two thousand feet, Gambetta and his assistants looking anxiously downward as Prussian rifles took pot shots at them. Impulsively throwing out ballast, the pilot rose to safer altitudes before any harm could be done. After a few hours, he opened the gas valve and attempted to land in an empty space, but peasants came running up to warn the balloonists that they were in Prussian-occupied territory. They took off and later, spotting a group of men who looked like French soldiers, tried to land again. These soldiers were in fact Prussians. Fortunately, their arms were stacked, and, by the time they could grab them, the balloon was rising rapidly once more; however, a bullet grazed Gambetta's hand. After this hair-raising escape, the pilot allowed some time to elapse before attempting a third landing. Eventually, they came down near Montdidier at 3:30 p.m. Gambetta's first decision, after he made the Delegation reverse itself over the question of elections, was to appoint himself minister of war. Installed at Tours, he sought to instill in the minds of all Frenchmen the idea that victory over Prussia was not only possible but an eminently realistic objective. One cannot read without feeling the flamboyant words of the circular addressed to this subject by Gambetta on 8 October: "We must set all our resources to work, and they are immense. We must shake the countryside from its torpor, guard against stupid panic, increase partisan warfare and, against an enemy so skilled in ambush and surprise, ourselves employ ruses, harass his flanks, surprise his rear—in short, inaugurate a national war. . . . Tied down and contained by the capital, the Prussians, far from home, decimated by our arms, by hunger, by natural causes, hunted by our reawakened people, will be gradually come to their senses."[51]

For Bismarck, Gambetta's accession to power could not have come at a worse time. The situation confronting him at the beginning of October 1870 was one that he was not happy to face, and it is easy to understand that he must have seen in it a real danger to his policies of the moment, not in the narrower sense but as huge and ponderous obstacles blocking the goal to which all his efforts were directed—ending the war promptly and on the terms he had outlined at Ferrières. It was by this goal that Bismarck's conduct was guided in the rather intense exchanges of views between the Prussian government and the representatives of the deposed imperial regime that marked the weeks around the middle of October and to which we must now briefly turn.

6

Bismarck, Bazaine, and Thiers

That the collapse of the negotiations at Ferrières had a profound effect on Bismarck has been the subject of considerable discussion in the preceding chapter. The failure of the talks marked the moment of lowest ebb in relations between the French authorities and the Prussian government, the time when the task of establishing relations seemed most delicate and difficult. But Bismarck, always conscious of his personal responsibility for the shaping of peace and always sensitive to other ways of keeping negotiations in hand, soon saw favorable possibilities of doing just that with another actor—Marshal François Achille Bazaine, commander of the Army of the Rhine—an army that had not yet been defeated, that still carried out its duties as the representative of the emperor, and that remained the only symbol of imperial authority in all France.

Bazaine himself was sixty years old at the time he caught Bismarck's eye. Although there were conflicting views among contemporaries, as there have been among historians, with regard to his character, the weight of the evidence reveals him as a healthy, honorable, and diligent figure—the product of a French military education, with all its advantages and drawbacks, full of life, straightforward—in short, in many ways an attractive personality. But an unpleasant experience in Napoleon III's "Mexican adventure of 1864–66," where he had been sent to shore up the troops, turned him sour, the more so when he learned that the government was attempting to pin upon his shoulders responsibility for what turned out to be an unmitigated disaster. The shock of this revelation never wore off. Thereafter, Bazaine's career went downhill, and his experience in the war that broke out in 1870 did absolutely nothing to improve it. After the war, there appeared, in 1873, sensational charges leveled against Bazaine by the senior officials of the Third Republic. He was alleged to have done nothing when the fortunes of the nation were at stake and, according to materials in the files of the French war ministry, to have contributed in a significant way to the French defeat—an accusation for which the government put him on trial for his life and later set him in condemnation for the remainder of it. The charges were not wholly unjustified. Bazaine's actions at Sedan were, as Geoffrey Wawro has convincingly demonstrated, confused and bizarre and undoubtedly contributed to the French defeat.[1] Perhaps character flaws entered in. Though by no means devoid of talent, Bazaine also possessed unquestionable personal deficiencies, and the most signal of these appears to have been an inability to distinguish the genuine from the false article in the company of those he admitted to his personal entourage. Like many other engaging and prominent personalities, he could easily be satisfied by a professed agreement with his own views and often neglected to look carefully at the person who was doing the agreeing. A somewhat greater interest in people might have warned him against the intentions of hangers-on and flatterers, one of whom, Edouard Regnier, we shall note in due course.

Like most other French military men, Bazaine had little sympathy for the provisional government in which such—to him—disreputable men of the left as Gambetta and Favre served, and he could not, he told his colleagues, pledge to it his loyalty until Napoleon III released him from the oath he had sworn to the empire. In any case, whatever sympathies to the new government he might have entertained were dashed by the selection of Trochu as president, a man for whom Bazaine had nothing but contempt, partly no doubt because of a scathing critique of Bazaine's performance in Mexico that Trochu had authored. In any case, on 16 September, Bazaine finally found himself obliged to address the question of the government's establishment: "Our military obligations toward the fatherland remain the same. Let us then continue to serve it with devotion and with the same energy: defending its territory against the foreigner and the social order against ill-conceived and unsuitable passions."[2] The statement was a masterpiece of equivocation. Was Bazaine loyal or independent? No one knew, perhaps not even Bazaine himself. But the declaration ended with words that expressed a belief that the army was a political force to be reckoned with—one from

123

Marshall François Achille Bazaine, defender of Metz. (von Pflugk-Harttung, *The Franco-German War*, 123.)

which the members of the provisional government could not fail to avert their eyes.[3]

But Bazaine was not the only Bonapartist personality who appeared on the stage at this time. Of all the imperial figures at London, the most interesting was the mysterious and enigmatic Edouard Regnier, a political agent and sometime adviser to the deposed emperor. Having played some role in imperial diplomacy in earlier years, Regnier was still a relatively unknown figure in France and elsewhere. A romantic, a dilettante, possessed of wide connections, Regnier was also something of a mystic and an evangelist. Born in Nice, in 1828, he worked as a journalist and publicist in Paris until 1866. He seems to have carried out this task with considerable satisfaction. But his greatest hankering in life after the debacle at Sedan was to play the role of confidential intermediary between the agents of the deposed empire and Prussia. After the French defeat, he crossed the channel and took up residence in London. He had not been there more than a few months before he found ways of involving himself personally in the exchanges between Bismarck and the figures surrounding the empress. For a few important weeks in September and October 1870, he was active as the unofficial go-between in the complicated diplomatic maneuvers surrounding a possible restoration of the Second Empire.[4]

But it did not take long before Regnier's relations with Eugénie went downhill. The source of the estrangement is not difficult to discern. In the middle of September, Regnier produced a long memorandum, which he forwarded to her residence at Chislehurst. The memorandum reflected Regnier's greatest enthusiasms and passions—a restoration of the imperial government under the empress herself. According to his plan, Eugénie would, at the first opportune moment, issue an announcement condemning the provisional government and, under the protection of the French fleet, return to the coast of France. There she would issue a call for the loyal sections of the French army to march on Paris, and, after having defeated the armies of the provisional government, the loyalists would then place her on the throne.

The plan might have appealed to the empress at an earlier time; before the news of Sedan, her behavior had verged on lunacy, as she screamed one day that she wanted to be a nurse, another that she wanted to ride through the streets of Paris as a new Joan of Arc.[5] Perhaps it was these memories that impelled Regnier to believe that she would accept his plan. If so, he was mistaken. The empress thought the scheme wild; she shook with fury when it was presented to her, and she refused even to grant its author the audience he had so ardently wanted to secure.

This failure did not deter Regnier. Quite the contrary. He now turned to the young prince imperial, whose acquaintance he somehow managed to secure, and persuaded the boy to write a note to his father on the back of a photograph of the Hastings sea front where he was living. Crossing the channel, Regnier made for the German headquarters at Versailles, where he appeared on 20 September. He was cordially received by Bismarck (himself now deeply involved in negotiations with Favre).[6]

During this interview, Regnier unfolded his plans. He assumed that the fallen Bonapartist empire was, in Bismarck's view, a preferable negotiating party to the provisional government, which still, after all, suffered from lack of international recognition. He therefore proposed that he be dispatched at once to Metz, where he could negotiate with Bazaine, whose distaste, he believed, for the Paris regime was no less intense than his own. Once at Metz, he would enlist the support of Bazaine, who in turn would put himself in touch with the empress. The latter would then summon former members of the *Corps législatif*, which would, under the protection of the Metz army, overthrow the provisional government and assume power in Paris. To this proposal Bismarck acquiesced, though not without misgivings. In the circle of negotiators to whom he expressed a sense of faith with the evolving concept of an armistice with France, Regnier fit only at the margins.[7]

In any case, the gambit bounced back on Regnier in the most painful of ways. Bazaine agreed to send an emissary, his subordinate, the dashing General Charles Denis Sauter Bourbaki, who had once commanded the national guard, to the empress. But Bourbaki soon became an unwilling participant. No sooner had he crossed the channel than he began to develop doubts about the wisdom of Regnier's plan. The empress did nothing to

General Charles Denis Sauter Bourbaki, first imperialist, then republican. (von Pflugk-Harttung, *The Franco-German War*, 506.)

dispel these doubts. Her anger was aroused not only by the fact of this renewed intervention by Regnier into the diplomatic arrangements on which the delicate relations between herself and Bismarck rested but also by the fact that the matter had become known to certain members of her circle in Great Britain who considered Regnier a character motivated only by financial distress and of a nature devious and secret beyond the limits of normal acceptability. Be that as it may, Eugénie did not wait for official notification of Bourbaki's arrival before taking action. She refused to have anything to do with any scheme that might hamper the efforts of the Government of National Defense, to the cause of which she now, for some reason, decided to commit herself (though the commitment was, one hastens to add, not to last very long). In any case, Bourbaki, disabused of Regnier's illusions, concluded that the game was not worth the candle. With Eugénie's refusal to see Bourbaki, Regnier's schemes and intrigues turned to smoke.[8] But this was not the end of the affair. When Bourbaki returned to Metz, the German commander, Prince Frederick Charles, refused to let him inside the fortress on the grounds that his pass had been dated in error. This, coming from a man whom Bourbaki cordially despised, was powerful stuff, and Bourbaki, fully sensitive to the implied slight, did not take kindly to it. The next several days were taken up with exchanges between the two men, which ended with the resignation of Bourbaki's commission and his departure to Tours, where he took control of the forces of the Government of National Defense.[9]

Bismarck, his distrust of the military growing deeper and wider with each passing day, was naturally stung by this news, and he wrote a long letter of scathing rebuke to Prince Frederick Charles's chief of staff:

> I appeal to Your Excellency's clear judgment and to your own perception so you will understand how discouraging it must be for me when, through this kind of failure to execute explicit royal orders, the danger arises that in the whole constellation of political calculations, one single cog which is necessarily in place will refuse to do its work. How can I have the courage to proceed with my work if I cannot count on royal orders . . . being faithfully executed? . . . Your Excellency knows that my whole energy has been devoted, and with some success, to providing for the victorious progress of our arms a free field, undisturbed by foreign

influence. I must then demand that the army show the same confidence in me that His Majesty the King has shown in his approval of my plans.[10]

In the meantime, the situation at Metz had become desperate. On 8 October, Bazaine sent an urgent message to his generals that outlined, in the starkest of terms, the gravity of the peril that menaced them: "The moment is approaching when the Army of the Rhine will find itself in perhaps the most difficult position that a French army has ever had to endure. . . . Supplies are beginning to run short and in what can only be described as a very short time they will run out completely."[11] Negotiations should therefore be resumed—and resumed immediately—to try to reach an armistice. Baron Napoleon Boyer, a trusted member of Bazaine's staff, at once set forth on a journey that was to take him not only to Versailles and then back to Metz but also, thereafter and most important, to London. Bismarck was not averse to receiving Boyer. This was just the moment of deep crisis in the relations between himself and the provisional government, when the task of successfully resuming negotiations seemed most sensitive and arduous. But Moltke, conscious as always of his personal responsibility for the shaping of Prussian military policy and sensitive to any attempt to force his hand by the pressure of special missions, would have none of this. Efforts by Moltke to quash the visit, including personal appeals to King William I through Prince Frederick Charles and by Moltke himself, were therefore put in hand. But Bismarck was able, though not without much difficulty, to defeat these efforts, and the king issued orders that the visit be allowed to take place. The proposal made by Boyer—and represented in the form of a letter from Bazaine—constituted a significant development in French thinking during this period. Bazaine's message to Bismarck in mid-October 1870 suggests a mind dominated, in particular, by three convictions—that (1) the army at Metz would be the perfect instrument to overthrow the revolutionary government in Paris and therefore should be released at once; (2) a restored empire offered the best chances for any future German-French relations; and (3) elections to a new national assembly would be the best way to bring this about.[12]

The first of these three convictions was wholly inaccurate. Bismarck, let alone Moltke, could never accept anything less than the surrender of the entire army and the fortress. As Bismarck put it, any discussions about a possible armistice must proceed in an environment in which the Prusso-German military position was in no way compromised. As for the second of Bazaine's impressions, the idea that Bismarck preferred a restored empire to a republic was, as Bismarck had repeatedly emphasized, the purest nonsense. What Bismarck wanted was a government that would conclude, in the fastest possible way, peace with Prussia and its German allies; though he had some sympathy for Napoleon III, the latter was by no means an acceptable negotiating partner in the absence of concrete sacrifices that would satisfy the German need for security.[13] As for the third, new elections were indeed indispensable if a new government was to have the legitimacy it needed to negotiate peace, but, until the first two of these problems had been overcome, the question was moot. After Boyer had outlined Bazaine's proposals, Bismarck unceremoniously dragged him into the garden, where there were no members of the General Staff. When asked by the stunned representative for an explanation of this breach of courtesy, Bismarck replied: "There are people in the next room who speak French. Walls, as they say, have ears."[14] His overall point was clear. Bazaine must decide what role the Rhine Army was to play in the negotiations between the two sides. He had asked for terms that were unacceptable in the extreme.[15]

What has been recounted earlier about Bismarck's views and policies would suffice to show that the fundamental points in Bazaine's letter, however well intentioned, bore very little relation to the facts. But there were other, equally important points of which this document failed to take note. Would the regent accept the peace terms upon which the Prussian authorities insisted? How would Bazaine's army be received by a French population whose leaders had now committed themselves—and it—to *guerre à outrance*? How permanent was a restored empire likely to be if it was seen to have been placed in power by the hand of the Prussian army? All this made it necessary for Boyer to return to Metz, to discuss the situation with Bazaine, and to find out what, if anything, could be done about the parlous condition of the French army—demoralized, starving, and on the point of defeat.[16]

Bazaine, it should be added, had gained from his talk with his corps commanders the impression that the army could be relied upon to carry out the mission he had in mind. This was the point he stressed to Boyer upon the latter's return to Metz on 14 October. But Bazaine suffered from excessive optimism—even his commanders made no secret of their belief that large chunks of the troops would break away once they were outside the fortress. The fact was that deep down Bazaine's subordinates had little faith in his plan.[17] In any case, nothing could be done without ascertaining the views of the empress, thus making it necessary for Boyer to set out for London, where he arrived on 22 October. Here he was not altogether disappointed, and the fact that he was not had perhaps something to do with Eugénie's personality as a political figure. Eugénie herself still remained a profound conservative. Intensely interested in politics, untainted by her husband's socialistic streaks, she nevertheless wanted to help her country, whose people, it must be added, had no special affection for her. But what peace terms was she being asked to accept? Boyer referred the question to Bernstorff, the North German minister, in London. The latter knew very well from his conversations with Bismarck that the Prussians would never allow the Army of the Rhine a free hand in France without concrete guarantees that would do nothing to damage the superiority of the military position their own army had, in the past six weeks, managed to achieve.

Eugénie, however, was concerned not to lose Bismarck's goodwill. And, behind the scenes, there were specific occurrences that suggest that it was a deal with the Germans toward which she was now steering her course. We have noted Eugénie's vacillations earlier—with Regnier in September, with Boyer a month later, when she was shaken by a curious determination to do nothing that would endanger the Government of National Defense. Even Bismarck had confessed himself bewildered by her reactions. Now, however, in late October, there were emerging faint but interesting signs that Eugénie was contemplating a return to France and, with a view to shoring up her position as the leader of a restored imperial government, engaging discredited and defunct organs of the Paris press. Apparently, she hoped to secure Bismarck's assistance in that effort. Here Boyer played a role. One is astounded to note in the papers of Bernstorff that two visits were paid to him by Boyer for the purpose of apprising him that he, Boyer, was in a position, through his Paris connections, to arrange for the purchase of the imperialist

131

daily *Opinion National* (which had been shut down by the Government of National Defense) and of inviting the Prussian government to take a share in the enterprise, the argument being advanced that this would be useful to Prussia. The ambassador, in reporting this to Versailles, expressed doubts as to the reliability of the visitor, and Bismarck refused to have anything to do with the proposed deal, arguing on the very sound grounds of principle against the buying-up of foreign newspapers generally.[18]

And Bismarck discovered other problems in dealing with Eugénie. Her advisers at this time were, in large part, reactionaries. But her chief fault in this respect lay not in the quality of highly placed persons who were given the privilege of personal access to her but rather in the narrowness of the circle into which they had been admitted. Eugénie saw and consulted with only an extremely small number of advisers, and her knowledge of developments in France, beyond what was relayed to her by this tiny group of intimates, was almost nonexistent. Through Boyer, she wired Bismarck, asking for a fourteen-day armistice during which time the Army of the Rhine could be replenished and during which negotiations could begin as well. What is more, she insisted that her title as Regent of France be publicly proclaimed. Once these terms had been granted, she promised to take action—promptly, boldly, and without backward glances. Armed with extravagant, erroneous, and positively surreal misinformation, she addressed herself to King William I, pleading with "his royal heart, his soldierly generosity," "implor[ing His] Majesty to accept [her] request," and ending with a bombastic flourish of almost religious fervor: "Your good will is the indispensable condition of the continuation of our negotiation."[19]

Bismarck viewed this offer with complete stupefaction. There was, in the first place, no quid pro quo, upon which he had insisted all along. There was also no recognition that the Army of the Rhine was itself on the point of collapse. Never mind that Moltke was about to take it. Never mind that the French had everywhere been defeated on the field. As for her letter to William I, the latter was no more inclined than Bismarck to give it the slightest attention: "I desire with all my heart to restore peace between our two nations, but to secure this it would be necessary to establish at least the probability that we shall succeed in making France accept the result of our transactions without continuing the war against the French forces. At pres-

132

ent I regret that the uncertainty in which we find ourselves with regard to the political dispositions of the Army of Metz, as well as of the French nation, does not allow me to proceed further with the offer proposed by Your Majesty."[20] To Bazaine at Metz, Bismarck was equally blunt: "The proposals which have reached us from London are absolutely unacceptable, and I declare to my great regret that I see no further chance of reaching a result by political negotiations."[21]

The negotiations between Bismarck on the one hand and Bazaine and Eugénie on the other thus ran into the sand, but their repercussions will be found in most of the relevant diplomatic and military correspondence of the period. Bismarck, in particular, was sharply affected. The episode was, to his mind, one more bit of evidence of the shakiness of the imperial position and of its growing unreliability as a partner in peace negotiations. Alone in his modest Versailles apartment, he wrote to Bernstorff on 15 October that the restoration of the empire was and never had been an end in and of itself but a means to an end and that—an equally important point—"the Paris government has made a mistake in forbidding elections and thus cutting off an expression of popular will."[22] For that reason, he vowed to keep in touch with other agents of the regency in London. His aim was to end the war on conditions that reflected the reality of the military situation—that and nothing else. The military situation improved markedly from the German point of view when, on 29 October, Metz fell and 170,000 prisoners, including Bazaine himself, were taken into German hands; demonstrations celebrating the news erupted all over Germany.[23]

Serious as were the complications that afflicted his efforts to negotiate an armistice with the figures of the overthrown empire, Bismarck was not significantly discouraged in his hopes for improvement in the relations between Prussia and members of the provisional government in Paris. So far, there had been no official recognition of its existence by any of the powers. The French authorities had yet to demonstrate, even to themselves, their ability to remain in power for any length of time. The immediate problems involved in completing the seizure of power had preoccupied them during the first

The capitulation of Metz, 27 October 1870. Color lithograph, 1871. (Bildarchiv Preußischer Kulturbesitz [BPK]. Used by permission of Art Resource, New York. ART428596.)

days following the September coup. But the main problem remained one of securing international recognition. It was with a view to doing so that, in the first few days following the disaster of Sedan and the establishment of the Government of National Defense, Adolphe Thiers, indefatigable and resourceful as ever, had embarked upon a mission aimed at appealing to the Great Powers of Europe. His mission may stand as one of the most difficult and demanding undertakings in the annals of modern diplomacy. The government, by the middle of September, was divided, the chief part of it shut up in Paris during the latter stages of his mission and able to communicate with the outside world only by means of balloons and carrier pigeons. No less a handicap were the chauvinistic pronouncements of Favre on 6 September. These produced unease abroad; it was felt, particularly in Petersburg, that if the young republic had inherited the warlike traditions of its predecessor, it must learn wisdom in the school of adversity. Finally, there was the problem caused, in the middle of Thiers's journey, by the collapse of the Ferrières negotiations between Favre and Bismarck and by the melodramatic announcements of the former and his colleague, Gambetta, about *guerre à outrance*.[24]

But Thiers had many qualities that commended him for the assignment he was about to undertake. More than any other man at this time, he represented France and a clean break with the man under whose rule it had suffered for the past twenty years. Aside from securing international recognition of the Paris regime, Thiers had a second aim, and this was to organize the neutrals for intervention in the war between France and Prussia. The neutrals had, he recalled, refrained from intervention in the wars of 1859 and 1866 by the announcement of quick armistices, and this led Thiers and his colleagues to the conclusion that they could somehow be drawn in by a prolonged military stalemate.[25]

At a meeting with Granville on 14 September, Thiers made a series of statements that may stand as one of the first responsible formulations by a republican spokesman on foreign policy. He began by recounting the highlights of the situation that existed during the ten days that had elapsed since the initial seizure of power. He discussed the reactions to the new French republic by the Prussians (which he found ambiguous) and by the other powers. Britain appeared to him to be the most hostile to intervention of all foreign countries. He pleaded that it was time to reverse this position. Asked whether

135

the British would put pressure on the Prussians, Thiers was told by Granville that "[the British government] would advise the Prussian Chancellor to grant an armistice so that the voice of France might be consulted as to a peace."[26]

This statement is of interest in two respects. It appears to be the first major statement by any power on the subject of a possible armistice. Coming just at the outset of Thiers's mission, it forecast the position that the British would later take on the subject of Alsace and Lorraine. It is significant that, as early as October, Gladstone had set his face against any peace proposal that would transfer the two provinces from France to Germany without first submitting this question to their inhabitants. But, beyond that, it reflected an illusion from which British diplomats, particularly those in London, parted only slowly and with great reluctance—the illusion that there was any significant chance that the Germans would ever seriously consider surrendering their goal of securing their borders.[27] Aside from the progress on Alsace and Lorraine, Thiers was unable to gain much of anything from his meeting with Granville. In fact, the two men did not see eye to eye. Granville let it be known that the government Thiers represented was no government at all, that it had been thrown together by the deputies at Paris in the middle of indescribable turmoil, and that it might, within the space of a single day, be swept away by the slightest adversity or reversal of fate. Aside from this, had it not been France that had been first to throw down the gauntlet against Prussia? Had it not grievously ignored the advice of Great Britain in doing so? Had it not richly deserved the condemnation it had received from the other powers for taking such precipitous action? At this point there ensued an altercation between Granville and Thiers, in the course of which Thiers claimed that he too had tried to restrain the ambitions of Napoleon and that *he* represented the *real* France— the France that had not desired war and that had done everything possible to prevent it from occurring. Granville was unmoved by this statement.

Thiers states in his *Notes et souvenirs* that he was instructed to depart London by Jules Favre,[28] but this claim may be taken with a pinch of salt. Favre was at the time a neophyte, hardly known outside Parisian circles. There is every indication that Thiers followed no instructions but his own unless orders from his nominal chief coincided with his strong impulse to push on toward Petersburg. The Baltic being too dangerous, Thiers had to travel via Cherbourg, Tours, Florence, north Italy, and Vienna. Late in the evening of 20 September, he stopped at Tours to report his observations to the Delegation.

To the members of this body Thiers relayed the proposition conveyed to him in his conversation with Granville—that the British were in a position to put pressure upon Prussia to agree to an armistice—and wondered whether there was any point in following up on their idea. One figure in the Delegation favored doing so. This was none other than Jean Baptiste, the comte de Chaudordy, the chargé d'affaires for foreign affairs and a diplomat of long experience and outstanding talent. Chaudordy proposed that the Delegation explore the matter further and address a series of questions to the British in the hope of making them more specific.[29] But in this he was opposed by all of his colleagues, Gambetta most strongly. In the latter's view, any delay in the energetic prosecution of the war could only play into the hands of the Bonapartists. Thiers did nothing to encourage Chaudordy; he was strongly anti-British, perhaps from his experience in 1840, and he believed it best to either open direct negotiations with the Prussians—this was already being done, one will recall, at the time by Favre—or to proceed directly to Russia, on whose goodwill for himself and for the French position Thiers depended. In the end, nothing came of the Tours meeting.[30]

On his way to Petersburg, Thiers stopped in Vienna in order to have an interview with Beust, whom he viewed as bitterly anti-Prussian. But Beust, despite his bias, was not the sort of person Thiers could bring himself to trust. For one thing, Thiers suspected him of having had a hand in aiding and abetting the headlong actions of the duc de Gramont that had done so much to bring on the war. Distrust of Beust was not the only reason why Thiers failed in Vienna. By the fall of 1870, the senior figures in the Habsburg monarchy saw the situation for what it was. Though not unfriendly to the provisional government, they realized that their independent existence rested on good relations with the new Germany. The atmosphere of the new situation can best be realized if one takes note of the comments made by Emperor Francis Joseph on 1 October to General Lothar von Schweinitz, the Prussian minister. Commenting on the victories of Prussia over France, Francis Joseph laid down: "You cannot expect me to be pleased about the thing itself. I shall not interfere at all. I shall let anything happen."[31] Even more striking was the remark made by Schweinitz to the Russian minister: "If you asked me what we

137

have promised Austria in return for her friendship, I should answer 'life.' She owes her preservation solely to our goodwill, for we are interested in maintaining her integrity, which in our view is more important to the equilibrium of Europe, than that of the Ottoman Empire."[32] The Austrians had by this time come to accept a Prussian victory as inevitable. The rapidly declining influence of Beust as prime minister in the councils of Francis Joseph did much to encourage a new line of policy; the Austrians had come to realize that their security lay in alliance with the new Germany, not in opposition to it. Nothing, therefore, came of the Vienna visit.[33]

That left Petersburg—the crucial destination of Thiers's mission. Had the Russians decided to engage Austria-Hungary and England, these three powers could then have forced a European mediation; if it appeared likely that they would take the side of Prussia, Bismarck could succeed in keeping the war isolated. The Russians were not to be shaken in their attitude. It was easier for them to adhere to it because they knew that Bismarck was in favor of their desire to free themselves of the Black Sea clauses of the Treaty of Paris. But there was, as yet, no direct agreement on that subject between Russia and Prussia. An effort to preserve good relations with France found support at this time both in Russian opinion and in the military high command, to say nothing of the foreign office officials by whom Gorchakov was surrounded. It found support with the tsar as well. But, for the moment, the Russians vowed to do nothing. Gorchakov said to Thiers: "We shall occupy ourselves later with uniting France to Russia," and Tsar Alexander added: "I should much like to gain an alliance like that of France, an alliance of peace, and not war and conquest."[34] This sentence, spoken on 29 September 1870, foreshadowed the Franco-Russian alliance that was to come into being twenty years later. It was of no help to Thiers at the time.

Thiers therefore returned home, only to find new problems.

For one thing, the majority of his countrymen, as his counterparts in the government were beginning to discover, still did not share (and never really would) in the great political ferment unleashed in Paris by the fall of the empire. Dissension between the capital and the countryside had become marked and menacing. This dissension found its expression in the increasing political isolation of the government from the provinces, in the growing restlessness and despair throughout moderate political circles, and in the creeping paralysis of the French war effort. For that reason, Thiers determined to make a new effort to end the war. His decision was supported by most of his colleagues, though it will come as no surprise to the reader that it was the occasion of decided friction and difference of opinion between himself and the hardliners of the Delegation at Tours. It was against this background—deep anxiety over the future course of the war, a fear that France's continuation of it would mean the removal of any trace of moderation on the part of Bismarck, and a realization that the existing position of the Germans with respect to the military situation was tending to strengthen their morale as it weakened that of France—that Thiers decided, on 28 October 1870, to proceed to Versailles to put out feelers to Bismarck.[35] It was here that he first learned of two stunning developments: the surrender of Metz and—still more important—the capture of Bazaine. After conferring with Moltke and Bismarck, Thiers returned to Paris, where, on a small boat on the river Sèvres over which there hung a destroyed bridge, he, at ten o'clock on the night of 30 October, met with Favre and Trochu. The little party then proceeded to the foreign ministry to discuss the terms they would present to Bismarck. Deeply shaken by what he correctly perceived was a rapidly deteriorating military and political situation, shaken too by his failure to extract from any of the powers of Europe even an inclination of a desire to intervene, Thiers advised the two ministers to accept any Prussian terms that enabled France to hold elections that would lead to the creation of a government authorized to make peace. But Trochu insisted on two conditions: the elections must be extended to Alsace and Lorraine, and Paris itself must be allowed to replenish itself during the period the armistice was in effect.[36]

A further event may very well have affected Thiers's thinking in the preparation of his negotiations with Bismarck—the famous insurrection on 31 October that took place in Paris against the Government of National Defense.

The causes of the uprising have been much discussed in the literature addressed to this period, but in general the revolt may be ascribed to three outstanding factors: (1) the steadfast refusal on the part of the Paris authorities to permit municipal elections (these doubtless would have returned a majority of Reds and socialists, seriously eroding the authority over the city that they had just managed to consolidate); (2) the announcement that Thiers was about to open negotiations with Bismarck the purpose of which was the conclusion of an armistice; (3) above all, the fall of Metz and the surrender of Bazaine. The news of these happenings, colored no doubt by the excited emotions of the more radical elements of the city's population—of whom the editors of the republican newspapers were the most conspicuous but by no means the only example—produced a violent reaction, partly of anger, partly of alarm, in Paris. So the radicals exploded, and for a time it appeared that they had indeed seized power and pushed aside the local authorities.

What occurred can be summed up in a few sentences. The radicals of about twenty *arrondissements*, assembling on the Place de la Concorde, decided to storm the Hôtel de Ville, the seat of municipal authority, and to proclaim the overthrow of the government and its replacement by a commune. Their leader, Gustave Flourens, had long wanted to have "a very serious talk with our friends in the Government of National Defense,"[37] and the march would give him the opportunity to do so. At the Hôtel de Ville, he found a huge crowd, some of whose members came out with fiery revolutionary statements, including *"Pas de l'armistice, guerre à outrance."*[38] The crowd burst into the room where the authorities were meeting and declared them overthrown. It took twenty-four hours before the more moderate members of the Garde Nationale were able to disarm and expel the rebellious agitators.[39]

It is easy to understand the concern with which the members of the government viewed the attempted coup, and it surely affected Thiers's thinking in the negotiations with Bismarck that resumed at Versailles on 1 November. Thiers outlined the French terms—elections and the replenishment of Paris—while Bismarck patiently listened and sized up his interlocutor. There can be no question but that, with respect to the first of these, Bismarck and Thiers were of similar minds, and Bismarck took pains to emphasize this, lest the impression be lost on Thiers. On the other hand, Bismarck was too good a diplomat to lay all his cards on the table at once. He was careful to sound out Thiers—seeing a man whose anxieties were at their highest pitch, whose nerves and energies were pushed to their utmost level of endurance. All in all, the first session of the negotiations seemed to go well, and Thiers lost no time in conveying this impression to the ministers in Paris.[40]

Discussions resumed on 2 November. It was here that Bismarck sought to pin down Thiers on the question of replenishment. What commodities of food did he want? What about fuel and resources? Bismarck listened patiently as Thiers spelled out the numbers: thirty-four thousand cattle; eighty thousand sheep; one hundred thousand pieces of salted meat; one hundred kilograms of meal; one hundred thousand tons of coal; five hundred thousand cubic meters of wood; food for the eight million Parisian animals, that is to say, hay or straw; and a pound of bread and a pound of meat for every citizen of a city whose population ran between 2.7 and 2.8 million.[41]

Bismarck was appalled and astounded when he learned of these numbers, and he had every right to be.[42] They seemed to him to reflect an attitude of a government more committed to war than one that sought to make peace. He thereupon asked Thiers if these figures could be scaled down. When told that they could not, he advised Thiers that he would have to take up the matter with the king. It had, in fact, been Thiers's aim to defeat the unreasonable ambitions of his colleagues and to engage their support for a program of more moderate aims. But he was handicapped in his attempts to achieve this by serious limitations on his own authority. The radicals at Tours, in particular, lacked sympathy for his position, and they did what they could to undermine it in the hope that he would be replaced by a tougher negotiator or, better still, by no negotiator at all. In Paris, the parties of the left were angered by Thiers's attempts to discourage discussion of war aims of their own, and they were suspicious that he harbored political ambitions for himself. In the country at large, he could count on broader support, but the disinclination of the Paris government to hold elections limited what he could achieve even here. And at the forefront of all his calculations there stood the specter of the uprising of 31 October. He and his colleague Louis Cochery had little excuse for any lack of awareness of what was going on, even if they did not directly control the situation. Bismarck, for his part, was sufficiently curious about it that he, in a further meeting with Thiers on 3 November, was moved to inquire if the Paris authorities had been able to restore order. Thiers himself was not sure and sent Cochery to the outskirts of the city to investigate. Cochery returned to report that the insurrection had indeed been defeated and that the government was in control.[43]

Not that this did Thiers much good. Bismarck roundly disappointed him when he, Bismarck, reported on 3 November that the replenishing of Paris was out of the question unless the Parisians were made to surrender the fortresses outside the city, this to compensate the Prussians for the military dangers they would experience by agreeing to these conditions. Bismarck saw no point in continuing the discussions if the French did not agree to these terms. The king and Moltke were of the same mind.[44] The question exhausted, Thiers, in a meeting with Bismarck on 4 November, proceeded to launch a discussion of the possibility of holding elections without an armistice if a quick peace could be arranged—a discussion that, considering that he had had no conversations on this subject at all with either Favre or Trochu, can be considered nothing short of astounding.[45] Thiers must have known in his heart how little promise there was in this effort. It was a confession of hopelessness and despair. But Bismarck, for his part, welcomed the offer and even promised to save Metz for France if such an arrangement could come quickly into effect.[46]

But it was not to be. This Thiers learned on 5 November when he returned to the same deserted and depressing spot under the bridge on the Sèvres to meet with Favre and Auguste Ducrot, the latter standing in for Trochu, who judged the situation at Paris too unstable to permit Thiers's entry. Before them, Thiers poured out the full measure of his aroused feelings and opinion. Continuation of the war was hopeless; it would result only in more severe terms. But his words fell on deaf ears. For Favre and Ducrot, there could be no question of an armistice without the replenishing of the city—besides, Ducrot argued, the war must continue, if only to erase the wounds of Sedan and Metz. Shaken, Thiers replied: "General, you talk like a soldier. All to the good, but you are not talking in political terms."[47] But Ducrot and Favre remained unmoved. It was in these circumstances that the negotiations between Thiers and Bismarck, much to the regret of both, ended, evidence of which was made clear by the publication by both sides, on 7 November, of circulars addressing the reasons for their collapse.

How to account for this? On both sides, it was the same thing: military considerations. Moltke (and Bismarck, too) would never agree to the replenishing of Paris without occupying the forts, and a strong case can be made for their position. While it may well be that, as Thiers and Cochery maintained, the measures being proposed by Trochu and Favre were not of such a nature as to presage any attack, they were still of such dimensions as to call, in Bismarck's eyes and those of the military figures at Versailles, for reciprocal measures of military security on the German side.[48] This consideration was particularly compelling at a time when the relationship between Thiers and the chauvinists at Tours seemed to be in tatters. The leading figures of the Delegation still believed that their hold on the reins of power depended, in the last measure, on success on the battlefield. Gambetta's brain, in particular, teemed with visions of glories just ahead; radical opinion in Paris had been roused to a fever pitch of anger and frustration. But this in no way alleviated the central French problem, which was one of surviving in a protracted conflict with a power that possessed superior resources and had military leaders whose minds ran circles around those of their own. Still, those who counted most in the echelons of power at this time were determined to press on. To what must be attributed so disastrous a miscalculation? The answer is clear: primarily to the spirit of nationalism that overtook so much of the educated portion of French society in the second half of the nineteenth century—a spirit that seriously distorted French policy, military and political, causing it to serve irrational, costly, and ultimately self-destructive purposes instead of those that a sober consideration of the highest interests of France would have indicated.

It says much for Thiers's courage that he did not capitulate before what was practically a united front on the armistice question. Yet Thiers was not without limitations of his own, and it is to these, too, that some measure of responsibility for the failure of the negotiations must be ascribed. Thiers came to the negotiations at the beginning of November 1870 profoundly disturbed about the French position and most eager to see something done that would put an end to war and bring the two powers to a peace settlement. So great was his anxiety in this regard that it led him to scrap the existing French negotiating plan, worked out in consultation with Favre and Trochu, and to substitute for it a plan of his own that, by any rational reckoning of the odds, had no chance of success at all. The result was to drive him further from his colleagues. Bismarck summed up Thiers's qualities in a note of 2 November to Paul von Bronsart, a staff officer: "He betrays his inner feelings and lets himself get pumped."[49] As for Bismarck himself: disappointed as he was, he pursued a policy of great prudence and reserve, not playing his cards all at once, professing confidence that the French would see the light of day, leaving it for them to respond to his proposals, but watching sharply and mistrustfully any evidence of their policy. Believing that some leading figures of the government then in power in France indeed wanted to end the war, he nevertheless viewed its most senior officials as chauvinistic, bent on *guerre à outrance*. The situation in France remained precarious in the extreme. To talk of anyone having full power in the country in November 1870 was to close one's eyes to the disastrous series of events by which the preceding days had been plagued—by the uprising of 31 October and the political confusion to which it had led; by the manifold disagreements between Thiers and the other figures of the Government of National Defense; and, above all, by the war weariness fast overtaking large parts of the provinces—all these were of dimensions so great as to make it literally impossible for anyone at Versailles to know what was going on. There was little Bismarck could do for the time being to affect the course of events in Tours or Paris. As one member of the Garde Nationale, Raoul B., put it on 1 November 1871: "Oh poor beloved France, today it would need a miracle to lift you from the abyss into which you have so permanently fallen. Today I hope for nothing more, I believe in nothing more on earth except God whose mercy is infinite. May he heed the fervent prayer of a believer that I addressed to him in the night. To have suffered so great a fall in barely two months—to fall from such a height—all because of one man [Napoleon III] to whom our cowardice made us accomplices."[50] Trochu is reported to have remarked upon hearing that peace sentiment was sweeping the country: "The people in some drawing rooms want peace; the man in the street wants war."[51] To which Thiers answered: "The Empire ruined us; the Republic keeps us from saving ourselves."[52]

7

Bismarck's Anxieties

The days following the collapse of the negotiations with Thiers were difficult ones for Bismarck, and he himself possessed few illusions about the number, the magnitude, and the complexities of the problems with which he was faced. But the thrust of his efforts never varied—to end the war quickly and in a way in which German aims, as he conceived them, were achieved.[1]

Bismarck's tasks were complicated by a sudden and adverse turn of events on the battlefield. On 9 November 1870, the French forces, operating under the name of the Army of the Loire, inflicted a serious defeat on the Germans at Coulmiers, a village approximately twenty-five miles west of Orléans, which itself duly fell to the French. The French victory, the first in the war, was viewed with the gravest of misgivings by Bismarck, not least because it fanned the passions of the chauvinists to a white heat. Particularly affected, of course, was Gambetta, who, with his boundless vanity and pride, saw this as the harbinger of still greater victories and who now vowed to continue the war until the German forces were completely exhausted. At Tours, he succeeded, by the middle of November, in producing a state of sharply enhanced nationalistic and militaristic fervor among the members of the Delegation. The republican agitators who were hired by his underlings and instructed to whip up agitation against the more moderate deputies did such a good job that it became difficult to control them. Their success, coming just on the heels of the Coulmiers victory, increased the republican tendency to violence.[2]

For Gambetta, the victory at Coulmiers was the first step on a path that led directly to Paris, and it quickly became the repository of all the hopes and dreams he had entertained since he made his first appearance at Tours.

145

This being the case, he wasted no time in making known his feelings to the senior Paris authorities. He and his confidant, Charles Freycinet—a brash and quixotic figure, originally an engineer specializing in problems of sanitation, now designated by Gambetta to address administrative matters—let Trochu know of the victory by carrier pigeon and pressed him to burst out of the capital to join the Army of the Loire. To the army Gambetta wrote: "You are on the road to Paris. Never forget that Paris is waiting for us and honor demands that we should wrest it from the barbarians who are threatening it with pillar and fire."[3]

Gambetta was also pleased that the elements had now turned against the German army. The long November nights had to be coped with at a time when mobile electrical illumination was not yet possible. The forces remained at their lonely outposts. Very soon, a terrible winter set in, with temperatures below zero and only a few hours of daylight out of twenty-four. Homesick and bewildered, these unfortunate men clung on in the desperate struggle with their environment. Labor, food, and fodder for draft animals all had to be imported from a distance of thirty miles. From the sky, there were intermittent bursts of rain and snow. And the Germans were now obliged to be constantly on the alert against the famous *franc-tireurs*—gangs of armed civilian mobs who clandestinely harassed an enemy against whom they would never have succeeded on an open field. As early as August 1870, the crown prince had spoken of this *franc-tireur* activity as becoming widespread: "Shots are fired, generally in cunning, cowardly fashion on patrols, so that nothing is left for us to do but defend ourselves by burning down the house from which the shots came or else by the help of the lash and forced contributions."[4] Bismarck had given it to Favre as his opinion that "these people are not soldiers, they are murderers. And we are treating them as such." And, when Favre countered that the French were only repeating what had been done to them by the Germans in 1813, Bismarck replied: "That is quite true, but our trees still bear the marks where your generals hanged our people on them."[5] *Franc-tireur* activity reached its peak around November, but Gambetta's preoccupation with lifting the siege of Paris diverted his attention from the guerrillas. Still, in parts of France, notably in Alsace and Lorraine, the number of civilian warriors grew. These groups endeavored to match the achievement of the regular army and to create an all-French military authority that could unite all anti-German forces throughout the country. The activities of the *franc-tireurs* naturally tended to excite the hopes and imaginations of the French leaders at Tours and at Paris who were seeking some nucleus around which resistance to the Germans on the eastern front could be planned, organized, and successfully waged.

In fact, the German position was considerably stronger than the French, and certainly Gambetta, had deluded themselves into believing. The Germans still controlled the vast majority of the countryside. In any case, the events of the next two weeks were to shatter Gambetta's illusion that a spectacular reversal of French fortunes was at hand. On 24 November, Gambetta's instructions for the army's next move fell into German hands. Armed with reinforcements and under the guidance of Prince Frederick Charles, who was fast making a name for himself as one of the most gifted of the German commanders, Hanoverian troops of the Prussian X corps routed the French on December at Loigny just north of Orléans; it was clear to Antoine Chanzy, the French commander, that Orléans could not be saved, and on 4 December German troops moved in. The French grip on the city was broken; on 5 December it once again, and finally, fell under complete German control.

The defeat shattered the fighting spirit of the French troops. Though Gambetta still continued to profess confidence in the Army of the Loire and continued to believe that it could relieve Paris, any sober assessment of the situation would have dismissed this as the purest fantasy. In any case, the members of the Delegation, shaken by this reversal, hurriedly left Tours on 5 December and made for Bordeaux, about two hundred miles to the south. Gambetta remained unmoved. He wrote to Favre: "At bottom, the whole country understands and wants a war to the end, without mercy, even after the fall of Paris if that horrible misfortune should befall it"[6] To Gambetta, a French victory was inseparable from the establishment of the republic, and from this it was a short step to believing that all those who stood in his way were either secret or open traitors. Again to Favre: "At bottom France is growing more and more attached to the Republican Régime. The mass of the people even in the countryside understand, under the pressure of unfolding events, what is at stake. It is the Republicans who are true patriots, true

147

Entry of German troops into Orléans, 4 December 1870. (von Pflugk-Harttung, *The Franco-German War*, facing p. 427.)

defenders of the nation and of the rights of man. . . . We shall prolong this struggle to extermination."[7]

It was just at this time of military uncertainty and diplomatic stalemate that there erupted at the Prussian headquarters at Versailles a struggle of the most bitter intensity between the two titans of the Prussian government—Otto von Bismarck and Helmut von Moltke. It might be convenient at this point to pause and recapitulate the positions in which these men found themselves in mid-November 1870, a little more than two months before an armistice was signed. There is good reason to do this because the following two months were to bring a confused welter of events in the relations between the two, and it is hard to understand the significance of these events without a clear understanding of the positions of each of the two parties.

It has already been noted that there was, as early as 1866, tension between Bismarck and Moltke and the men around each of them. These differences surfaced in July of that year at Königgrätz, when Bismarck prevented the victorious Prussian forces from doing what Moltke wanted—that is to say, driving to Vienna and occupying the Austrian capital. Moltke never forgave Bismarck for what he regarded as a monstrous intrusion into military policy. The gap in understanding between the two men was greater, the measure of anger more profound, and the time it persisted longer than Bismarck suspected. This was apparent as early as the third week of July, one week after war with France broke out. One source of grievance, felt and expressed on the military side just at this time, was the presence at the front of Roon, the minister of war, whose proper place, Moltke and his colleagues believed, was in Berlin. More serious was the immediate and total exclusion of Bismarck from daily military conferences and a deliberate decision to keep him in the dark as to what objectives were agreed on and the strategy by which the military meant to achieve them.[8]

For the most part, Bismarck, at first inclined to allot a higher priority to military considerations than to political ones, took these slights in stride. It was only natural for the Prussian government to focus its activity on the war effort, the aim of which was the engagement and destruction of the French armies. Bismarck's attitude, however, underwent a marked change after the battle of Sedan and the collapse of the Ferrières negotiations, when it became apparent to him how urgent it was to end the war before there was foreign intervention. He was unaware, for example, of the decision to invade France and then to besiege Paris, and the news of these developments, colored no doubt by the studied condescension with which they were delivered by Moltke's subordinates, produced in him a violent reaction, partly of alarm, mostly of anger. On 10 October, the papers carried sensational reports of the German successes, including the allegation that the provisional government in Paris was about to agree to peace terms. Bismarck wrote an angry note to Moltke to ask that "I receive continuous information concerning military proceedings and if this does not seem possible in any other way that [I receive it] by means of simultaneous communication of the telegrams designed for the Berlin press the content of which is still of news to me when I read it five days later."[9]

Then there was the matter of the *franc-tireurs*. Bismarck believed that the most vigorous measures should be taken against them—a belief reinforced by his wife, who demanded that the Prussians "shoot and stab all the French down to the little babies."[10] He could not understand why Moltke and his staff dismissed, supposedly out of humanitarian concerns, his demands for a concerted and energetic response to these horrors. Bismarck regarded this reaction as a smokescreen to hide Moltke's real intention—to slow down the pace of operations and deal with the French the way he wanted to. In Bismarck's view, brutality was justified because it was the only way to convince the French that the war could not be won and to stave off what was and remained his nightmare—an intervention, in one form or another, by the neutrals.[11]

Bismarck's worries over Moltke's conduct grew almost daily, and they soon clashed again over who had responsibility for conducting Germany's affairs. A good illustration of this dispute and of its implications for policy concerns one Wilhelm Stieber, head of the *Feldpolizei*, and the orders he received from Bismarck to rebuke the mayor of Rheims, who, after the Paris revolution of 4 September, renounced his allegiance to the empire and threw his loyalty to the provisional government. Stieber had been placed under the authority of the General Staff, but, since what was at stake here was clearly a political matter, Bismarck decided to intervene. Stieber's preoccupation with ingratiating himself with his superiors led him to make known to Moltke the instructions he had received from the minister-president, which in turn led to charges by Moltke that Bismarck could not keep his hands off the conduct of military affairs. The result was an explosion on Bismarck's part and a bitter exchange of notes between himself and Moltke. And there soon followed efforts by leading members of Moltke's staff not only to disrupt relations between Bismarck and the king but also to deflect the king's policy in a direction that could only be favorable to a prolonged war.[12]

As we have seen, relations between Bismarck and Moltke did not improve after the Prussian forces took Versailles on 20 September, and the depth of their estrangement is abundantly clear from all the available evidence. By mid-October, people in the entourages of both men noted and were hardly surprised by signs of enhanced antipathy on Bismarck's part toward the chief of the General Staff. Beneath all the embittered tenacity that six months of war had bred, Bismarck was gripped by a dull apprehension of the stalemate on the battlefield. Not all was bleak, to be sure. Bismarck realized that Coulmiers was France's only successful effort, and if it was successfully contained (as he believed it would be—and was), the worst would be over.[13] But it promised at least another month of further casualties on a dreadful scale. This appalling prospect, together with the breakdown in the negotiations with the Paris authorities and the representatives of the imperial government, told heavily on the nerves of those concerned with the conduct of the war. The long exertion was now taking its psychic toll. Bismarck and, of course, Moltke, too, were both wretchedly overworked and overwrought. Tempers were frayed, sensibilities chafed and tender.

Beyond this, there was growing disagreement between the two men over the wider questions of policy involved. As Moltke's enthusiasm for the conflict increased, along with the depth of his desire to bring the French to the point of ruin, his suspicion of Bismarck became highly inflamed.[14] Bismarck, of course, was determined to end the war as quickly as possible with the territorial arrangements that he considered necessary for the security of the new Germany. On his mind always was the possibility of foreign intervention. He was keenly aware, for instance, of the desire expressed early in September by the Russians to end the war through the agency of an international conference.

Though this came to nothing, it was one of the reasons that Bismarck had opened negotiations with Bazaine and Bourbaki at Metz (see chapter 6).

Moltke came to the question from a diametrically opposed point of view. He believed that the best way to deal with the French was to treat them as eternal enemies, and he regarded any comments by Bismarck on military affairs to the king or to anyone else as an unforgivable infringement of his authority. The war, in his view, "was a duel between two determined nations in which Great Power responsibilities play no part."[15] Believing this, he considered that to trifle with international matters was simply to play into French hands. Thus, the difference between the two men soon attained that portion of the personal and the ideological that often produces the most violent of human antagonisms. Bismarck, feeling the supreme responsibility resting on his shoulders, poured out his frustrations in a letter to his wife: "The military men make my work terribly difficult for me. They lay their hands on it, ruin it and I have to bear the blame."[16] But Bismarck could make no headway. According to the Grand Duke of Baden, it was Moltke's opposition to the fallen regime that definitely set the king's face against the possibility of the restoration of Napoleon III, and it is no exaggeration to say that if the negotiations with Bazaine had not collapsed for other reasons, the weight of Moltke's influence might of itself have been enough to cause their failure.[17]

As for the old king: he was now intensively belabored by Moltke with data about the French military plans and intentions and steadfast assurances that both would collapse under a sustained German initiative. Moltke himself later denied in his memoirs that he was trying to deliberately delay operations so as to thwart a quick end of the war, as Bismarck strongly suspected.[18] But that he thought diplomacy out of place, that he ardently wished for the utter destruction of France as a Great Power, and that he did his best to bring the king to a similar view cannot be doubted. Worse still, Moltke had many sympathizers in the king's entourage for whom he was a putative messiah. And he had gained such an ascendancy over William in the first months after the war that there was no telling what plans of his the monarch might feel obliged to entertain.[19]

Bismarck, of course, was under no illusions about the state of affairs that prevailed on the battlefield, and he was anything but insensitive to its implications for Prussian policy. He was fully aware of Gambetta's determination to pursue *guerre à outrance* against the Germans and of the helplessness of the provisional government in the face of it. Not only that, but the defiant tone of the Parisian press was no longer confined to those papers that expressed a Germano-phobic line; it pervaded the entire spectrum of Parisian journalism. And the provisional government's failure to curb these manifestations continued to loom large in Bismarck's eyes as evidence that it could do nothing to curb the excesses of Gambetta's policy.

Thus, the months of November and December were ones of extreme tension and excitement over the whole course of the war effort. It was, it will be recalled, on 5 September that Moltke made his decision to advance into France and encircle the capital. But the encirclement had proceeded slowly, so slowly that by January no preparations had been made to bombard the city. Bismarck viewed this snail-paced operation with mounting horror, and it brought to high relief the conflicting views held by Moltke and himself over the proper course to be followed against the French in these difficult and unprecedented conditions. Bismarck, for his part, had developed a feeling that the entire future of the German war effort, if not the result of the war itself, was at stake. He argued that bombardment must commence at once, believing that it would finally bring the French to heel and would lead them to request an armistice that would then be followed by elections and a treaty between the two powers, thus averting outside intervention. Moltke, on the other hand, could see no reason for haste at all. He noted: "There is no need to hurry. When the war is decided, it will be decided decisively."[20] Siege warfare was repellent to him. It evoked the specter of the Crimean War and a treatise of his on that subject in general in which he had written that "cities of half a million population will certainly not be taken by force of arms, but must fall by themselves."[21] He let the king know in no uncertain terms that it was most unlikely that such an operation could be undertaken with anything less than a loss of men in appalling and wholly unacceptable numbers. To support this opinion, Moltke offered the following considerations:

1. The Germans had, until Coulmiers, unparalleled success on the field of battle. The General Staff was confident that it could, without great difficulty,

arrange the affairs of France to its own liking, and the French would not be inclined to go too far out of their way to offer resistance.

2. It was clear from the repeated failure of negotiations and the declarations of Gambetta that flowed from this that the French were not interested in either elections or peace. The only way to bring them to heel was by the complete destruction of their army and the total conquest of the country.

3. No matter that the Delegation had fled to Bordeaux. It was still white with the hope of those who sought to bring ruin to the enemy and, more important still, was—through its agents, especially in Alsace—at this very time busily enlisting *franc-tireurs* for that very purpose.[22]

In Moltke's view, the conflict must avenge itself completely upon its authors, but there was no hurry; the struggle could be waged methodically, almost casually, until that goal had been achieved. Bismarck could only bridle at the unconditionality posed by such a wild scheme and the stupefying naïveté on which it rested. Here he was attempting to bear the burden of negotiations, while Moltke and his allies permitted themselves to seek relief in reactions of bluster, petulance, and hysteria. For the statesman and military leader, these new and unprecedented possibilities stimulated a new set of ambitions and a new set of anxieties. Of these, the anxieties were often the more dangerous, for they could lead to defensive reactions (or what were conceived as such) even more savage, more open ended, and more destructive than those inspired by ambition. And the military leaders and particularly the military planners were especially vulnerable to both sets, compelled as they were to deal with hypothetical military contests divorced from any and all political background, charged as they were with the responsibility of figuring out how wars could be "won" and not how they could be avoided, compelled as they were to postulate the prospective adversary's total hostility and to ignore the political considerations that might alter his behavior.

Events in France strengthened Moltke's hand. For all his bluster, Gambetta found his hands tied by internal problems: the not infrequent breakdowns in communication, the serious deficiencies in supply, the cases of confusion and panic normal to any force battered by six months of war. That the war must go on, however, that the defeat at Loigny had merely been an unpleasant episode that could easily be set right, that fresh resolve could now be demonstrated from his new position at Bordeaux—all these Gambetta never for a moment doubted. To sustain the morale of the home front and to search out and eliminate elements of weakness in the national consciousness were the principal objectives developed in his wartime domestic policy. What Gambetta wanted was "political situation reports" by agents who were to keep their ears open in markets, in public houses, and in small shops. Gambetta's directive to those who compiled them emphasized the importance of completeness, objectivity, and unvarnished truth in the preparation of these reports—they were not to be retouched or have their colors softened by ideological brushes—and this was taken seriously, so much so that, as the war went on, the reports began to annoy and alarm the leading figures of the Delegation, who saw them as inconsistent with his policy of *guerre à outrance*. This did not trouble Gambetta. In interpreting the course of the war to the French people, he had generally, even in its first phase, always told those under his command to avoid excessive bombast and to observe Talleyrand's maxim, *"Pas de zèle."* But, as the war dragged on and spilled into the new year, his scheme for dealing with the enemy became ever more exaggerated, ever more shrill, and he offered the French people the prospect of a glorious victory by evoking the psychic satisfactions of the Great Revolution. Gambetta's scheme—a great offensive in which the armies of Paris would meet the armies of the Loire and the combined forces would together drive the enemy from the soil of France—was a scheme that was bound to be attractive to anyone who did not stop to inquire how it was to be achieved. This image, if applied seventy-eight years earlier to the France of, say, Dumouriez, might not have been so far from reality, but, as applied to the French position in 1870–71, it was grotesquely overdrawn, a caricature rather than a reflection of what really existed, highly misleading and pernicious as a foundation for French policy, and a grievous and needless underestimation of the capacity of the adversary.[23] No matter. Gambetta's agents were, in all their undertakings, "to make clear this essential truth, that the Republic alone, by its institutions, can assure the liberty, the greatness of the future of France."[24]

In the meantime, the differences between Bismarck and the military continued to grow. Moreover, as the war spilled into winter and the activity of *franc-tireur* operations expanded, the full cup of German resentment for the French nation boiled over. "The war," wrote a German soldier, "is now gradually acquiring a hideous character. Murder and burning are now commonplace on both sides, and one cannot sufficiently beg the Almighty to make an end of it."[25] In the words of another: "We are learning to hate them more and more every day. I can assure you that it is in the interests of the civilization of our own people that such a racial struggle be brought to an end. Atrocious attacks are being avenged by atrocities which remind one of the Thirty Years' War."[26] Not surprisingly, as the struggle dragged on, Moltke showed himself more and more inclined to intervene in what to Bismarck were political matters that did not concern him. Particularly outrageous, in the minister-president's view, was Moltke's attempt to negotiate directly with Trochu, who, after Coulmiers, construed a plan by which forty thousand men in Paris would break out of the city, burst through the Prussian lines, join forces with the Army of the Loire, and drive the Germans out of France. It was with a view to dissuading Trochu from going forward with this plan that Moltke, on 5 December, addressed the following letter to the French leader:

> Versailles, 5 Dec. 1870
>
> It may be useful to inform Your Excellency that the Army of the Loire was yesterday defeated near Orléans and that this town was occupied by German troops. If Your Excellency sees fit to convince himself of this fact through one of his own officers, I should be happy to furnish him with a safe conduct for his passage.
>
> Accept, dear General, the expression of the high consideration with which I have the honor to be your humble and immediate servant,
>
> Chief of Staff, Count von Moltke[27]

To Bismarck, this communication presented the most serious sort of danger to his ability to conduct the kind of diplomacy with which he was charged. Trochu was president of the Government of National Defense, and Moltke's letter could be construed as an instrument for the opening of negotiations— this at the worst possible time. Not only was it intolerable from a political standpoint, but also the structure of thought addressed to it was so bizarre and distorted that it called for an immediate protest. This Bismarck drew up in a memorandum to the king titled "Initiative on Negotiations with the

Enemy." Bismarck laid down: "Every new German initiative for negotiations creates in Paris a false impression and understanding."[28] Moltke was not slow to respond. "In affairs political as well as military," he groaned, "the Federal Chancellor is disposed to decide everything himself without paying the smallest heed to what the responsible military experts have to say."[29] Thus, at the end of 1870, relations between Bismarck and Moltke, far from improving, were subjected to further strains, much worse than anything that had occurred up to that point.

The major issue remained what it long had been, that is to say, the bombardment of Paris. As noted, Bismarck was eager that operations begin immediately, and his view was supported by Roon, who let Bismarck know that the guns and ammunition for this operation were and for some time had been abundantly available. Bismarck had two motives for pressing for the immediate commencement of the siege. He wanted to convince the Paris population of the hopelessness of the situation with which they were now confronted. Moreover, there was an international consideration. The Russians had, in October, suddenly announced that they would no longer consider themselves bound by the Black Sea clauses of the Treaty of Paris of 1856. The full story of how this news was received by Bismarck and the steps he took to defuse the international complications over Petersburg's decision will be recounted in due course. For our purposes here, it is important to record that the Russian decision provided additional impetus for Bismarck to urge that the siege begin at once. Successfully conducted, it would, he hoped, compel the French to sue for peace before the Black Sea issue developed in a manner unfavorable to Prussia.[30]

In this struggle, the military—with the exception of Roon—fought him every step of the way. Particularly outspoken was the crown prince's chief of staff, the able General Leonhard Count von Blumenthal, by whose hands the siege would be conducted. Clearly considering the effects that an unsatisfactory bombardment would produce, he wrote: "Politics should have nothing to do with this question . . . it is a military one and the honor of the army is at stake." He would, he announced, surrender his command rather than heed the "infantile counsels" that came from the chancellor.[31] One sees in the annals of European history few parallel writings that approach, in cynicism, if not in heartlessness, this appalling attitude.

To Bismarck's mind, Blumenthal's words represented only an unquestionable and fatal delusion. So preposterous, so monstrously destructive, and so lacking in any conceivable necessity or advantage to anyone at all were these arguments that it was impossible to imagine any rational explanation for them, even from the standpoint of the most fearful, hateful, and suspicious of tyrants. The reasons for Bismarck's reactions were logical and obvious. He wanted, if at all possible, to avoid a prolonged war. He wanted to retain any and all levers that would permit him to obstruct the soldiers in their efforts to establish the conditions in which this could take place. In an earlier memorandum to the king, he insisted that he at once be given "the fullest and most up-to-date information on all military plans. I need this in view of the eventualities posed by the prospect that neutral Powers may try to affect the outcome of the war. . . . Knowledge of our military strength and aims will allow me to assess the proper approach to adopt in negotiations with England, Russia, and Austria."[32]

It is amazing to note the total failure of Moltke and Blumenthal to understand this rationale for Bismarck's policy. Constrained by their simpleminded notion that a war of destruction against France was inevitable (or, in their case, desirable), they saw in Bismarck's behavior only the evidence of a fatuous and suspect dilettantism and comforted each other (neither of them knowing remotely as much about France as did their antagonist) with mutual assurances that Bismarck was naïve, that it was pointless to try to deal with the French, that the French understood nothing but brute force, and so on. This lack of understanding flowed not from failure on Bismarck's part to explain his policy; this he had set forth in great detail in letters to the king such as the one just quoted. The cause lay, rather, in a total inability of the two men to grasp the subtleties of a policy that aimed to handle the situation by any means short of a war of annihilation.[33] To thwart their obstructionism, Bismarck pulled out all the stops; one of his most striking efforts was the campaign he began to wage in December 1870 in the German press.[34] Articles demanding that the siege begin at once filled the air. Popular songs were composed to the effect that Moltke should undertake operations at once. One ran:

Lieber Moltke, gehst so stumm
Immer um den Brei herum?

158

Bester Moltke, nimm's nicht krumm:
Mach' doch endlich Bumm, Bumm, Bumm.[35]

[Dear old Moltke
what's up with you
pussyfooting around so silently?
best of Molkes, don't begrudge me,
just go and do it, boom boom boom.]

The stroke succeeded, but only at the cost of further infuriating military opinion at Versailles. Blumenthal, ever the admiring underling, again took up the charge for his chief: "If we allow ourselves to be driven by the so-called 'Voice of the People,' as the newspapers call it, to adopt measures in opposition to reason and to all military science, it will be an end to generalship. The people will have to try us by court-martial, turn us out, and appoint in our places lawyers and newspaper correspondents."[36] As for Moltke: though finally consenting, under pressure from the king, to begin the Paris bombardment, he regarded this operation as only the first step in a wider campaign that would be waged throughout the entire country. In his view, the surrender of Paris would be no different from that of Metz. The city would be occupied, its fortresses captured, its garrison hauled off to Germany and thrown in jail, and its administration taken over by a German military government. For Moltke, the siege was to be a military matter in which the politicians should have no say. In his own words: "The question when artillery or military attack should begin can only be decided on the basis of military views. Political factors can find consideration in so far as they do not demand anything militarily inadmissible or impossible."[37] In Bismarck's eyes, Moltke's words represented a distortion prevalent in the military mind, always given to extremism when it came to the relation between military and political objectives. Moltke, on the other hand, saw the struggle as a war of annihilation, and he refused to listen to any ideas that ran counter to that purpose. It was also becoming apparent to Bismarck and others that Moltke and his staff, in addition to being all-powerful, also considered themselves to be both all-virtuous and all-wise. They, it was inferred, would know exactly what to do with the conquered French and with all other post-hostilities problems. France, supposedly hopelessly benighted and wrongheaded, would be totally

159

excluded from participation in the fashioning of the regime of peace under which it and its people would be obliged to live. Moltke's mind was obsessed with the concept of destruction—sheer destruction, destruction for its own sake—as the central aim of the war.[38]

Bismarck nonetheless was able to secure the support of the king when bombardment commenced on 27 December, but the antagonism between the two men had become so deep that Frederick William, crown prince of Prussia, seeing the two most active and high-powered figures in Germany going off in diametrically opposed directions, decided to do what he could to compose their differences. On 8 January, Moltke received an urgent request from the crown price to come see him. The two met over dinner, during which the prince endeavored, with minimal success, to bring a friendly influence to bear upon the general. In later years, he came to regret this misspent effort. And no wonder. Moltke had not lifted his fork before he began breathing fire. Independent, insolent, brutal, and even cruel in his methods, he announced that, after the siege, the liberated forces would sweep southward with a view to capturing the resources of the enemy. As he put it: "We must fight this nation of liars to the very end. We will stop at nothing to despoil them. . . . Then we will dictate whatever peace we like."[39] This immediately raised in the mind of the crown prince the specter of the Germans possibly tied down in a foreign country and waging war without end. The plan also involved the removal from Bismarck's hands of control over Germany's policy toward France and the assignment of it to Moltke. Doubtless with this fear in mind, the crown prince asked about the political dimensions of such an action. Moltke replied that he knew nothing about politics and added: "I am concerned only with military affairs."[40] Though shaken by what he heard, the crown prince did not give up, and five days later he invited both Bismarck and Moltke to dine with him. Despite his sincerity, he immediately ran into hopeless difficulties. Whoever might have thought that Bismarck's bitterness over the policies being urged by Moltke had reached the saturation point was sorely mistaken. Bismarck used the occasion to launch an attack not only upon Moltke and upon the latter's subordinates on the General Staff but, more sweepingly, upon the whole course on which the military had, in the four months that followed the fall of Sedan, embarked. Moltke, stung to the quick, furiously insisted that Bismarck was again attempting to intrude into military

160

The War Council at Versailles in November/December 1870. Painting by Anton von
Werner, 1900. (Photo: Elke Walford. Hamburger Kunsthalle, Hamburg, Germany.
Bildarchiv Preußischer Kulturbesitz [BPK]. Used by permission of Art Resource, New York.
ART428957.)

matters. There followed an exchange between the two that, as a source of violence in the interpersonal relations between two senior figures of the same government, can rarely have been exceeded. The dinner broke up, Bismarck tearing for the door and remarking that Moltke was behaving like a child.[41]

The failure of Crown Prince Frederick William to reconcile Bismarck and Moltke had wide ramifications. Above all, it revealed that the gap separating the two men went beyond the issue at hand—namely the bombardment of Paris.[42] This and further meetings between the two not only led to deadlock but also ushered in a period of extreme conflict the intensity of which may be judged by the fact that Bismarck at one point felt obliged to leave the palace and take up residence at a chateau five miles away with a view to protecting himself against a military-inspired coup against his person. As for Moltke: whatever his other faults, he was not lacking in either courage or power of decision. After a bout of anguished reflection in the privacy of his study, where, according to his admiring biographer, Verdy du Vernois, he paced up and down with folded arms, he emerged and, on 14 January, formally put forward in a memorandum to the king his ideas on postbombardment operations that he had broached with the crown prince five days earlier. Here, however, he went further and made it clear that he fully expected to be put in charge of the negotiations for the surrender of Paris as he had of Sedan. Once again, he described himself as uninterested in politics, which, he said in a conversation with one of the crown prince's advisers, would be left to Bismarck. Seldom, however, does one find a plan that was more likely than this to have sweeping and unquestionable effects in the field of politics and diplomacy.[43]

Bismarck was stunned and intensely angered when he learned of this dispatch. Moltke's memorandum touched off further exchanges between the two men. On 14 January, Bismarck sent a memorandum to the king in which he gave a detailed and frightening picture of Germany's political and international position should Moltke be given his wishes and in which he insisted that the question of the fall of Paris was inextricably bound up with that of peace—a peace that, though it would give the new Germany new territory and a large indemnity, must not be so punitive as to add significantly to Parisians' already deep feelings of humiliation and resentment. Moltke and the members of his staff had, Bismarck conceded, more reasons than he had to

Frederick William, crown prince of Prussia (future Emperor Frederick III). (von Pflugk-Harttung, *The Franco-German War*, 74.)

be oblivious to these realities but insufficient reason for ignoring them altogether. The Danish War of 1863–64 and the Austrian War of 1866 had both revealed situations that should have given pause to even the most sanguine of military chauvinists. There flowed from Bismarck's untiring pen a further memorandum five days later. Here he took up the issue, already referred to, of Moltke's dealing with Trochu, noting that his anger was aroused not only by the fact of the abrupt and unexpected intervention by Moltke into diplomatic arrangements on which the relations between two governments then rested but also by the fact that the matter had, before he could do anything about it, become known to the public on both sides. Bismarck politely but clearly expressed his view that Moltke had overstepped his authority, and he asked the king to issue orders the effect of which would be to bring the general immediately to heel. He particularly emphasized his belief that no negotiations between Paris and Versailles should occur to which he had not first been made party.[44]

One can easily imagine the anguish and despair Bismarck's memoranda evoked in the mind of his sovereign. He was old and tired; his nerves were strained; his health was poor. Yet, it was for him to decide. In the duel between his two great opponents, he was inclined to side, as a military monarch, with Moltke. But Bismarck had raised unanswerable arguments, and in the circumstances of the time—particularly in view of the arrangements for the establishment of a new German empire that were now being worked out—Bismarck's services would be more indispensable than they had been before. William therefore came down on Bismarck's side. Evidence of this first became apparent on 20 January, when Bismarck let the king know that the French were expressing a desire to renew talks, and William issued instructions to inaugurate them—a decision that foretold the end of Moltke's plans to continue the war. It was with a view to making this decision clearer that the monarch, on 25 January, issued two peremptory and explicit orders, the first of which barred Moltke from entering into any discussion with the French authorities, either at Paris or Bordeaux, without first ascertaining from William whether Bismarck should be informed and the second forbidding him to execute further military plans without consulting the chancellor and giving the latter the opportunity to make known his views with respect to these.[45]

These instructions infuriated Moltke. After receiving them, he went off to attend a meeting of his staff on 26 January, at which the royal orders were extensively discussed. The reaction to William's messages were what one might expect; Verdy and Bronsart were disagreeably impressed by what they regarded as an unquestionable slight against their master and poured out the full measure of their bitterness against Bismarck. Whatever the thrust of William's messages, the bulk of the meeting was devoted to a continued exploration of the steps that might be taken to exclude Bismarck from military deliberations. Moltke, whose back was stiffened by the reaction of his subordinates to William's messages, now began to suffer a degree of humiliation that approached hysteria. An angry reply was worked out that evening, the purpose of which was clearly to change William's mind. The reply minced no words. It expressed Moltke's amazement that William could entertain, much less accept, accusations that his, Moltke's, conduct with Trochu had been anything but correct and proper. All he had done was to suppress information on military operations that would be needed only if Bismarck as well as Moltke were advising the monarch on the siege. William's suggestion that he had acted improperly was one he found "*ungnädig*," ungracious. In any case, to admit Bismarck to the councils of war would be to place the army under a dual authority that he could not conceive as possible—something that, if it were to come into effect, would cause him to resign, leaving "the relevant operations and responsibility for them to the Federal Chancellor alone. I await," he announced pointedly, "Your Imperial Majesty's most gracious decision on this matter."[46]

When discussions resumed the next day, circumstances had changed in important respects. The sheer emotional spasm that had made the letter attractive had dissipated, and Moltke's earlier hope for a change of heart on William's part had cooled. The historian is at a loss to explain the reason for this change. There are some vague references in Moltke's correspondence to words having passed between himself and members of William's staff that might have served to soften his attitude. Or it may have taken him some time to understand the full measure of William's commitment to the decision he had made and to realize that any attempt to alter it would be pathetically unperceptive, naïve, and misconceived. In any case, the letter was not sent, and its place was taken by a considerably softer and more restrained one, but one that still left no doubt that he considered Bismarck's accusations against him

165

thoroughly wide of the mark, that requested William's good offices to prevent further abuse from the minister-president, and that asked for a clarification as to the relationship between Bismarck and himself. On this last, Moltke showed that he had no intention of surrendering the prerogatives over strategy that he believed only he could exercise. He noted: "To give information concerning operations planned or in the course of being planned to anyone other than the generals I would consider a breach of duty."[47] William's staff drew up a polite response to this second memorandum of Moltke's, but they never sent it. They had no cause to. On 28 January, an armistice was signed between the provisional government of the French and the new German empire. But its signing in no way ended the bitterness felt by Moltke and his subordinates toward Bismarck. That the military leaders had not changed their opinion of the chancellor, that they regarded him as unsuited to conduct negotiations, that they remained suspicious of his motives as he pursued these, cannot be doubted; for evidence of their attitude one need only point to the devastating words of the passage addressed to this subject in the memoirs of Albrecht von Stosch, the normally dispassionate intendant-general: "I have never known such bitterness against any man as prevails against Prince Bismarck at this moment."[48]

It is not normally within the province of historians to occupy themselves with what-might-have-been questions. But it is surely not unduly speculative or extravagant to suggest that, had Moltke's influence been allowed to prevail on William I in the winter of 1870–71, the course of history would have been drastically changed. Bismarck's influence on the peace negotiations would, to all intents and purposes, have been eliminated. There would have been no attempt by the new Germany to enter into any negotiations with the French with a view to rapidly concluding a peace. The Great Powers of Europe, we may be sure, would have been loath to leave further initiative to Berlin. The success of Moltke would have been warning enough to them. Even as it was, Bismarck began, by the beginning of 1871, to hedge his bets and to take precautions against the possibility that the worm might turn in such a direction. Had it done so, these efforts would have gone into high gear, impelled by a fear that German ambitions were boundless and that the destruction of France could be prevented only by help from the outside.

The forces that move men and governments to action in the field of international affairs are not always logical ones, nor do they always operate directly. Thus, the impulses that were destined ultimately to play a primary role in Bismarck's decision to end the war as quickly as possible and to open new negotiations with the French, besides those already recounted, were also ones that had little to do with France and Germany, and not even much to do with the states of South Germany, with which Bismarck was now concluding treaties that would bring them into the new empire. His decision, in the main, grew out of the experiences suffered by the Russians in their attempts to annul the Black Sea clauses that had been set up by the Treaty of Paris of 1856. For this reason, anyone interested in tracing the negotiations that led to the armistice of 28 January 1871, which is discussed in the following chapter, has no choice but to chart the course of events as reflected by the Russian experiences with that treaty and the effect these had on Russian policy.

Let us return to the year 1856 and recall, at the risk of slight repetition, that the Treaty of Paris, which ended the Crimean War of 1853–56, forbade the Russians to maintain war ships in the Black Sea. The restriction was imposed largely on the insistence of the British out of the belief that its existence would prevent Russia from threatening Turkey. Though the treaty contained other provisions offensive to Petersburg—notably the creation of two new independent Danubian principalities over which the Russians had hitherto exercised a preponderance of influence—it was these Black Sea clauses to which the Russians took the greatest exception and to the abrogation of which all Russian policy for the next fifteen years would be directed. Whether Tsar Alexander II had ever really abandoned, in the back of his mind, the idea of destroying the Black Sea clauses of the Treaty of Paris by seizing Constantinople and taking control of the Straits may be doubted. But there can be little question that the international upheaval of 1870 confirmed his belief that he had to do something about this perceived injustice. These hated provisions of the treaty of 1856 were more than a diplomatic offense;

they deprived Russia of the right to defend its borders and thus struck directly at its sovereignty. It was with a view to abolishing these restrictions once and for all that the Russian foreign minister, Alexander Gorchakov, in a circular of 31 October 1870 addressed to the Great Powers, announced that Russia would no longer consider itself bound by the Black Sea clauses of the Treaty of Paris.[49]

For Bismarck, this announcement could not have come at a worse time. There was, first of all, the problem of Moltke, which was just then beginning to reach its highest intensity. Second, there was the problem of France. The French government that had signed the treaty was that of the Second Empire, which had been overturned by the Paris revolution of 4 September 1870. It no longer existed. But the Government of National Defense by which it had been replaced had yet to secure from the other powers of Europe anything resembling formal declarations of their recognition of its existence, this in spite of the friendly reception they had, one month earlier, given Thiers. Worse still was the fact that it was this government that was now at war with Germany.[50]

And, as if this were not enough, Gorchakov's announcement opened the door to the prospect of an Anglo-Russian confrontation. For the British were insistent that, because the Treaty of Paris had been an instrument to which all the Great Powers had set their hands, there could be no question of the nullification of one of its most salient clauses by a unilateral statement. At the head of the British government there stood William Ewart Gladstone, a liberal whose sympathies for Russia were not unknown. At the same time, however, there was ferment, too, on the right wing of the political spectrum. Among this faction, more than twenty-four months of exclusion from power had bred no small measure of desperation and much questioning as to whether anything less than the toughest of lines on this question was really the right one. Of outstanding importance in this connection was the press. Gorchakov's announcement touched off a stampede in the newspapers seething with bitterness over the Russian decision, as well as warnings that anything less than the strongest of actions would be enough to unseat the entire British cabinet.[51]

In the wake of these smoldering discontents, the political atmosphere of Europe during the last three months of 1870 was one of much nervousness, uncertainty, and potentially explosive combinations. It was to tamp down international tension that Bismarck's efforts were now addressed. He had, as we have seen, let the Russians know, as early as 1866, that Prussia had no objection to the annulment of the Black Sea clauses; he had done so again before the war broke out in 1870, and he assured the Russian government that the intimacy that existed between them because of monarchical ties continued unabated.[52] Still there existed in the mind of Gorchakov, a man of unbridled vanity and dizzy from the profound popular acclaim he hoped would now become his lot, a profound suspicion that Bismarck would not keep his word—could not keep it—seeing that all his efforts were addressed to the war with France, to say nothing of the fact that there was still no formal binding agreement between the two courts on the subject. All the same, Bismarck was too astute a diplomat not to detect the signs of continued uncertainty in the mind of the Russian foreign minister. On 7 November, he telegraphed to Heinrich Reuss, his minister to Petersburg, that there was no doubt that "the King could be expected in his royal communications to give pronounced consent" to the Russian decision.[53] This intention Reuss confirmed the next day at a palace ceremony, at which he spoke with great effusiveness and cordiality about the state of Prusso-Russian relation in the eyes of William I, who was obliged to see in Alexander II Germany's sincere ally and warm friend, a disposition that the tsar cordially reciprocated.

Reassuring as these words may have been, it was only natural that the increasing evidence of tension between Russia and Britain should be highly disturbing to Bismarck. Of particular concern to him was, once again, the prospect of foreign intervention. He noted, on 7 November: "The favorable position we have taken toward Russia will after several weeks not loom as large as it does now in the calculation of the Powers."[54] Resolving the crisis quickly became a matter of the highest priority. Negotiations were put in hand, as a result of which a representative of the British government, Odo Russell, visited Versailles. How serious the British were about the matter was shown on 21 November, when Russell declared that, if the Russians did not withdraw their circular, the British, with or without allies, were ready to take up arms. This was probably an exaggeration. As Jonathan Parry has so persuasively observed, much of Tory jingoism in the Victorian era was for domestic political purposes. There were sober Tory influences to hold the conservatives back even when they were in power, and, most of the time, when they threatened war, it was more in the spirit of urging Austria (or, later, Germany or both) to wage it against Russia, with British help—never an attractive proposition for them.[55]

Still, the conservative attitude could not but alarm Bismarck in the highest degree. And this was only natural, considering the problems now looming on the horizon. First, there was the obstreperousness of the Russians in insisting that they and they alone had a vital interest in the Black Sea, even if this position led to a possible confrontation with the British. The effort to avoid complications in Anglo-Russian relations had lain at the heart of Bismarck's policy ever since the outbreak of the war, in July. The present Russian behavior was jeopardizing that policy. Particularly galling and even more menacing was the evidence that the Russians, caught between the anti-German tendencies of the nationalists at court and those who favored Bismarck's pro-Russian policy, were rooting for the former and were thus straining Russo-Prussian relations. The outstanding figures in the pro-French party, while admittedly a minority, could easily be brought into a position to exercise stronger influence on Russian policy. They were prevented from doing so partly by Tsar Alexander, but only partly. The tsar was no great friend of Bismarck's, but he had high regard and affection for his own uncle, King William I of Prussia, to whom he was related by marriage. He accepted a reasonably close relationship with the North German Confederation as something flowing naturally from a common interest in sustaining the principle of inherited monarchy as the linchpin of any proper political system.[56] Still, Alexander was dismayed and unnerved by the implications of the Prussian victory in 1866 and the extent to which this had a revolutionary impact—overthrow of dynasties, great territorial expansion by right of conquest, and so on. This reaction could only add to the uncertainties Bismarck faced, for Prussian power was now much greater than it had been then.[57]

And others, notably the Pan-Slavists, had even stronger views. They looked to the Straits and Turkey not only as a region of Balkan Slavdom in which they could now begin to exert their own direct influence but also as a staging area for intrigues and operations against the Austro-Hungarian and Turkish empires generally, and they viewed Bismarck's policies with the darkest suspicion. Besides, there were other problems elsewhere, not the least of which were Vienna's difficulties with the Hungarians, who had set their faces against any attempt to cooperate with Russia. But not only was Austria a signatory of the Peace of Paris; it had also, together with Great Britain and France, signed, on 15 April 1856, a treaty that guaranteed the integrity of Turkey and that the Russian action now threatened to undermine. This treaty formed the basis of a tripartite relationship and was to come into operation when such a threat to the independence of Turkey arose. A central element of Bismarck's policy was the preservation of a reasonable equilibrium between Austria and Russia and the avoidance of any major conflict between these two powers. Now the Russians were taking actions that infringed Turkish independence. Finally, there was the new situation that confronted Bismarck on Germany's western border—namely the prospect that the French would use the crisis as a means of breaking out of their isolation and appealing to the powers to end the war on terms much different from those that Bismarck had envisaged.[58]

This was the situation—in Russia, in Great Britain, in France, and in Austria-Hungary—that Bismarck faced as the year 1870 drew to a close. He must have seen in it a real danger to the policies that formed the pillars of his statecraft, and he now threw himself into the task of seeing to it that these were not weakened.

To the Russians, in the first place, Bismarck made it crystal clear that they could, as he had promised before, count on Germany's support in relation to the Black Sea clauses of the Treaty of Paris of 1856.[59] But this was not enough. A primary source of anxiety among the figures in Petersburg was that Bismarck's preoccupation with the war against France would tie his hands and give him second thoughts. Bismarck therefore resolved to act at once, since he believed that any hesitation on Germany's part would strengthen the hands of the Petersburg chauvinists who were quietly working behind the scenes for France. If they were to initiate action for the French, Germany would be deprived of a valuable ally, and the risk of neutral intervention of some sort would be correspondingly increased. In addition to this, Bismarck set about, quietly and with great skill, to create a situation in which Russia and Great Britain could compose their differences. In the end, the Russians and the British agreed, the former somewhat unhappily, to submit the entire question to a general European conference under the chairmanship of Granville, the foreign secretary, at London. The British laid down one condition: that the conference meet without any decisions about the subject being made beforehand. But the Russians had been assured by Bismarck that the clause of the Paris treaty to which they objected would be annulled. On 2 December, the Austrian government, prompted by Bismarck, agreed. Though within the Austro-Hungarian bureaucratic structure distrust of and antagonism toward Russia was of long standing, particularly on the part of the Hungarians, there was no particular animosity between the Austrian and the Russian emperors, and Bismarck took advantage of this fact to secure a commitment from Vienna to attend the meeting.[60]

The immediate problem was thus solved, but there remained one great danger, namely France. Not only was France a signatory of the Treaty of Paris of 1856, but also Paris was the city where the instrument had been signed. Bismarck was well aware that the British government wanted a meeting at which all the powers that had signed the 1856 treaty would be present. That meant that French representation was essential. On 14 December, Granville had written Bismarck a note stating that he expected Favre to take his seat at the upcoming deliberations in London. As for Bismarck, his reasons for suggesting and supporting an international conference were related strictly to the Black Sea clauses of the treaty and had no wider implications. But the French, of course, saw the whole matter very differently. This was particularly true of the minister in charge of foreign affairs for the Delegation, Jean Baptiste, comte de Chaudordy, of whom mention has already been made in chapter 6. Of all the personalities at Bordeaux in the hectic months leading up to the conference, Chaudordy was the most able and, from Bismarck's point of view, the most dangerous. A cultivated man of charm and cynical wit, with the ability to ingratiate himself with people from widely different milieus, this quintessential diplomat possessed cold political intelligence, strategic gifts of the first order, and great resources of courage and patience. His salient weakness was a desire to avoid the limelight and to rely on others to execute his designs. This weakness was very much in evidence as the list of conference participants was being drawn up. It was Chaudordy's intention to use the conference as a framework for taking up a whole range of problems, not the least of which was the fashioning of an armistice on terms favorable to the French government. But Chaudordy, true to form, was content to assign the burden of this task to Favre, who, at Paris, needed Bismarck's permission to cross the Prussian lines that ringed the city.[61]

At first, Bismarck was willing to allow this because the British made no secret of their belief that French representation at the conference was indispensable if it was to attain international legitimacy.[62] But, of course, the provisional government had none. Moreover, Bismarck was, as will be seen shortly, deeply engaged in supremely sensitive and delicate negotiations with members of the regency; the prospect of a member of the provisional government at the London conference could undercut the progress he was making with its predecessor. And what if Favre was successful in discharging the designs that loomed so large in the eyes of Chaudordy? All Bismarck's efforts to end the war quickly would receive a terrible blow, bringing anguish and disheartenment.

Bismarck therefore determined to reverse field. Pulling out all the stops, he cut off all communications between the Prussian outposts and the surrounded city on the excuse that French artillery had opened fire on the designated *parlementaires*.[63] Because of this, the invitation to the conference sent to Favre by Granville never reached the former's hands. The conference convened on 3 January 1871, and Bismarck saw to it that the invitation came to Favre only on that day. On 10 January, the conference was adjourned for another week. During this time, Bismarck used a plethora of procedural arguments surrounding the granting of safe passage to wear down Favre's eagerness to attend, and he managed to make Favre's anxieties all the more acute by pointing to the situation inside his stricken city and the difficulties of maintaining public order if such a senior official were now suddenly to disappear from the scene. Favre himself would later write that, as of this juncture, "civil war was a few yards away; famine a few hours."[64] Bismarck was only too willing to accommodate these fears when, on 16 January 1871, he addressed a long letter to Favre in which he underlined the gravity of the peril that now menaced the great French capital. "I would permit myself to inquire whether it would be a good idea for Your Excellency to leave Paris now to attend a discussion on the subject of the Black Sea. . . . I can hardly believe that Your Excellency, in the critical situation to which you so have effectively contributed, would wish to deprive yourself of the opportunity of collaborating in a solution for which you must bear a share of the responsibility."[65] This was too much for Favre. He decided to remain in Paris.

But, for Bismarck, the whole episode showed just how important it was to make a quick peace, lest a new and deeply troubling stage unfold between the new German nation and the other Great Powers of Europe.[66] Let us once again step back in time to see how he tried to resolve that overriding anxiety.

The reader will recall Bismarck's problems in October and November of 1870. The negotiations with Thiers had failed utterly. The defeat of the French forces at Loigny on 2 December did nothing to weaken Gambetta's determination to continue the war at all costs. A conference was soon to take place at London at which the British were determined that the French be given a voice. It was in these circumstances that Bismarck's attitude toward the imperialist émigrés once more began to change. On 5 December, he wrote a note to Reuss in Petersburg: "Up to now there have been no negotiations with Napoleon. But we cannot exclude that possibility if we wish to close the Pandora's box that intervention would threaten."[67] Even before he wrote these words, Bismarck had received from the deposed emperor what he could only take to be encouraging news. On 27 November, there came into his hands a memorandum from Napoleon the purpose of which was to outline a plan for the reestablishment in France of the empire overthrown by the Paris revolution of 4 September 1870. The contents of this memorandum are worth reviewing at this point both because of their lasting influence on Bismarck and as a reflection of the political atmosphere of the time.[68]

The memorandum began with a somewhat plaintive acknowledgment of the exceptional influence that Bismarck had come to exercise on European affairs. At the same time, Napoleon was careful to assure Bismarck that he regarded a German victory as imminent and found himself obliged to ask how a peace could be quickly concluded. Napoleon thought he knew the answer. He was reasonably confident that the vast majority of the French people wanted to bring the war to an end. This could, he argued, be done through the creation of a new *Corps législatif*. Once this assembly had been created, it could put in hand negotiations for peace on a basis that Bismarck believed possible. After the fall of Paris, William I could issue an appeal to the French people for the restoration of Napoleon and Eugénie.

This memorandum received, we may be sure, Bismarck's most careful attention. Napoleon's attempt to reclaim power clearly presaged a situation in which the Germans would soon expect to enter into diplomatic intercourse with the deposed emperor. But the situation was still too confused and the position of Napoleon, with respect to the other powers of Europe, too uncertain to permit useful recommendations on a policy toward the fallen regime.[69] All the same, Bismarck determined to resume discussions with Napoleon through a channel to which he had full access—that of General Adjutant Henri Castelnau, Napoleon's personal emissary, who had placed the original memorandum in Bismarck's hands and with whom Bismarck had, on 16 December, an extended conversation.[70]

Bismarck reacted to the memorandum he had received from Napoleon in a conciliatory manner, recalling, as he did to Castlenau, the respect that the North German Confederation had shown the emperor after Sedan but pointing out the difficulties posed by the prospect of an imperial restoration. For one thing, the defeat of Bazaine at Metz removed from the scene the possibility that an army favorable to Napoleon could somehow be used to place him once again in power. And this was not Bismarck's only concern. Napoleon had expressed his preference for a reconstituted *Corps législatif*—but using such a body was bound to be cumbersome; locating its members would not be easy, and, in any case, there would be no guarantee of the political direction they might now favor. But the worst feature of this scheme lay at the end. After the surrender of Paris, the King of Prussia would appeal to the people of France to make their voices known through this body. As was the case with the scheme involving Eugénie described earlier, for the Germans to accept such a proposal would be foolish and shortsighted in the extreme. How could it fail to arouse opposition from the republicans who had been fighting the war for four months? Napoleon and Eugénie would appear as the puppets of the enemy, and for Bismarck this simply would not do.[71]

Bismarck proposed to scale down the size of Napoleon's plan. As a beginning, only the governors-general of Rheims, Strasburg, and Nancy—all areas under heavy German control—would convene and call for an assembly of former prefects to deliberate on their part in sharing responsibility for the war's results; in reality, the true meaning of their assemblage would be to put out feelers for peace; there was a growing popular desire in these areas to see hostilities brought to an end.[72] Yet, any hopes Bismarck may have entertained with respect to a successful execution of this plan were quickly dashed by the arrival, in the middle of December, of a long telegram from Bernstorff, who recounted the points of a memorandum addressed to him by the duc de Persigny, former minister of the interior, with whom he had maintained close relations since the September revolution. What Persigny produced in that memorandum were four pages, the lines close together, of the bleakest prose the files of the North German Foreign Office could ever have accommodated. Persigny minced no words. There was in this plan nothing in which he could see the slightest merit. For one thing, the prefects had no legal powers of any kind; for another, they were too insular in outlook to execute an operation of this sort. And, as if this were not bad enough, they could implement the plan only through administrators appointed by the Delegation, who could surely be counted upon to thwart any chances of success it might have had. The only former imperial official who could summon an assembly, argued Persigny, was Charles Guillaume Palikao, the last prime minister of all France. Persigny thereupon elaborated a new plan that he believed likely to prove thoroughly more viable. As the most senior official of the last legitimate government, Palikao would, immediately after the fall of Paris, without any participation of the emperor or empress, summon an assembly that had been deliberating without interruption the fate of the country since the revolution of 4 September. This assembly would appoint a provisional *Corps législatif* and set up a structure for elections to create a final one.[73]

Bismarck was not unimpressed by this plan. Persigny was close to Napoleon and had the greatest familiarity with the leading figures of the Second Empire. Though hardly a man of deep integrity and character, he was unquestionably a skilled political operative. As minister of the interior, he had had responsibility for propaganda (wartime and otherwise) and censorship; he had had several other functions, as well, and these were in a constant state of flux and change, but always of outstanding importance. His responsibility for censorship had carried him deeply into the field of espionage, and he evidently had entered also, in ways that flowed from his tenure in this office, into

176

the military and political fields. Persigny's vigorous and outspoken nature, his impatience with governmental red tape, the unusual nature of his undertaking, his understandable eagerness to get on with it—all these features were, as we shall see, bound to place him at odds with his former colleagues and to guarantee him a significant, if tenuous, place on the supremely important but treacherous and difficult path to ending the war. And his plan was simple enough—or so it seemed on the surface.

But difficulties soon arose. Persigny and Palikao soon developed the opinion that the time was not ripe for their plan to succeed. They came to feel that the willingness of the French to accept that plan would depend on misery and suffering, the full measure of which the population had yet to endure. It was to this end that they soon began constantly and systemically to stress the idea that there was a "lack of moral depression" in France. Here their fundamental motive was the protection of their respective personal positions in the France that would grow out of the war. It was the protection of these positions that came first, and this was the key to their diplomacy. This entire argument struck Bismarck as bizarre. If they are waiting for a moment of even greater moral depression in France, he noted, "then I leave it to these gentlemen to judge for themselves, but we must note that in case different circumstances obtain, we would not feel ourselves bound to be responsive to their enterprise. . . . We have declared ourselves ready in the present situation to be receptive to the desires of Persigny and to allow him to go through with his idea of convening the full *Corps législatif*, but if, after the fall of Paris, this situation changes, and the idea of convening the *Corps législatif* no longer commends itself to us, we reserve the right to take any other path that may lead to the achievement of our aims."[74] In these new circumstances, Bismarck's enthusiasm for Persigny's plan began to wane.

In the meantime, Bismarck soon found himself confronted by a third Bonapartist proposal. From London, the Empress Eugénie proposed to end the war by ceding to the new Germany territories equivalent to those of Nice and Savoy, which France had taken from Sardinia a decade earlier. Then, Prince Napoleon, inserting himself into the picture, would, at Versailles, sign a peace with Germany in his own right. Bismarck had earlier rejected this scheme for a variety of compelling reasons, the primary one being that he suspected (correctly as it turned out) that Eugénie was bent on securing easier terms than he was prepared to give the republic. Now, however, she asked only that she be given a chance to establish herself in France. These terms now made sense to Bismarck because they seemed to resemble the ones he had offered Thiers: an indemnity, the ceding of territory, and occupation of French territory by German forces until the debt had been repaid. The offer would be presented to the French as soon as the fall of Paris had taken place.[75] An imperial agent, Clément Duvernois, was dispatched from London to secure the approval of the emperor at Wilhelmshöhe and the imperial representatives in Brussels, from whence he would proceed to Versailles. Not the least of Bismarck's reasons for preferring to negotiate with the regency at this time was his belief that it offered a clear vision of what an armistice would be. The composition and structure of the provisional government, on the other hand, so full of discordant voices and personalities struggling to get attention and geographically divided, part at Paris, part at Bordeaux, made it difficult, if not almost impossible, for him to fathom just who was in charge or what vision of a settlement its members might be inclined to accept. Bismarck therefore minuted: "I would not like to see this project damaged by others. Whatever project offers the best prospect of success may be judged when these are presented to us; for that reason I wish to hear from Clément Duvernois himself. If the negotiations with the Empress lead to a fruitful result, we can, after the fall of Paris, accept her terms, provided these are faithfully adhered to."[76] But he added: "It is imperative that neither side takes us for granted."[77]

But complications immediately arose. On 12 January, Bernstorff announced: "Duvernois will leave tomorrow evening."[78] Three days later, there had been no departure, and Bernstorff found himself writing his chief: "Duvernois will depart tomorrow morning; he still has business to finish with the Empress, but he is certain that she will give him complete powers to negotiate, and these will be confirmed at Wilhelmshöhe."[79] Only on 16 January could Bernstorff confirm that Duvernois was on his way. The intricacies of Duvernois's travel plans did nothing to encourage Bismarck to believe that his mission would be a successful one, and with the news of each delay he became more impatient and critical. He could see the French desires only as confused and contradictory. He wrote to Bernstorff on 22 January: "The recognition of the Emperor has for us so many difficulties with respect to England and Russia that we may be justified in excusing ourselves from believing that this is the shortest way to peace. The capitulation of Paris will present us with an opportunity of finding a shorter path to realizing that goal, without consideration of dynastic and monarchical questions, as to how to achieve our interests."[80] His patience with Eugénie, Napoleon, and all their hangers-on was now quite played out.

That left the provisional government. Favre, for his part, needed no prodding. On 23 January, he signed an agreement stipulating the following—there would be an armistice of twenty-one days; the army would be disbanded and its soldiers would remain prisoners of war; France would cede territory and pay a heavy indemnity; and German troops would occupy Paris until the indemnity was repaid. The negotiations had ended, though not before the hapless Clément Duvernois, breathless from the journey he had made from Wilhelmshöhe, at last appeared, on 28 January, at Versailles. When told of his arrival, Bismarck could only remark: "Clément Duvernois. Twenty minutes too late."[81]

8

Armistice

Negotiations with Favre meant that the scene of the drama had shifted to Paris, where it was to remain until an armistice was concluded, on 28 January 1871. The situation was becoming intolerable. The Prussian rain of ruin engulfed the city. On 19 January, bread was rationed for the first time, this despite previous assurances from the government that the stock of flour was almost unlimited. The same day, there was a sudden thaw that turned the frozen ground to glutinous mud, hampering the French army as much as the usual incompetence of the high command. Food supplies dried up, as cats, rats, and newts were slaughtered and served up to the population as daily fare. There was, as well, a staggering increase in civilian deaths: 8,238 in December, 11,885 in October, 19,233 in January. Rupert Christiansen has provided a vivid description of the ghastly conditions:

15 January
Firing from the heights of Châtillon, to the south of the city, the Prussians continued to bombard the Left Bank, as well as firing heavily on the forts. The newspapers reported daily laconic catalogues of shell damage to buildings and their inhabitants. A shell fell on the barracks in the rue de Babylone, on the Sorbonne, in the rue de Rennes, on the Bibliothèque de Sainte-Geneviève. There were few casualties, much broken glass. There were horror stories, too (a little girl sliced in two on her way home; six women killed in a queue outside a shop; ten children blown to pieces at their boarding school in the rue Oudinot, their palpitating flesh pasted against the wall of the dormitory) and tales of miracle escapes (hurrah for the brave *curé* of Saint-Sulpice, who kept his calm when a bomb interrupted mass, begging the faithful to depart quietly and walking up and down the aisle like a sea captain pacing his deck in the midst of a tempest).[1]

The times were no easier for the politicians. Favre had begun his tenure at the Paris foreign office with few enemies, but, as he became involved in negotiations for peace, he began to develop new opponents. Chief among them was, of course, Gambetta, whose reaction to the whole idea of negotiating with the Prussians was that it represented the kind of unwise concession to frantic opinion that encouraged, rather than prevented, civil war and that, moreover, offered aid and comfort to the enemy by making it appear that the government feared it was losing popular support. The fact that the French armies upon which he had placed such great faith—the north army, the Army of the Loire, the east army, Bourbaki's army—all had experienced total defeat after having gone on the offensive at the beginning of 1871 did nothing to discourage the grandiose ambitions he harbored and his belief that somehow the people of France would rise to the occasion and drive the enemy across the border.[2] Gambetta's reaction to these reverses throws light upon the qualities he displayed in his role as minister of the interior, in which position he took not inconsiderable pride and satisfaction. That he possessed undeniable political talents is attested to even by those who resented his heavy-handed manner in personal dealings. But offsetting this was his tendency to overemphasize the power of the will to master difficult situations, and this made him disinclined to admit that space and time and the strength and morale of the enemy imposed limits on the nation's military capabilities. He had laid down on 30 October: "There is one thing that cannot capitulate and that is the French Republic . . . so long as an inch of sacred soil remains beneath our feet, we shall hold firm the glorious flag of the French Revolution."[3]

In Gambetta's eyes and those of his followers, victory in war was the prerequisite for a French Republic, and they began to see as either traitors or enemies those of their colleagues—whether at Bordeaux or at Paris—who felt themselves obliged to question this view. He noted: "The combination of the military and political situation of the country demands that the system of toleration . . . give place to a more energetic program of a type to upset the supporters of the fallen régime."[4] Goaded by Gambetta, the members of the Delegation began to take more extreme measures. Citizens' councils were dissolved; teachers who questioned orthodox beliefs were systemically removed; and a government newspaper was put in hand "to spread into every commune the news of official decrees and to help in the political education of the people." The teachers were instructed to exploit to the fullest this invaluable organ, whose goal was to pound home a simple truth—that "the Republic alone by its institutions can ensure the liberty and the greatness of the future of France."[5] Gambetta's hostility to negotiations with the enemy was based less on his belief that the French armies were capable of fulfilling their mission—by the end of January 1871, hardly anyone believed that—than on his conviction, unshakable if unfounded and untenable, that the psychological effect of opening negotiations on friend and foe alike would be unforgivable, unthinkable, unimaginable.

For Trochu, too, the situation was fast moving from difficult to intolerable. Concerned with the burning and immutable problems of daily existence, his febrile mind produced in December a scheme for the dramatic breakout from the city of the national guard—an operation that, once accomplished, would enable it to unite with the nonexistent armies of the east.[6] Whatever doubts he may have developed over the feasibility of such a plan—and, from any military point of view it was sheer lunacy—were drowned out by the cries from the editors of the radical newspapers. These last were by this time beginning to suffer a degree of frustration and desperation that approached hysteria, and their panic led them to demand action that would bring the siege to an end once and for all. This escape was to take place in the western section of Paris, near Versailles, which the guard would attack. The plan (involving ninety thousand men) was duly implemented on 19 January, but the whole operation at once fell apart, ground down under the weight of the Prussian guns.[7]

The Paris cabinet met the next day. The writing was on the wall for anyone who cared to see it. Trochu had failed. The Prussian siege could not be broken. To entertain any doubts to the contrary was madness. But there still existed in the population mass anger over the disaster that had taken place, and clearly someone must be made to pay the price for it. There could be no mistake: it had to be Trochu. But Trochu refused to resign. He mumbled, "I am the Jesus Christ of the situation" and on 21 January mounted his horse and galloped off toward the German lines to seek a death that eluded him in Paris.[8] Poor Trochu! Even this escape was denied him. But the provisional government had a solution. Trochu was pushed aside; he stayed on as president of the council, but the post of governor of Paris was abolished. The governor of Paris could not capitulate, as the authorities had defiantly proclaimed two weeks earlier, because there was no governor of Paris. Trochu quickly passed out of events.[9]

Trochu's departure set the stage for a new bout of social unrest. On 22 January, three hundred members of the red brigade of the Garde Nationale—seizing upon the weakness of the government in the wake of Trochu's demise—marched to the main prison house of the city and demanded the release of those jailed. The governor of the prison, whether sympathetic or intimidated, succumbed at once. The marchers discovered two hundred bottles of wine and two thousand bread rations, and they made off with these without incident. Marching through the streets, shouting imprecations at the leaders of the city, they drank themselves silly and soon fell off to sleep.[10]

On the following afternoon, there occurred an even uglier incident. A crowd of about two hundred, led by two female rabble-rousers, one dressed in a man's uniform with underwear to match, marched to the Hôtel de Ville. What they intended is not entirely clear. But the government's nerves were now strained to the utmost level of endurance. A shot was fired—by whom it is not clear—and panic ensued. This incident caused intense pain and anger on both sides. The reaction of the republicans was to launch a campaign of terror as savage and bloody as anything contemporaries had ever seen. But retribution was left to the government. Loyalist troops soon stormed the building, and the rebels hastily dispersed, using as shields omnibuses and street furniture. When the air had cleared, five bodies and eighteen wounded lay on the square outside the Hôtel de Ville. For the first time since the siege began, Parisians had fired on Parisians.[11]

This new shock could not fail to affect the opinion of Jules Favre. Shaken and horror-stricken at the flood of events, he knew the city was on its last legs, and, with a view to ending the bloodshed, he secretly summoned as emissary the Comte d'Hérisson, instructing him to seek a meeting with Bismarck and request an armistice before he and his colleagues were hammered into unconditional surrender. It was a dangerous decision for Favre to make. Neither Gambetta nor the other members of the Delegation at Bordeaux was told of it. But Favre was able, though not without considerable difficulty, to rally the support of the cabinet, itself surrounded by hostility in virtually every quarter of the city. In horror, Favre contemplated: "God only knows what the people of Paris will do to us when told of the truth."[12]

Still, Favre's position was clear. On 1 June 1872, testifying before the commission of the French legislative committee charged with investigating the conduct of the war by the provisional government, he described the situation in which the country found itself at the end of January 1871: "The negotiations—which can be criticized by anyone—took place when we were masters of nothing. We were absolutely at the mercy of the conqueror. . . . I say this with absolute certainty. I am not giving excuses—it is difficult to understand this time, especially for those who did not live through it. But those who were in Paris will not, I know, dispute this assertion."[13]

Favre, in any case, was determined to negotiate. Through the protocols established under a flag of truce, d'Hérisson described the state of affairs to the Prussian outpost and arranged for a brief ceasefire. He returned to Paris to gather up Favre in the late afternoon of 23 January, and the two of them thus forlornly crossed the Seine in a leaky little boat whose holes they sought to stop up with strips of paper and tattered handkerchiefs; a tin saucepan helped to bail out the water. The night was moonless, illuminated only by a fire at the Palace of Saint Cloud, which threw on the water a brilliant red-colored gleam. Disembarking, Favre was taken to the modest house occupied by Bismarck, whom he met at 8 p.m. Two conditions Favre had already ruled out beforehand. There could be no question of concluding preliminaries of peace with the provisional government. Equally, no German soldiers could occupy Paris.[14] What Favre envisaged was the election of a national assembly before which time the city could be replenished. Though most of Favre's colleagues in the Paris provisional government supported this plan, they did not wish to commit themselves to anything concrete. What they wanted was an armistice limited to Paris. Before he separated from Favre, Bismarck promised to put in writing the conditions that seemed to him to reflect the points on which both sides had agreed.[15] Favre thereupon took his leave. The next day, he returned and was immediately drawn into conversations with the German chancellor.

Bismarck took great pains to see to it that, in these conversations, there could be no occasion for misunderstanding. Though his command of the French language was perfect, he believed it indispensable to bring in interpreters. As Favre's knowledge of German was less than perfect, this made all the more sense. There thus took place at the end of January 1871 a series of conversations between Bismarck, leaning back in his chair with his eyes closed, an interpreter pouring translation into one ear, and Favre, a second interpreter doing likewise for him—a series of crucial discussions that would eventually become the preliminaries for peace. Unfortunately for the historian, no written record of these discussions exists. The recollections of the conversations appear in the memoirs of Jules Favre; though recounted circumstantially and not without a certain bias on the French side, they constitute the most reliable source we have of the talks between Bismarck and the French minister; the defects of these volumes are more than compensated for by an almost startling lucidity of such scrupulous subtlety and precision of expression that this narrative could only with great peril fail to make use of them, containing as they do notes Favre sent to his ministerial colleagues in Paris and the responses of the latter to him. Mention should be made that when these volumes made their first appearance, in 1871–72, they drew no fire from Bismarck, who certainly would have been the first to contradict anything he found faulty or misleading. It is therefore from Favre's memories that the following account is drawn.[16]

Favre's pages show that Bismarck was determined, not surprisingly, to conclude no armistice that did not have attached to it suitable military and political conditions. There were two extremely sensitive points. Bismarck knew that there existed within the Paris cabinet controversy and acrimony over the whole question of peace, and he knew as well that there was among the city's authorities a veritable army of intrepid mayors of whom Georges Clemenceau (the future prime minister, just now rising to a position of prominence) occupied the most conspicuous and influential position. All the same,

Favre sought to paint as favorable a picture of the situation as he could. Trochu had resigned; further French offensive action would be difficult, indeed impossible.[17]

This argument left Bismarck unimpressed. He was becoming increasingly worried about the risks of holding elections throughout the country. In view of Gambetta's defiance, he did not see how this was possible. For this reason, he let Favre know that he had made contact with representatives of Eugénie with a view to restoring the fallen empire; that it was by no means impossible to bring back the dethroned sovereign and impose her on France; that she would easily find a hundred thousand devoted men among the French prisoners detained in Germany who would provide ample support when the Germans pulled out; and that, at worst, there remained, as a final resort, the possibility of convoking a certain portion of the *Corps législatif* and entering into negotiations with it.[18]

Against this, Favre protested indignantly and invoked a wild and alarmist image of a France under representatives of such a discredited and widely hated figure. It was at this point that Bismarck sat down to spell out for Favre his feelings about a possible course of action that he believed would be acceptable to each side. Favre listened intensely and then proposed one of his own. It did not differ to any appreciable extent from Bismarck's: an armistice of twenty-one days; the army to be disbanded and its soldiers to remain prisoners of war in Paris; the old battalions of the Garde Nationale, sixty in number, to remain armed for the preservation of order; the remainder, with all free corps, to be broken up; the army to surrender arms and *couleurs*; officers to retain their swords; the armistice to extend to the whole of France; the respective positions of the army to be marked out; Paris to pay a war indemnity and to surrender the forts to the Germans; the Germans not to enter the city while the armistice was in effect; and parliamentary elections to be held for the return of an assembly charged with the making of peace.[19]

Much now seemed resolved, but one question of outstanding importance remained on Bismarck's mind, and he bluntly put it to Favre on the night of 23 January: "Would the Delegation and the few scattered armies that remained in the provinces honor the terms of the armistice?" To this question Favre replied with a flat "No."[20] This, said Bismarck, was a matter that he, Bismarck, would have to take up with the king and the military chiefs. It says much for Favre's courage that he did not try to conceal from Bismarck the realities of the situation at Bordeaux. He had, in fact, become increasingly comfortable with Bismarck as a negotiating partner, though he knew the peace Bismarck would offer would be a painful and harsh one. Still, despite their differences in outlook, both had essentially the same aim—a quick end to the war. But the entire situation received a new dimension of seriousness by Favre's admission.

On the afternoon of 24 January, Favre left Versailles for Paris in order to report to his colleagues. He took with him the document that he had worked out with Bismarck. The desiderata were considered at a meeting of the cabinet on the evening of the same day. The cabinet professed itself satisfied with most of the terms. They debated intensely the amount of the indemnity Paris was to pay (Favre's papers left some doubt as to what the figure was to be). Recognizing, as most of them did, that the situation in the city had in many respects become more complicated during the preceding few days, the members agreed that an armed guard was necessary to preserve order.[21] But the major problem they encountered concerned the question of who would deliver the announcement of the capitulation to the representatives of the population and, more important, by whom the accord should be ratified. Surely the Parisians would never agree. And the government itself had been suppressed—that is to say, it existed only as a shadow of its former self, this as a result of the decision of 21 January.

Still, the cabinet gave Favre complete powers of negotiation, and, together with his son-in-law, he returned to Versailles on the afternoon of 25 January. Eventually, it was agreed that the Garde Nationale would keep its weapons; the regular army would surrender all of its arms (except for the officers' swords); an indemnity of 200 million francs would be levied; and the forts around Paris would be surrendered, but no Germans would be allowed to penetrate beyond the city walls during the three-week period of the armistice. In the meantime, a newly elected assembly at Bordeaux would debate the merits of peace or war.[22]

On the evening of 25 January, Favre again saw Bismarck, and the two of them spoke for more than an hour. Whether the armistice was signed on 25 or 26 January is a matter of controversy to this day. The official date is, however, the latter.[23] Two points remained to be settled. Favre had negotiated the agreement as the vice president and foreign minister of the Paris government. There was no military counterpart, and no one in the French military was particularly eager to set his hand to so stinging a document. After much discussion, it fell to one General Valdan, a decent and considerate officer who had taken over affairs in the wake of the resignation of General Trochu, to assume this role. On 28 January 1871, the military convention was signed—Moltke, Bismarck, and Theophil von Podbielski, the forthright and energetic quartermaster general, representing the Germans; Favre, the newly appointed Valdan, and a staff officer signing for the French.[24]

Of far greater concern was the situation in eastern France, where Bourbaki had undertaken to relieve the fortress of Belfort, to which the German armies had laid siege. Moltke saw no reason why the armistice should apply to this part of the country, which was continuing to resist his own armies. He pressed this view behind the scenes with great energy and persistence and, one may be sure, not a little satisfaction. Favre would have liked to include eastern France in the armistice, but Moltke, supported by Bismarck, was too strong for him, and the French delegation at Versailles was simply in no position to resist. It was therefore determined that the entire area of eastern France would lie outside the area encompassed by the armistice. In later years, Favre was severely taken to task for allowing this clause to be part of the agreement.[25]

Yet, this criticism is lopsidedly hostile and unenlightened. In order to give the reader a clear understanding of why this is so, it may be useful at this point to interrupt the narrative and jump back to the last days of 1870, when the French military made its last stand against the enemy.

At the end of December of that year, an army under the command of General Bourbaki set out to lift the siege of Belfort. But it was checked in this effort by the Germans at the battle of Héricourt (15–17 January 1871). The defeat devastated Bourbaki's army, and the Germans were in hot pursuit as Bourbaki made for the Jura valley and sought safety in Switzerland. Bourbaki's superiors at Bordeaux were furious at this reversal, and they let him know so in no uncertain terms. The great strains that worked upon the poor general's nerves were too much for him to bear. On 26 January, he put a gun to his head, but, like Trochu, was unable to pull off the suicide; he succeeded in grazing his neck.[26] Still, he was out of commission. On 31 January, he was replaced by Justin Clinchant, but the replacement had even less desire to fight the Germans than did Bourbaki. On 1 February, Clinchant concluded a convention with the Swiss under the terms of which eighty thousand French soldiers would be interned in that country.[27]

Two further criticisms were directed at Favre in concluding the armistice—that he had failed to (1) insist that Bourbaki's army be included in its terms and (2) notify the Delegation at Bordeaux the moment the document was signed. Again, neither of these criticisms is acceptable without major reservations. Favre himself knew almost nothing about the condition of Bourbaki's army, and what he did know came from the wildly exaggerated and flagrantly distorted reports of Gambetta concerning the progress of French arms in the provinces.[28] Furthermore, the criticism ignores the element of time. At Versailles, Bismarck had, it is true, let Favre know that Bourbaki was indeed in dire straits, but the French military representatives at Bordeaux (and some in Paris) were fully aware of what was going on and had wholeheartedly endorsed the campaign Clinchant was thought to be waging.[29]

The apparent breakdown in communication between Favre on the one hand and the members of the Delegation on the other was not as pronounced as it might appear. The dates themselves bear witness to this. Favre had dutifully telegraphed to Gambetta about the armistice, and his message was received in Bordeaux on 29 January at the latest. Gambetta had kept abreast of developments in the field through mail, through telegraph, and through carrier pigeon, and he received a steady stream of visitors who made the pilgrimage to his house to gain his ear for their views on the military problem. On 29 January, Clinchant received from Gambetta a telegram that contained the text of Favre's message. More important, he also received from Edwin Manteuffel, the German commander in the south, a note to the effect that the armistice exempted from its purview the eastern departments of the country, and confirmation of this came to him from Bordeaux two days later.[30]

That Favre was an imperfect and somewhat emotional man, accustomed to theatrics, is clear from a number of sources. But, in the present instance, the evidence supporting him is so formidable in its totality and the absence of any direct refutation from any quarter so notable that one can conclude only that the charges against him were bogus from start to finish. To begin with, one must consider the state of the French army. As Geoffrey Wawro magisterially declares, *"l'armée Bourbaki* would, as late as the 1960s, survive in France as a reproach for mass disorganization."[31] When the eastern army began to move—"crawl" would be a truer word—to the Swiss frontier, it was in desperate shape. Assailed and threatened on all sides, cut off from any source of reinforcement, sick, tired, hungry to the point of starvation, the army to which the commission drew attention in condemning Favre was a pathetic and miserable collection of men, a ragtag operation, incapable of taking any initiative whatsoever. To imply that it was anything more than that is to indulge in the purest nonsense. The reason for Favre's omission of it in his telegram to Gambetta remains a matter of conjecture. He may simply have forgotten. It may have been that he distrusted Gambetta, who he feared would use the exclusion as excuse to call for further fighting. Favre's account sheds no light on the matter. But the importance of the eastern army as a fighting unit can be dismissed with great definiteness, its value in the negotiations for an armistice equally, indeed, even more so.[32]

The remaining history regarding the conclusion of the armistice flows plainly from Favre's pen and needs no extensive recapitulation. Shortly after five o'clock on 28 January, two copies of two documents were laid before the chancellor and the French minister by Bismarck's secretaries. One document addressed the armistice and the second the capitulation of Paris. The documents were drawn up in German and French. Only Bismarck and Favre signed, thus strengthening the impression that the matters to which they pertained were political, not military, in nature. Indeed, Moltke and the rest of his staff had nothing but contempt for them, believing, as always, that Bismarck had gone too far and had let the French off too easily. Never one to give up lightly, Moltke continued to breathe defiance toward his hated enemy, and he remained as determined as ever to launch a new campaign that would sweep through France and destroy it as a Great Power. For the moment, however, he could do nothing except to condemn Bismarck as vehemently as ever to the members of his staff.[33] Bismarck, for his part, had reason to be pleased. The British diplomat Odo Russell, a fair and impartial observer who was present at the ceremonies, described Bismarck's accomplishment as a "master piece of statecraft that will live for the ages,"[34] and one can be sure that these sentiments reflected the views of the senior diplomatic officials in Europe, who, though clearly worried over the extent of the new empire's victory and its implications for European stability, were eager for the war to come to an end.

Yet, it is axiomatic in the world of diplomacy that methodology and tactics assume an importance by no means inferior to that accorded to concept and strategy. Over the next weeks, Bismarck experienced anxiety not only about the naïveté of Moltke's grandiose ideas for a conquest of France but also about two other matters that deserve special attention.

First was the question of the strength of the provisional government. Was it strong enough to confront the radicals? The mayors, it was reported, were still pining for *guerre à outrance,* and a series of blood-curdling pronounce-ments from the editors of the Parisian nationalist press echoed their sen-timents to the letter.[35] Aside from, or along with, these editors, there was naturally no other group of people in Paris whose enthusiasm for this cause was greater over the entire period of the war, but especially—"ironically" would be a truer word—in its final weeks and days, than the chauvinists who, against all odds, still lived and worked for the liberation of French soil from German troops. Of these, one, presumably the most impassioned, a figure who was becoming increasingly familiar to German intelligence, was Madame Juliette Adam, and of her brief note must be taken at this point.

Sprung from a well-known, rather well-to-do provincial middle-class fam-ily, Juliette Adam (née Lambert) was a woman of fiery political temperament, indefatigable energies, broad interests, and varied tastes. Her opportunist-republican salon was one of the leading literary and political meeting places in Paris during this period. Her second and much beloved husband, Ed-mond, was a prominent figure in Paris during the war—prefect of police, as a matter of fact, during the siege. Of all her enthusiasms and passions, the strongest and deepest was her hatred of the new Germany and Bismarck (whom she had never met), coupled with an equally strong adulation for Gambetta.[36] Throughout December 1870 and January 1871, Madam Adam exercised her considerable influence over the Paris chauvinists to encourage defiance to any terms the Germans might propose and to urge prolongation of the war, come what may. News of the armistice shocked and devastated her. She wrote, "I would like to die,"[37] but quickly directed her efforts toward organizing a prolonged resistance.

What disturbed Bismarck was not so much the fact that Juliette Adam and people like her held such views as the fact that the government was obviously either unwilling or too weak to prevent their emergence. He knew that Favre, in his occasional conversations with him or members of his staff, pooh-poohed the importance of such persons; it was not these irresponsible scribblers but the government itself that exercised authority. But Bismarck was not reassured. If the Parisian authorities did not really approve of their attacks, why could they not stop them?[38]

Even the details of the armistice as released in the government's statement of 29 January were cause for concern, concluding as it did with an announcement to the effect that "Paris has suffered much but the Republic will profit greatly from a struggle so nobly sustained."[39] Such language, intended to assuage the chauvinistic faction, alarmed many foreigners in the country, and we find Tommy Bowles writing: "The idea of presenting the Republic as a consolation for the sufferings and fall of Paris is one which would just now be extravagant in the wildest burlesque; but it is surpassed in folly by the second phrase I have cited, which seems to have been purposely designed in order at once to irritate the Prussians when they have their foot on the neck of the country, and to maintain the country itself in an attitude of resistance which is now no longer possible."[40]

Finally, there was (or remained) the problem of Gambetta. Bismarck could not forget that he, along with some of the other delegates at Bordeaux, had, against all odds, dreamed of raising new armies with a view to rescuing Paris and driving the German forces across the Rhine. Concerning the armistice itself, Gambetta had no reservations whatsoever, and the reason for his attitude was not hard to understand. He hoped to use the interval to accomplish two objectives. The first of these was to raise a new army, "a school for instruction of our young troops,"[41] as he called it, for the purpose of liberating Paris and defeating the German invaders. His second objective was no less daring than the first—namely to see to it that the elections for the national assembly produced a collection of republicans seething with anger and determined to pursue *guerre à outrance*. But here he found himself in a predicament. He knew in his heart that most of the inhabitants of the provinces were heartily

Les franc-tireurs du Nord, Gambetta's partisans, after the defeat of the Prussians, 10 January 1871. Color etching. (Bildarchiv Preußischer Kulturbesitz [BPK]. Kunstbibliothek, Staatliche Museen, Berlin, Germany. Used by permission of Art Resource, New York. ART428971.)

sick of the war and wished to end it as soon as possible. The only way, therefore, for him to achieve his objective was through an order that restricted the
franchise to the most radical of the country's inhabitants, and he now threw
himself into the task of finding the means to accomplish that objective.[42]

That Gambetta took the steps he did was not merely the product of his
own diligence and the fire-breathing intensity of his hatred for the Germans.
The real fault lay with Paris and the failure of the senior members of the
provisional government to act with alacrity in informing him about the steps
necessary to implement the election procedures. Favre himself had wasted
no time in telegraphing the news from Versailles: along with the armistice,
there would be elections, set for 8 February, and a member of the provisional
government should be sent to Bordeaux and so inform Gambetta. It took the
Paris authorities some time to make up their minds as to who would undertake this disagreeable mission. In the end, it was decided that the task should
fall upon the shoulders of Jules Simon, a moderate man endowed with formidable powers of persuasion and one who understood, like Favre, the need for
speedy acceptance of the armistice terms by Bordeaux. Simon determined to
show resolve. Should Gambetta reject the terms of the armistice, he would
be immediately declared a traitor and dismissed along with those members
of the Delegation who found themselves obliged to lend him their support.[43]

It was a dangerous situation. Not until 1 February—four days after the
armistice had been signed—did Jules Simon embark on his mission to Bordeaux. The chauvinistic utterances of Gambetta, stimulating members of the
Delegation to new hopes for help from the outside, seemed to Bismarck to
heighten the urgency of clarifying the future of the armistice terms. Doubts
about its fate were already in the air and were spreading—to the delight of
Moltke and his staff.[44] Bismarck had foreseen some of these difficulties. No
sooner had he signed the armistice with Favre than he, on the evening of
28 January, held a meeting with Clément Duvernois, mentioned in chapter 7,
who steadfastly represented the empress, so as not to completely foreclose
the possibility of negotiating with the figures of the fallen empire. It was, to
be sure, not a very high card, but Bismarck believed that he might yet have
to play it. The failure of the Paris cabinet to secure the acceptance of the
armistice from Bordeaux was leading to the impression that its members
lacked the strength to do so. It was dangerous to let things go on this way.[45]

But the question may well be asked: *why* were they permitted to go on this way? Why did the Paris government not do more to rein in Gambetta? Here the written record fails us. Some members of the cabinet were figures not distinguished by political deftness. The days after the signing of the armistice were ones of extreme tension and excitement over the course of the war. There was anger in the population, fury in the press, hunger everywhere—a city buzzing with resentment over the unexpected announcement that an armistice had been signed with the enemy.[46] Still more important was the failure of Favre to impress upon his colleagues the need for quick and decisive action. But this was perhaps forgivable. It must be recalled that Favre was negotiating with Bismarck under difficult and unprecedented conditions. He traveled almost daily from Versailles to Paris. It was by no means impossible that an overwrought mental and physical state had worn him down. Sixty-five winters had crossed his brow. He often worked long into the night. He was a tired man who was performing immensely exacting duties. Between the diverse pressures on the part of adversaries far younger, more active, better informed, and intellectually more agile than himself, this wearied, beleaguered figure did his best to discharge the duties with which his colleagues had entrusted him. It is difficult to retrace his adventures and activities in that terrible winter of 1870–71—to note his varied reactions, his maneuverings among his impetuous associates, and even his frequent vacillations—without being moved to sympathy for him in his difficult and unprecedented position and to admire his courageous persistence in the face of much frustration and adversity.[47]

In the late afternoon of Tuesday, 31 January, while radical circles in Paris were still buzzing with excitement over Bordeaux's defiant gestures and calling for breaking off the negotiations, Gambetta and three members of the Delegation met in Gambetta's offices and there hotly debated the terms and the significance of the armistice and the imminent elections. Out of these discussions came three electoral decrees that excluded from participation in the upcoming elections all persons who had any official connection to the Second Empire—these wrung from the others only after Gambetta had threatened to resign if they were not immediately adopted. Shortly thereafter, Simon appeared on the scene and demanded that the decrees be nullified. For the moment, all seemed lost. Gambetta stood impregnable. Throughout the morning and afternoon of 3 February, the telegraphic correspondence between the offices in Bordeaux and Paris was replete with reflections of the tension between the opposing factions of the French ministers. Gambetta resolved to let the elections take place in the manner he had prescribed. His attitude toward them remained marked at all times by extreme nervousness and an almost panicky determination not to permit the procedure to end in any expression of popular opinion that could weaken or deprive him of what he was determined never to yield.[48]

At Versailles, nerves were no less strained. Gambetta's actions aroused Bismarck's fury to a fever pitch, for it seemed to confirm to the letter all the doubts he had held about the ability of Paris to control Bordeaux. Again, all this was understandable. And, again, one must make allowance for the extreme tensions, the wartime feelings, and the highly charged political atmosphere of the time. Bismarck believed that it was critical to end the war through the election of a new assembly, and he did not take kindly to the prospect that Gambetta and his cohorts now were threatening to destroy all the progress he had made in that direction. Yet, he dared not counterattack too publicly, for to do so would unleash the fury of the Parisian radicals, whose tactics were playing directly into the hands of Moltke and the soldiers, for whom the war was a prize fight, a slugging match that had to go on until France fell down from exhaustion. At the same time, Bismarck was at pains not to alienate Moltke now that he had the terms he wanted. Stosch, the intendant-general, noted: "Bismarck was trying to stem his earlier arrogance and was, during these days, constantly obliging and amiable. The old proverb has been proved true. 'Idleness is the root of all evil.' The waiting has gone on too long."[49]

Just at this time Bismarck took two critical steps that he knew could not fail to jolt Favre into action. First, he warned Favre that, if Gambetta were allowed to get his way, the Germans would have no choice but to support the Bonapartist party, which had called for the resurrection of the old *Corps législatif*; if worse came to worst, the war would be renewed. At the same time, he appealed to Favre's sense of loyalty. Gambetta was deliberately trying to smash all progress toward ending the war; diplomatic relations, he pointed out, were not usually strengthened by kicking people in the face. The annulment by Favre and his colleagues of Gambetta's decrees was the only way to set matters straight.[50]

Favre could not fail to feel the weight of Bismarck's arguments. Just at this time, an appeal from Simon calling for reinforcements reached Paris. At ten o'clock on the evening of 3 February, Favre and his colleagues met to work out a common course of action. The following hours were taken up by agitated debate among the Parisian leaders over the position to be taken in light of Gambetta's uncompromising stand. A clear majority of the Parisian leadership now favored defiance of Gambetta, and they determined to make this known to him in the most explicit terms of which they were capable. This they did through a public announcement late that evening stating that they regarded Gambetta's election decrees as null and void and through a further directive to him to immediately relinquish his office. The instructions given Gambetta faithfully reflected the political interests of the members of the provisional government and the country, and the decision was clearly the right one to make.[51]

The Paris cabinet determined to subject Gambetta to additional pressure. Bowing to the wishes of Simon, three of its members were dispatched to Bordeaux with instructions to outvote the Delegation and annul the exclusionary decrees. Their mission was indeed a sensitive one. None of its members doubted for a moment that many Bordeaux officials were still solidly behind Gambetta and determined to defy Paris even if this meant, as it surely would, plunging the country into civil war. This did not trouble Gambetta. He said: "There is a voice calling for definitions of principle and purpose which is thrilling and moving. It is the voice of the French people. We will respond to this voice. In place of the reactionary and cowardly assembly of which the enemy dreams, let us install an Assembly that is truly national and republican, desiring peace, if peace assures our honor, but capable also of waging war, ready for anything rather than lend a hand in the murder of France."[52]

This statement, treating at one and the same time the motives of the spokesmen at Bordeaux and the state of mind of the French people, was, despite its eloquence, inaccurate and unrealistic in the extreme. Gambetta, it will be noted, identified his statements about the armistice with the voice of the French people. Actually, the Bordeaux delegation had no mandate from

197

the people. The passages in the statement faithfully reflected the political interests of the Bordeaux faction at a particularly desperate moment in its history, and nothing else. This was a faction that was never supported by a majority of the French people and never would be. Its leaders expressed a strong contempt for the negotiations between Bismarck and Favre and professed to understand better than the French people themselves what their true interests were.

In addition to misidentifying these two voices, Gambetta also misinterpreted them. The French people were presented in the Delegation's statement as a people preoccupied with national humiliation at the hands of the enemy, united in their resentment of what was being done to them. Actually, as we have seen, great portions of them, and particularly those portions for which the Delegation purported to speak, were preoccupied primarily with internal dissensions and the passions of the time. Nor was it correct to say (or imply) that the Bordeaux outlook was marked by largeness of view or generosity of spirit. Surely, this outlook, whatever virtues it may be conceived to have had, was, from its inception, one of the most narrowly and intolerantly exclusive of all political ideologies.[53]

In any case, it was Paris that triumphed over Bordeaux. Gambetta, believing that Simon enjoyed only shaky support among the officials in the capital, had sent the minister of justice, Isaac Crémieux, to Paris to ascertain more fully the views of Simon's colleagues. Along the way, at a railway station at Vierzon, on the icy banks of the Loire, Crémieux crossed paths with the three members of the Paris cabinet who were making their way to the south. A stormy meeting thereupon ensued. It was left to these members to complete the destruction of Gambetta's hopes of obtaining their support or even sympathy. Like a steamroller, the trio flattened to the last detail every aspect of Gambetta's scheme. Crémieux thereupon decided to cancel his trip to Paris and return immediately to Bordeaux, where he let Gambetta know what he had been told. For Gambetta, this was the last straw. With the receipt of Crémieux's message, he lost all further stomach for leading the French. He had misjudged the situation; he had misjudged Paris; he had misjudged Favre; he had misjudged Bismarck. In the face of continuous opposition in the capital, he could not face a continuation of the struggle for power in France. On the morning of 6 February, Gambetta resigned. His decision to do so removed the last great barrier on the path to peace.[54]

In tendering his resignation, Gambetta did no more than see, at long last, what writing was on the wall. In that sense, he may be said to have bowed to the inevitable. Yet, certain of Gambetta's personal qualities contributed to his downfall. Prominent among these was his extreme "ungovernmental-ness"—his lack of understanding of or patience with the strictures of governmental operation; his reluctance not only to go through channels but to pay any attention to them; his belief, common to many of his colleagues of that day, that the lower echelons of the governmental apparatus were there only to be bypassed. To be sure, some of Gambetta's broader judgments on the nature and situation in the France of 1871 were well taken, but, in receiving and interpreting the stated position of the Paris leaders on specific matters at issue between themselves and the Germans, he was impulsive, careless, and repeatedly inaccurate.

Added to this were Gambetta's deplorable high-handedness, tactlessness, and personal insensitivity vis-à-vis other Frenchmen in positions of power. One senses, in examining his activity and statements, that he was, as a rule, more interested in people in the mass than in people as individuals. In any case, his attitude toward the other members of the Paris government was often marked by a remoteness that smacked of arrogance and contempt. Not all of these instances of tactlessness or discourtesy were serious lapses, and, as always, one must allow for the passions and excitements of the time. In the years 1870–71, many people had the intuitive feeling that they were passing through one of the decisive moments of history; beliefs and convictions were put to the ultimate test, and the urge to action was permitted to override many normal inhibitions. But, by his underestimation of his official associates in France, by his lack of interest in them—and lack of consideration for them—as human beings, Gambetta may be said to have contributed to his own undoing.

Gambetta had, moreover, certain broader deficiencies of understanding of

199

the political and military scene that, though they probably did not enter into the actual causes of his failure, heightened quite needlessly his enthusiasm for his undertakings and increased the cruelties of the disappointments he was destined to suffer. Horrified by what he saw transpiring, he tried his best to reverse the ghastly plight into which the war had brought his country. Still, he exaggerated the extent of French power after Sedan and tended to ascribe the evils and resentments of the 1870–71 period to previous political oppression, even when they were primarily the reflections of the inadequacy of the new republican system when faced with the strains of modern war. In this way, Gambetta was carried into a somewhat uncritical acceptance of the republican thesis and of the need and popular demand for *guerre à outrance*.

Yet, the historian cannot follow without a deep sense of sadness Léon Gambetta's tragic and stormy passage across the scene of this inquiry. About his devotion to the French cause there can be no question. Whatever else he may have been, he was an orator with few equals in the history of nineteenth-century Europe. Despite the exuberant and uninhibited political bias they display, Gambetta's speeches about the events of this time rise above every other contemporary record for their literary power, their penetration, and their unrivaled capacity to excite, if not always to inspire. And, through this tale, as through the whole bizarre record of his adventures and mistakes, there runs the reflection of a blazing honesty and a purity of idealism that did unstinting credit to the French society that produced him and the merits of which he never failed proudly to assert. He was *one* French way of reacting to the war. That there is much in it to criticize is undeniable, but it deserves not to be forgotten or ridiculed.

To Bismarck, the news of Gambetta's resignation was heaven sent, for it gave him renewed energy to combat the desires of the military, which was bent on continuing the war until France was destroyed as a Great Power. But the days following the resignation constituted a second period of high tension in the relations between Paris and Versailles. Until peace preliminaries had been signed, renewal of the war could—and Bismarck brutally pounded home this point to the French at every turn—not be ruled out. The German military had, for reasons that need not be gone into, allowed two French generals, Louis Léon Faidherbe and Antoine Eugène Chanzy, both of whom it had taken prisoner, to proceed from the German headquarters to the French capital. Their appearance resulted in a new flare-up of German attention to the Paris situation. Faidherbe was gloomy about the chances for renewing a campaign. But Chanzy swept all such reserve aside. He had no doubt about resuming the war as soon as the armistice had expired, and, with a view to doing just that, he demanded that the ministers in Paris produce the needed armies. Favre and his colleagues dismissed such schemes as phantasmagoria. But behind Chanzy there stood, as there did behind Gambetta at Bordeaux, a number of mayors, editors, and chauvinists like Juliette Adam who were bent on pursuing just such a course.[55]

This made it all the more important for Favre to get on with the business of holding elections for a national assembly. To him, the assembly appeared as a re-insurance against the establishment of any sort of militarist or radical dictatorship capable of suppressing the provisional government. Article II of the armistice charged the provisional government with implementing the procedures for the elections in those areas of France where they were to take place. In these areas, no one was to be barred from participation. But here there were three obstacles over which the French officials found themselves obliged to jump. The first was the abject misery into which the France of 1871 had fallen. More than one-quarter of its departments were occupied. In those departments, postal communications were forbidden, and it fell to the German troops to post the election notices themselves. No less serious was the divergence of outlook that still existed between the Delegation at Bordeaux and the senior figures of the provisional government in Paris. In such circumstances, there was no clarity of leadership. The voters were simply urged to choose "men of good reputation and independent character."[56] Absent a recognized national government, leadership would have fallen to established political parties. Again, owing to the condition of the country, political organization was not to be found. Finally, the situation was made immeasurably worse by the use of a procedure known as *scrutin de liste*, which facilitated the crossing of party lines, thus making it possible for men of vastly different political points of view to be elected on the same ballot.[57]

Adding to the confusion was the lack of formal machinery in the selection

General Antoine Eugène Chanzy, opponent of the armistice. (von Pflugk-Harttung, *The Franco-German War*, 428.)

of candidates. In each department, self-selected committees drew up names of candidates without taking the time to notify the officials so chosen. It was also difficult for voters to discern the principles for which a given candidate stood beyond the question of peace or war. The candidates were required to issue no statements by which their views could be determined, though in some parts of France the designation "peace" or "war" was affixed to the name of each candidate. Still, the elections took place as scheduled on 8 February 1871 in the great majority of the electoral districts throughout the country. They represented the first sounding of popular will conducted in France since the war. That they were, in general, honestly held and that they constituted a faithful reflection of the feelings of the voters has never been seriously challenged by historians of the war.[58]

The result was highly unfavorable to the advocates of war. Out of a total of 676 deputies elected, more than 400 were monarchists of the Orléans-Bourbon bloc; only 200 were republicans of all factions. The Bonapartists fared worst of all, carrying only 30 constituencies. Even with the addition of some disgruntled monarchists who split from their own party, the republicans had the support of less than a third of the electorate; as was to be expected, they did their best in the big cities, where moderate conservative parties ran them a close second. But the peasantry, by far the largest segment of the population, voted almost solidly for the monarchists.[59]

Two unmistakable conclusions emerged from the elections. France might not have spoken about its political future, but it had resoundingly spoken in favor of peace. The electorate had punished the republicans who insisted on continuing the war and the Bonapartists who had started it. There was no further visible reason for prolonging the spilling of blood. No less obvious a conclusion was that the elections had put Thiers at the forefront of French politics. He had opposed the war. He had toured Europe in the hope of securing help for his country while it was being waged. Of all the official personalities, aside from Favre, he had a background in negotiating with the Germans, an onerous task that no faction was willing to gladly undertake and the miscarriage of which could spell instant political ruin—and renewal of the war. In addition to this, he enjoyed among his colleagues almost universal respect. His was undoubtedly the finest mind on the spot; he was eager to get on with the negotiations and wasted no time in letting Bismarck know that the political complexion of the new assembly was thoroughly congenial to bringing to an end the terrible war that had been waged for some eight months.[60]

After some dissension and hesitation, the decision was taken by leading figures of the provisional government to convene the assembly at the Grand Théâtre in Bordeaux. On 12 February 1871, about two hundred members convened for the opening session, and the next day Favre appeared to submit the resignation of the members of the Government of National Defense. Five days later, on 17 February, there arose the first great debate when a deputy, Émile Keller, purporting to represent the members of the extreme republican left, demanded that the assembly commit itself to a refusal to cede Alsace and Lorraine without the prior consent of the inhabitants of those provinces. This painful motion produced the first serious crisis in the assembly. The battle was now on. Thiers himself was present and acted as master of ceremonies for his faction. It was plain to observers that every nerve of his politically impassioned being was aroused by this supreme parliamentary contest. His face deathly pale with tension, his burning eyes darting constantly over the scene and absorbing every detail, he announced that such a declaration would be sheer madness: "I could not accept a mandate that I would not be able to carry out as an honest man and good citizen."[61]

From that moment on, the situation in the hall became very ugly. With no visible reason for restraint, the leftists began to show increasing signs of truculence and impatience. To quell the demands of Keller's supporters, the deputies decided to appoint a committee to study the merits of his motion and to recess in the meantime. The committee, with one dissenting vote, offered a substitute resolution that, while sympathizing with Keller's position, resolved to rely on the "wisdom and faith of the negotiators."[62] The measure met with the assembly's overwhelming approval, despite a crescendo of threats and imprecations from Keller's supporters. Thereupon, the members of the assembly chose to make Thiers the head of the government and to confer upon him the title of *"chef du pouvoir exécutif."*[63] To Thiers, the situation was now resolved. He left the assembly around seven in the evening, satisfied of his ultimate triumph and convinced that the crisis had been surmounted. On 19 February, he departed Bordeaux with his new foreign minister, Jules

Favre. The next day, he sent word to Bismarck that he would arrive in Versailles on the morning of 21 February.[64]

Thiers had no illusions about the gravity of the peril that menaced France. Renewal of the war was unthinkable, and Bismarck held all the high cards. Still, Thiers did his best. It was his hope to obtain a peace on the basis of the terms he had negotiated with Bismarck in October and November, but Bismarck had no intention of granting such a peace. Thus, when Thiers asked for an extension of the armistice, Bismarck flatly refused. But, replied Thiers, as the armistice was to expire on 24 February, it would be impossible to draw up a peace in so short a span of time. For this reason, only preliminaries of peace could be determined, and it was to these that Thiers, accompanied by Favre, and Bismarck now addressed themselves. As a gesture of courtesy, Bismarck and the emperor agreed to extend the armistice to 26 February.[65]

The first issue to arise was that of the entry of German troops into Paris. Thiers left no doubt that this would be a "catastrophe."[66] But on this point Bismarck would not be moved, insisting that such an honor, done in accordance with the customs of the day, was due the German army. Thiers then asked that he be allowed to present his case to William, and this, it was agreed, he would do the next day when he went to Versailles by himself. Bismarck and Thiers then turned their attention to the fate of the great French fortress of Metz. This had been the subject of considerable controversy among the German leaders. As early as August, Bismarck had made plain his intention to demand the fortress for German security.[67] But, as the year turned, he began to develop serious doubts. The demand had been made in circumstances that had changed in important respects. He questioned the value of Metz as a military advantage. More important still was Metz's population; entirely French, it would be an indigestible morsel in the new German empire. Included in it, its inhabitants would prove a constant source of trouble.[68] The point is one that deserves emphasis. Bismarck knew that the German empire in the ensuing decades had no need of more wars, of external adventures, or of more territories. On the contrary, no country would ever have a more urgent need for a long period of peace. Taking the territory would indeed prove to be a folly of the first order. And the subsequent treatment of its inhabitants by the German authorities would be one of a long series of neglected opportunities and mistakes.

Unfortunately, Bismarck's views on Metz stood in direct contradiction to those of Moltke and his chiefs. The taking of Metz, as noted in chapter 6, had been *their* great achievement. It was a success they had pictured *themselves* as achieving, thereby earning the admiration and gratitude of peoples all over Germany. Returning Metz to the French would be a national humiliation. Besides, the city had already been organized by the Germans as the new department of the Moselle. Moltke's communications to Bismarck buzzed with indignant protests over the prospect of its surrender, and these protests found strong support and expression in the mind of William I himself. A warrior king, he came down wholeheartedly on Moltke's side.[69]

Bismarck was outnumbered, and he knew it. He put forward the demand for Metz at the meeting with Thiers and Favre on 22 February. Thiers was all but resigned to the loss. He scarcely needed to be told Bismarck's reasons for wishing to keep the city. He had told Favre that, before its capture, Bismarck might have been content with Alsace and part of Lorraine, but no longer. He therefore offered little resistance when the demand was made. Much sharper was his reaction to the indemnity of six billion francs that Bismarck put on a piece of paper, the sight of which caused Thiers to "jump as if he had been bitten by a mad dog."[70] The sum was indeed exorbitant, and Thiers's reaction was to plead for more time. Thereupon Bismarck repaired to the vast but chilly apartments of William I, and Thiers and Favre took leave for Paris.[71]

On 22 February, Thiers was back at Versailles, this time alone for his interview with William concerning the entry of German troops into Paris. He was brusquely received by Bismarck and pointedly warned by him not to push the emperor too far. In fact, Thiers congratulated himself that William appeared to be cheerful and relaxed as the interview ran its course. This Thiers attributed to the emperor's charm and warmth of character. (William, for all his faults, was indeed not devoid of these qualities when he wished to display them.) But Thiers's view took no account of the depths of William's emotional constitution. He was a military king—first, last, and always. The German army, said he, must be permitted to enter Paris; its honor demanded no less.

A more plausible hypothesis would have been that the evident improvement in William's spirits, as the interview progressed, was induced by the pleasing awareness that it was closer, with each passing moment, to its termination. Indeed, some of the adjutants who were present at the interview came away believing that William's treatment of his French interlocutor and, indeed, the entire atmosphere of the interview itself had been distinctly cool and perfunctory.[72]

A further meeting with Bismarck was equally barren. Over the ensuing two days, French desperation mounted with the revelation of the implacable determination of Bismarck and the German high command over the terms of the preliminaries of peace. But Bismarck was being implacable for a good reason: he wanted the negotiations to end and to end them quickly. If, by Sunday, 26 February, there were no preliminaries, hostilities would be resumed, as Moltke had hoped, and would grow to absurd and monstrous dimensions—far beyond what the most sanguine military logic could justify. When Thiers again brought up Metz, Bismarck snapped: "In Germany they accuse me of losing battles that Count Moltke has won. Do not ask me for impossibilities."[73] Metz must remain in German hands—there could be no question of any kind about this. Thiers had, as noted, come to believe that Metz was a lost cause and raised no further objection.

On the question of the indemnity, Bismarck was prepared to show some flexibility, though not much. Thiers complained that French financial experts found it difficult to gauge the totality of the demands made on their country. Bismarck replied that France was a land whose indigenous sources of accumulation were many and that there was a strong tradition of private industrial initiative and investment. On the German side, a great and bewildering variety of expenses had to be met—war costs, widows' and orphans' pensions, funds for maintaining prisoners, and a share for the South German states. Heavy though these needs were, he was now authorized to reduce the indemnity to five billion francs. This revelation, obviously conceived by Bismarck as a way of demonstrating to Thiers and Favre that he had succeeded in obtaining from William a concession that no one else ever could have done, produced a most salutary effect on the two French diplomats. Thiers at once accepted it, delighted to be spared a billion francs.[74] Bismarck welcomed Thiers's reaction. Not one predisposed to uncritical enthusiasm for any foreign statesman, he had nonetheless come to appreciate Thiers, now seventy-three years of age, and to regard him as a force for peace and stability, as someone who was due respect, even affection. As he put it a week later in a letter of 27 February 1871 to his wife: "My little friend Thiers is very witty and amiable but no businessman when it comes to verbal negotiations. Thought bubbles incessantly spill from his mouth as from an open bottle and tire his interlocutors because he impedes them from getting to what's really drinkable. But at that he's a decent little fellow, white-haired, respectable and agreeable [he has] good old French manners, and it was very hard for me to be as hard on him as I had to be."[75]

On one important point Thiers managed to get his way. The garrison of Belfort, under a gallant French commander, had withstood the German advance—an oasis in a wasteland—until 15 February, when, on orders from the war ministry of the French government and with the full approval of Bismarck, it had given up the fight and retired—with full honors of war. If the capture of Metz meant so much to the Germans, the retention of Belfort meant even more to the French, and to the accomplishment of this objective Thiers addressed himself with a dedication, a persistence, and an unflagging energy and attention that have few parallels in diplomatic experience. If Bismarck would grant France the right to keep Belfort, peace would follow. If he did not, Thiers would resign, and Bismarck could run the country. This was not an idle threat, and Bismarck knew it. Absent Thiers, forces beyond Bismarck's vision would be guiding Bismarck's footsteps in shaping Germany's relations with France. The military men would get their way. The door to foreign intervention would open. Fortunately, assistance came to Thiers from a wholly unexpected quarter. Moltke and the General Staff attached little importance to Belfort; it would be of no use in another German invasion of France and of little use to the French if they chose to invade Germany. The emperor, amazed at Moltke's generosity, gave the transaction his blessing.[76]

On 26 February 1871, the preliminaries of peace were signed at Versailles. An initial article delineated the rough outline of the new frontiers, the boundaries of which were to be drawn up by a commission. France surrendered all lands east of that line to Germany. Two villages in the department of the Moselle were ceded to Germany, as well. Belfort was to remain French. A second article bound France to pay Germany five billion francs, at least one billion during 1871 and the rest within the space of three years from the ratification of the preliminaries. A third article limited to thirty thousand the number of German troops that would enter Paris and specified the area where they were to march—an area bounded by the Seine, the avenue de Ternes, and the rue du Faubourg Saint Honoré—territory that was sufficiently upper class to satisfy German pride and far enough away from the working-class quarters where disturbances could be expected. French forces, except for the forty thousand that were to remain in Paris, were to retire behind the Loire until a final peace treaty, the negotiations for which were to begin in Brussels, had been signed.[77]

All in all these terms, received by Thiers and Favre over the nine-day period from 19 to 28 February 1871, were undeniably severe, and they evoked hysterical indignation and defiance on the part of the more radical sections of the Paris population. The nationalist press broke out in torrents of bitter recrimination against the Germans for depriving France of its sacred soil, against Bismarck for having been the author of the agreement, and, by implication, against Thiers and Favre for having been party to it. Yet, the peace, for all its harshness, was not quite the prize example of the German mailed fist as is sometimes alleged. The Treaty of Tilsit, imposed by France upon Prussia in 1807, went a good deal further and was a good deal harsher. The 1871 agreement contained no provisions that limited the size of the French army, none that gave Germany the right to intervene in French domestic affairs, none that required the French to destroy their naval vessels or surrender any of their colonies. The France of 1871, unlike the Prussia of 1807, remained a Great Power.[78]

On 28 February, Thiers read the terms of the treaty to the assembly at Bordeaux. He was keenly aware of the urgent need for immediate ratification. Much of the country, notably the eastern and northern portions, had been greatly destabilized—socially, spiritually, and politically—by the experiences of the war. Large parts of the French population were dazed, shell-shocked, uncertain of themselves, fearful of the future, highly vulnerable (as we have had occasion to see) to pressures and enticements from radical minorities in their midst. The German army at the time was a unified, disciplined movement under the total control of Moltke and the emperor. Not only that, but the German army had emerged from the war with great prestige because of

Otto von Bismarck dictates peace terms to Adolphe Thiers and Jules Favre, 26 February 1871. Painting by Carl Wagner, ca. 1875. (Bildarchiv Preußischer Kulturbesitz [BPK]. Used by permission of Art Resource, New York. ART428995.)

its immense and successful effort. The German high command was, for this and other reasons, in a position to manipulate the peace process effectively for its own purpose.[79]

Thiers's reading completed, the assembly took up debate. The left wanted examination of the treaty deferred until the next day; the right wanted it considered that very evening. Thiers then shuffled to the podium—a frail, bespectacled, stooped figure, with a small head that caused him, at times, to look strangely like a young student. He then proceeded to speak for an hour, without the use of notes but with such startling lucidity and such scrupulous subtlety of expression that when he finished, only a handful were unsure that he had answered every possible point. The assembly voted to consider the treaty in committee that evening and to meet in public at noon the following day, 1 March. On that day, the assembly overwhelmingly ratified it by a vote of 546 to 107.[80]

While the debate was proceeding at Bordeaux, the Germans were making their way into Paris. Under sparkling skies and in mild air, the army marched down the race course at Longchamp, after which it entered the city via the Pont and Avenue de Neuilly, then turning to the Porte Maillot and the Arc de Triomphe. But the city was barren. Canals were frozen. Food was short. In any case, the parading Germans now received some unpleasant news. The quick ratification of the treaty had given the French a card to play. Its terms required the Germans to withdraw from Paris as soon as ratification took place. At eleven o'clock on 1 March, Favre received a telegram from Bordeaux confirming that the treaty had indeed been ratified. Himself unable to pass the German lines at that time, he wired Bismarck the following morning with the news, requesting the immediate evacuation of the German troops. Not satisfied with this, Favre now managed to go directly to Versailles with the official ratification documents that had been sent to him from Bordeaux. Finding the French papers to be in good order, Bismarck reciprocated with imperial ratification. Instructions were issued to the effect that the German troops now in Paris should at once be evacuated.[81]

William I was not pleased by what had happened, and he let those around him know it. Bismarck, in a conversation with a subordinate, discussed what he believed to be the reasons for the unhappy and personal state of mind of the emperor: his abnormal life; the tradition of psychic eccentricity in

211

the Hohenzollern family; his anxiety about his children—all this added to the unwillingness to bear unwelcome developments or to delve deeply into questions he had before him. It rendered him vulnerable, as Bismarck saw it, to flattery and opposing influences. In any case, it now fell to Moltke to break the news to William, and this he did in an off-putting and stiff way that undoubtedly contributed to the monarch's annoyance. Moltke failed to act as Bismarck would have acted. Bismarck, whenever he gave William unwelcome advice, adjusted his pressure very sensitively to what he knew to be the limits of the latter's emotional and intellectual patience; also, when he did give unwelcome advice, he was much too wise a man to boast about this, as many others would have done, to outsiders. But no matter. The German army withdrew from Paris and began to make preparations to return home.[52]

The events just recounted—Gambetta's resignation and the ensuing ratification of the preliminaries of peace by the National Assembly on 1 March—form, in combination, a suitable point for the termination of the examination of the background of the diplomacy of the Franco-Prussian War. For Gambetta's retirement, marking as it did a turning point in the history of the struggle, removed from the scene the last great personal opponent of peace between France and Germany, and with the conclusion of peace preliminaries there disappeared the last serious formal impediment to the final treaty, signed in Frankfurt on 10 May 1871.

Conclusion

We have had occasion to observe in the preceding narrative the processes by which the two parties conducted the conflict that plagued their relations for nine tortuous and bloody months and that would continue to burden those relations for the next eighty years, right down to the middle of the century that followed: the Franco-Prussian War of 1870–71. Certain of the conclusions to which this event leads, particularly those relating to questions of historical fact, have been brought forward in the narrative itself. There are, however, certain broader reflections to which this account gives rise, and these, too, deserve a word of mention before the narrative is brought to an end and permitted to take its modest place among the multitude of studies addressed to the subject of recent international history.

No sooner had the Franco-Prussian War ended and the new German empire been formed than Benjamin Disraeli, a former British prime minister (and a future one, as well), declared: "This war represents a German revolution, a greater revolution than the French Revolution of the last century. . . . Not a single principle in the management of our foreign affairs, accepted by all statesmen for guidance up to six months ago, any longer exists. There is not a diplomatic tradition which has not been swept away. You have a new world, new influences at work, new and unknown objects and dangers with which to cope."[1]

Disraeli's statements almost certainly went too far, and we must remember that his words were directed more at his opponent, Gladstone, who had been prime minister when the war occurred, than they were at foreign courts. But they had in them an element of truth. Prussia now stood at the head of an empire that was incontestably the mightiest power on the continent, one whose

213

rise had been achieved in a remarkably short space of time. Where would the new Germany expand next? The Netherlands? Belgium? Switzerland? The Baltic provinces of Russia?

Bismarck was by no means oblivious to the concerns of Germany's neighbors, and he saw only too clearly the difficulties they foretold for the new Germany. Out of fear of the new German empire, the states of Europe might band together with the recently defeated foes of Prussia to offset and maybe reduce the gains the victor had only so recently and spectacularly acquired. Fear and embitterment directed at Germany seemed palpable on almost every hand. The deep-seated embitterment, in particular, that marked educated French opinion in the immediate aftermath of the war and that came so prominently to the fore in the fulminations of the French press of that period produced profound effects on the relations between the two powers. We take note of certain features of these effects in the following paragraphs.

The taking of Alsace-Lorraine is often pointed to as the source of Franco-German enmity and of Germany's new problems in Europe. Obviously, this interpretation contains an element of truth. For the French, the loss of these two provinces would in future years certainly be the cause of much resentment and bitterness, as symbolized by the black draping of their respective symbols on the Place de la Concorde. Strangely enough, however, for the Germans, Alsace and Lorraine were to bring more headaches than satisfaction, for the government in Berlin was never able to make up its mind about the relationship of the two provinces to the remainder of the German Reich, and its policies were often hamstrung by this vacillation.[2] Moreover, there was in Great Britain and in liberal parts of Europe much resentment against Germany for having annexed the provinces without first resorting to a plebiscite.[3]

But here some words of qualification are in order. As we have seen, for Bismarck as well as for Moltke, the security of Germany's borders was, almost from the beginning of the war, a paramount consideration, since each recognized that the French would never accept their defeat as had the Austrians. Bismarck was not wide of the mark when he said: "French bitterness will exist in the same degree even if they came out of the war with or without cession of territory. . . . Even if our victory at Königgrätz roused bitterness in France, how much more will our victory over themselves."[4] The record

214

bore him out. Bismarck and Moltke, too, were, in a word, right to be concerned about border security, and there was a watertight argument that the two provinces were strategically vital. Alsace and Lorraine both had been routes through which a succession of French invasions of Germany had, in the two hundred preceding years, taken place. Security aside, many Germans regarded the provinces as prizes that they deserved for the success of German arms. It is difficult to see how Bismarck could have resisted such pressure—even had he wanted to do so. Still, though Alsace and Lorraine constituted a heavy and perhaps irremovable mortgage on Franco-German relations, they never constituted the major source of Franco-German antagonism. Even their return by Germany to France in 1918 did nothing to ease relations between the two powers.

The main problem that made France and Germany such irreconcilable antagonists after 1871 was French insecurity, of which Alsace and Lorraine were a symbol, not a cause. The security dilemma was the great result of the Franco-Prussian War, and it could be reversed only by French armaments and alliances that would in turn make Germany insecure. Such alliances developed over the next twenty years: in 1892–94 between France and Russia, in 1904 with the signing of the entente with Great Britain, and in 1907 with the creation of the Triple Entente comprising these three powers. The only other two ways France and the new Germany could have been reconciled to each other were impossible—France, like Austria, could have turned to Germany for support, but the legacy of the war, to say nothing of French pride and independence, ruled this out completely; financial and economic cooperation between France and Germany could have accomplished this, but this, too, was a pipe dream. The French were a frugal people, and the accumulation of small savings was favored both by custom and by the social institutions that governed French life. The result was the existence in the France of that day of a host of small savers whose savings represented a major source of investment capital. Some of this capability was revealed by the success of state loans issued to cover the indemnity payments after the war. By 1873, the indemnity was paid off, well before the Germans had expected. French bankers had not failed to note the implications of this achievement for the success of foreign investment generally, but they regarded this as a source of strength to use against Germany, not to cooperate with it.[5] The only other way that France and Germany could have been reconciled was by military parity—that is, by a rough equivalence in armaments and armies on each side. This was the situation created by the settlement of 1866 and destroyed by the victory of the Germans in the war of 1870–71.

The preceding sentence suggests another way of looking at the Franco-Prussian War of 1870–71. There is something odd about the way we remember the war of 1870–71. The Austro-Prussian War of 1866 stands out in our minds chiefly for the exclusion of Austria from Germany, for the annexation by Prussia of all the states north of the River Main, as well as the cities of Hannover, Nassau, and Frankfurt, and for the establishment of the North German Confederation under the tight control of Berlin. Italian unification ended Austrian rule in Lombardy-Venetia, the papal states, and Rome. The Napoleonic wars destroyed the Holy Roman Empire in 1806 and put the Confederation of the Rhine in its stead.

But the controversies over the war of 1870–71 almost always emphasize what was created—Prusso-Germany, Bismarckian Germany, united Germany—and the impact each had on the international system. When we think of what was lost, it is invariably Alsace and Lorraine, the fortress of Metz (as well as imperial rule in France), and the destruction of the Paris commune. Yet, no one, before Paul Schroeder at any rate, seems to have realized that the Franco-Prussian War ended the independent international existence of four states south of the Main: Bavaria, Württemberg, Baden, and Hesse-Darmstadt. Their disappearance and their inclusion in the new German Reich had consequences at least as profound not only for the creation of the German empire itself but for the European international system as a whole.[6]

That this was so can be seen from a number of standpoints. First, these states were—and had been throughout the early years of the nineteenth century—geographic, military, and political buffers that made the rivalry between France and Prussia politically manageable, even if they were only the focus of that rivalry. Eliminating them as actors made Franco-German relations exponentially worse; in any future conflict German forces would be poised directly on the French frontier, upending the previous system not only (nor mainly) by the impact of this elimination on the overall distribution of power but also (and more important) by their removal as buffer states.

Second, taking in these states added to the new German Reich millions of Catholics for whom Bismarck had only contempt, and this made governing Germany all the more difficult. Complicating this problem was the fact that there were other peoples in these states who were not German by nationality and with whom Bismarck would have to deal—Danes, Poles, and now French. Paramount among his anxieties—today seemingly implausible, but real and feared at the time—was that the new Germany would break up.

In other words, the victory over France in 1871 and the resulting terms of the Treaty of Frankfurt gave Germany more power than it needed and, as just noted, raised questions as to where Germany planned to expand next. The settlement of 1866 and the North German Confederation that created it gave Prussia all the power that it really needed—military, political, and economic. Despite occasional setbacks and disagreements with Prussia, all the states south of the River Main were tied to it. Not only did their acquisition work against Bismarck's goal to free Prussia from competing obligations and secure it against an attack, but it made it indisputably a Great Power. Moreover, the victory in 1871 deprived Prussia of something it had in 1866—a sense of purpose, an aim to achieve, a principle to fulfill and discharge. By absorbing more Catholics and ending the existence of the South German states, Prussia had compromised its older historic mission of representing and defending Protestant interests and individual state patriotism in Germany against the Catholic imperialism and selfish domination of Austria, while also, through its too-complete military victories, territorial expansion, and latent, labile hegemony in Europe, ruining its chance to be accepted generally as the guarantor of an independent, nonthreatening center for Europe that prevented the dominance of either flank (France or Russia)—Metternich's *rocher de bronze* and Bismarck's own ideal of Germany as *das Bleigewicht am Stehaufmännchen Europas*.[7]

Any reader of these lines about Bismarck will find them harsh compared to what was said about him in the preceding chapters of this narrative. In fairness, one must say that few statesmen ever experienced such a wide array of problems as Bismarck did in the years 1870–71. No human hand will ever sort and weigh with any degree of precision the ingredients of the complex causes and motives that governed his policy in those two years. Yet,

217

certain achievements of his policy are undeniable, and it is only fair, for this reason if for no other, to terminate this study with some examples of those achievements.

In the first place, Bismarck succeeded in limiting the war to the two belligerents. In so doing, his diplomacy defeated what desires existed on the part of the neutral powers to intervene in the conflict. During the initial stages, defeating those desires proved relatively easy, if only because of the overwhelming consensus on the part of the European powers that the rulers of the Second Empire had put themselves incontestably in the wrong by declaring war on Prussia on 19 July 1870. But that soon changed. The members of the provisional government who came into office (if not into total power) after the empire's overthrow on 4 September were determined (initially almost to the man) to avoid losing any territory—the cession of which was a fundamental German war aim—and thus escape the fate of other powers that had lost wars in the middle of the nineteenth century—as Russia had in 1856, as Austria had in 1859 and 1866.[8]

Their intention to do so was not apparent to Bismarck until some days after Sedan. It will be recalled that he had tried to test French feeling when he accosted Napoleon III on the road to Donchery in the hope that peace negotiations would swiftly follow military defeat. In this he was roundly disappointed, to the delight of Moltke and members of the military. It was just at this time that a number of situations came into being that served to fix the French leaders in an attitude of resistance and to stimulate in them the belief that they could end the war without losing any territory. These included:

1. The downfall of the Second Empire itself and the readiness of those who took positions of leadership in the new provisional government to believe that the source of difficulties in the relations between the two powers had now been removed and, with it, all reason to penalize their country.
2. (What was thought to be) the greatly improved strength of the French forces themselves, invigorated by new leadership—a development that meant they had a better chance to defend Paris and repel further German attacks.
3. Clear signs of a possible deterioration in the Prusso-Russian relationship in the face of which the senior officials of the Russian government, particularly the Russian chancellor, Alexander Gorchakov, bitterly jealous of Bismarck and acutely conscious of the strength of nationalist opinion at home, might be

218

expected to persuade their master, Tsar Alexander II, himself already upset over the upheavals caused by the Prussian victory in the war with Austria in 1866, to react violently to any further extension of Prussian power.

Many of the French political leaders were overcome—"deluded" would be a truer word—by these developments, and this undoubtedly is what led them to believe that they could withstand the Germans and, what is more, persuade the other powers of Europe to intervene on their behalf. Bismarck, of course, was under no illusions about the state of affairs that now prevailed in Paris, and he was anything but insensitive to its implications for German policy. All his diplomacy after Sedan was directed toward ending the war as soon as possible with the German war aims, as he conceived these to be, satisfied. His success in doing so was an achievement of a wholly superior order, the more so because it was achieved only after he had won a battle of titanic proportions against the chief military figures of his own government.[9]

Here was the second achievement with which Bismarck must be credited—his handling of the problems with the military men, from Moltke on down. These problems reached a boiling point at the end of October, when Metz finally fell and Moltke determined to exclude Bismarck from any military deliberations regarding the siege of Paris, which had begun the previous month. For this reason (and for the others already discussed), Bismarck determined that the war must end and end fast, even if this meant, as it did, bludgeoning the French ruthlessly into surrender. "Here," Geoffrey Wawro observes, "was a textbook clash of civil-military decision making."[10] Had Moltke had his way, the war would unquestionably have been prolonged. Bismarck's strategy would have suffered a catastrophic defeat. Bismarck's steadfast opposition to Moltke's tactics resulted in a series of fateful communications in December 1870 and January 1871 between himself and the king by means of which Bismarck managed, but only after a prolonged suspense and a number of apparent reversals of fate, to secure the latter's support. His efforts in this regard, which heightened the ill will that already existed in higher German military circles and particularly within Moltke's inner circle against his person, may well be said to have constituted a feat of Herculean proportions on the part of the chancellor's statesmanship—a feat upon which the general peace of Europe unquestionably depended.[11]

219

The points Bismarck stressed to the king have already been noted (see chapter 7) but they are, if only because of their importance in ending the struggle just recounted, worth repeating here. A military victory over France of the kind of which Moltke dreamt would, Bismarck repeatedly stressed, not solve any of the new Germany's problems or those of Europe. It would only sow seeds of future troubles. Any of these troubles would be even more serious than any the war had been intended to remove. A war of conquest against France would inevitably lead to war with Russia, and perhaps even Great Britain and Austria-Hungary, as well. Such a war, regardless of its military outcome, could only be, in its consequences, a calamity for all Europe. Its consequences would present the most serious dangers for the survival of the new Germany itself.[12]

These were, of course, farseeing views. But they found little echo anywhere in German circles, with the possible exception of Roon, the minister of war. The military view—which assumed the war would be easy and, after its having been launched, now sought only the most favorable way of prolonging it—was being put forward among all members of Moltke's staff, and it seemed easy for many people to understand. But winning a war, Bismarck soon learned, was one thing, ending it something quite other. Ending the war was a problem with which Bismarck was constantly preoccupied; it raised questions Moltke never had to answer or even to ask.[13]

Further worthy of commendation is the skill with which Bismarck handled relations between the provisional government and the fallen empire. This perhaps was his greatest achievement, and for that reason it deserves, at the risk of slight repetition, further recapitulation here. In the five months between the downfall of the Second Empire and the conclusion of the armistice, it fell to Bismarck to negotiate a possible peace with two sets of parties, one composed of the representatives of the empire that had been overthrown, the other comprising the members of the provisional government who had contrived to overthrow it. It is sometimes said that Bismarck pursued this course purely for tactical purposes—namely to raise the specter of a restored empire as a means of bustling the officials of the new regime into a settlement of the kind he envisaged. There is no evidence for this and a decisive argument against it.[14] Bismarck's eye was always on the political plane. To him, it was a matter of indifference with whom a peace was concluded; the question was always who would be able to conclude peace most quickly and conclude it in a way that satisfied the fundamental German war aims. He had, in dealing with each side, to measure the relationship between public feeling and stated policy, between motive and action, between cause and effect.[15]

Negotiating a peace with the members of the provisional government proved, right down to the day when the preliminaries of peace were signed, on 26 February 1871, a demanding and nerve-wracking undertaking, and it is not difficult to understand why this should be so. Misled by various distorted impressions they had gained of the state of popular morale in the country, its leading figures felt themselves in possession of a political lever by means of which they could end the war on the terms they wanted because—or so one can only conclude—their country, France, was unique. She was sui generis. She stood alone.[16]

For Bismarck, this view presented a host of problems, the solutions to which often seemed to verge on the impossible. Rarely, if ever, can a statesman have had to deal with situations more complex, chaotic, fluid, and obscure than those that prevailed in France during this time and particularly at the end of 1870 and the beginning of 1871, when the French attitude began to change. It is impossible to understand Bismarck's actions and decisions in regard to these problems without some sort of picture of the developments to which they were conceived as pertaining. Above all, there was (it might be called) a split-mindedness now running through the entire fabric of French politics and attitudes toward Germany. One part of the French government in Paris professed to be seeking peace with the new empire, while another part of it at Bordeaux appeared to be acting on the assumption that the war should continue and not end until the German armies had been driven from the sacred soil of France. Here is where the formidable figure of Gambetta played so prominent and, for Bismarck, so frustrating a role. During this time, the pages of the Parisian press, as well as official reports received by German intelligence, were full of items extolling the virtues of this most flamboyant and charismatic of men, portraying him as a powerful center of resistance to the German armies, in fact, as the likely source of their expulsion, as well as the possible nucleus of a revived eastern front against Germany. These reports had been filtered through many mouths and inflated many hopes, this in spite of their wildly exaggerated and grossly overly optimistic character. But they were, for various reasons, calculated to arouse the most eager enthusiasm in republican circles, and it cannot be said that they failed entirely in their purpose. The sentiment they evoked was undoubtedly behind the collapse of the negotiations in November 1870 with Thiers (and perhaps those in September at Ferrières with Favre). Gambetta—how his personality haunts these pages! It is hard to visualize the tremendous head of emotional and political steam he produced during the whole of this period. The great power of his oratory, his prevailing love for ostentation wherever it could be displayed, raised, with respect to the conclusion of peace, the specter of false standards, set up painful contrasts, heightened differences, inflamed sensitivities, and created sources of innumerable tension—both for his counterparts in Paris and for Bismarck himself.

Because he could not be certain of the intentions of the members of the provisional government—one side of it waging war demonstratively out of one pocket, the other side waging peace, clandestinely out of the other—Bismarck, after the failed negotiations with Thiers, seriously explored the possibility of making peace with the members of the fallen empire. But making peace with the Bonapartists presented obstacles that turned out to be every bit as cumbersome as those he faced in dealing with the Paris authorities. That Bonapartists were likely to satisfy what Bismarck regarded as the essential German war aims he was never really inclined to doubt. But how were they to regain power? Here was the crucial question. Clearly, they could not do so under the force of Prussian arms and still retain the confidence they would need to win support in the elections that were the indispensable condition of the ratification of any peace settlement and the establishment of its legitimacy. How could they be expected to muster that support if they were seen as or appeared to be merely puppets of the German empire?[17]

Not until January 1871 did some republicans in Paris—including, most strongly, Jules Favre, the minister in charge of foreign affairs—come to realize that continuation of the war would be suicide, that it would play into the hands of Moltke and the military leaders who were determined to wage it until French power had been reduced beyond recognition, and that the time had come to settle with Germany before events spun totally out of control. At this very time, however, a new problem made its appearance. The Russians began to act up. On 31 October 1870, Gorchakov had repudiated the Black Sea clauses of the Treaty of Paris of 1856. That repudiation raised the specter of a confrontation with the British, who saw the Russian decision as an attempt to undo a treaty by a unilateral statement and demanded that the issue be submitted to an international conference.

That demand, to which the Russians found themselves obliged to agree, though somewhat angrily and unhappily, raised a host of problems for Bismarck, for the British were insistent that France, as a signatory to the 1856 treaty, be represented at any conference addressed to its alteration. Bismarck viewed French representation at such a conference with the highest alarm. Among other things, it would open the door to a discussion of the war whose end he was actively engaged in negotiating with none other than Favre himself. Any such discussion could only lead to the war's prolongation. Through the skillful set of maneuvers recounted in chapter 7—exploiting the divergent perspectives of Paris and Bordeaux on the proper approach to this issue; raising difficulties about the procedures to which Favre would have to submit himself if he was to obtain the papers he would need to pass through the German lines; seeing to it that Favre's invitation to the conference was delayed until its deliberations had already begun; exploiting Favre's understandable reluctance to leave Paris in the wake of the Prussian siege and the catastrophe to which that siege had brought the city's fortunes—through all these maneuvers, Bismarck was able to prevent Favre from ever attending the conference at all. But, always careful never to foreclose his options, he agreed to see Clément Duvernois, a representative of the empress, while he negotiated with Favre. This decision did not, Eberhard Kolb has pointed out, in any way signify a preference for the Bonapartists over the republicans.[18] It was designed as a precaution in case the negotiations with the latter, for some reason, did not bear fruit. In any case, as we have seen, a whole series of factors—Eugénie's mercurial temperament; the bewildering series of predicaments into which her advisers habitually fell; and, not least, the repeated and inexplicable delays in the departure of Duvernois for Versailles—all these factors conspired to keep the Bonapartists away from the scene where the crucial discussions regarding an armistice were unfolding. By the time Duvernois arrived at Versailles, the clock had run out. A deal had been struck between Bismarck and Favre.

Entry into the Potsdamer Platz in Berlin, 16 June 1871. (von Pflugk-Harttung, *The Franco-German War*, following p. 650.)

The way was now clear for the signing of an armistice and the holding of elections. Once Gambetta's obstructionism with respect to these had been removed through his resignation on 6 February, the war could proceed toward its formal end—through the signing, in Versailles, on 26 February, of a preliminary peace and the ratification of that peace, on 1 March, by the National Assembly, the members of which had been elected on 8 February and had now convened at Bordeaux. The negotiations then moved to Brussels, where the last details of the peace settlement were to be worked out. But the conclusion of the final peace was itself delayed by yet another difficulty. On 18 March, there broke out in France a civil war that resulted in the establishment, by radicals, of a Commune in Paris, with the avowed aim of destroying the new French government. The features surrounding that event have been bypassed in the narrative because they affected the peace negotiations only episodically and tangentially. But certain of these features may briefly be taken note of here. The violent ideological preconceptions of the Commune's leaders; their hatred of the capitalist world; the churlish delight they took in taunting and insulting not only the government of France but the governments of the other powers; the cynicism, opportunism, and absence of good faith that marked their methods of dealing with non-communard officials everywhere—these were the traits that marked the communards and brought about their downfall. The French authorities, feeling as they did the pressure not only from the Germans but from all the governments of the powers of Europe to establish order, quickly took steps to do just that. It was quickly arranged that the number of troops the French would be allowed to maintain north of the Loire should be revised upward to eighty thousand from the original forty thousand and that the return of French prisoners of war in Germany should be hastened so as to permit the formation of an army necessary to crush the uprising. On 10 May, Bismarck and Favre, the latter bypassing Brussels entirely and coming directly to Germany, signed the Treaty of Frankfurt; eleven days later, on 21 May, the two exchanged the ratifications of the treaty, which had been approved by their respective governments. It was those ratifications that brought the Franco-Prussian War to an end.[19]

The German empire thus came into being, and Bismarck at once had a new mission to conceive and carry out: the search for a new international stability. Aware of the unease caused all over Europe by the creation of the new German empire and the dangers that this implied for the stability of Germany itself, he threw himself into the task of making the system he had created work. "No one else," Paul W. Schroeder has observed, "was available for this managerial task; it is doubtful that anyone else would have tried."[20] Who indeed?

Abbreviations

AHR	*American Historical Review*
AMAE-CP	Archives du Ministère des Affaires Etrangères– Correspondance Politiques (Paris)
APP	*Die auswärtige Politik Preußens, 1858–1871*
BN NAF	Bibliothèque Nationale nouvelle acquisition française (Paris)
BURS	*Bibliothèque universelle et revue suisse*
CEH	*Central European History*
DDI	*Documenti Diplomatici Italiani*, prima serie, 1861–70, Ministero degli affari esteri (Rome, 1952–63)
DG	*Dual of Giants*, by David Wetzel (Madison, 2001)
DO	*Enquête parlementaire sur les actes du Gouvernement de la Défense Nationale: Dépêches télégraphiques officielles*, 6 vols. (Versailles, 1875)
DR	*Deutsche Revue*
DT	*Enquête parlementaire sur les actes du Gouvernement de la Défense Nationale: Dépositions des témoins* (Versailles, 1873)
EHR	*English Historical Review*
EK	*Europa vor dem Krieg von 1870*, ed. Eberhard Kolb (Munich, 1987)
ER	*Europa und die Reichsgründung*, ed. Eberhard Kolb (Munich, 1980)
F	*Francia*
FBPS	*Forschungen zur Brandenburgischen und Preußischen Geschichte*

GND   Government of National Defense

GP   *Die Große Politik der europäischen Kabinette 1871–1914*, ed. Johannes Lepsisus, Albrecht Mendelssohn Bartholdy, and Friedrich Thimme, 40 vols. in 56 (Berlin, 1922–26)

GStAM   Geheimes Staatsarchiv (Munich)

GW   Otto von Bismarck, *Die Gesammelten Werke*, ed. Wolfgang Windelband and Werner Frauendienst, 15 vols. in 19 (Berlin, 1925–35)

HHSA PA   Haus-, Hof- und Staatsarchiv, Politisches Archiv (Vienna)

HZ   *Historische Zeitschrift*

JBZ   *Jahresbibliographie: Bibliothek für Zeitgeschichte*

JMH   *Journal of Modern History*

MMK   *Moltkes militärische Korrespondenz: Aus den Dienstschriften des Krieges 1870–71* (Berlin, 1896)

MGM   *Militärgeschichtliche Mitteilungen*

NA-PRO-FO   National Archives, Public Record Office, Foreign Office (London)

NFA   *Neue Friedrichsruher Ausgabe* [new ed. of *GW*], ed. Konrad Canis, Lothar Gall, Klaus Hildebrand, and Eberhard Kolb (Paderborn, 2004–)

OD   *Les origines diplomatiques de la guerre de 1870–1871*, ed. Le Ministère des Affaires Ètrangères, 29 vols. (Paris, 1910–32)

PA   Politisches Archiv des Auswärtigen Amts (Berlin)

PJbb   *Preussische Jahrbücher*

QuFiAB   *Quellen und Forschungen aus italienischen Archiven und Bibliotheken*

SSS   *Systems, Stability, and Statecraft: Essays on the International History of Modern Europe*, by Paul W. Schroeder, edited and with an introduction by David Wetzel, Robert Jervis, and Jack S. Levy (New York, 2004)

VSWG   *Vierteljahrsschrift für Sozial-und Wirtschaftsgeschichte*

ZBLG	*Zeitschrift für bayerische Landgeschichte*
ZfG	*Zeitschrift für Geschichtswissenschaft*
ZGORh	*Zeitschrift für die Geschichte des Oberrheins*

Notes

CHAPTER 1. POLITICS AND PERSONALITIES

1. Quoted in Alistair Horne, *The Fall of Paris: The Siege and the Commune, 1870–71* (Garden City, NY, 1967), 42.

2. Ibid., 43.

3. Ibid.

4. On all this see Pierre de la Gorce, *Histoire du Second Empire*, 6 vols. (Paris, 1894–1905), 6:310–13.

5. Barthélémy Louis Joseph Lebrun, *Souvenirs militaires, 1866–1870* (Paris, 1895), 181.

6. Horne, *Paris*, 43.

7. Geoffrey Wawro, *The Franco-Prussian War: The German Conquest of France, 1870–1871* (Cambridge, 2003), 79–84.

8. Rothan to Gramont, 17 July 1870, *OD*, 29, no. 8619.

9. Ludwig Bamberger, *Bismarcks grosses Spiel: Die geheimen Tagebücher* (Frankfurt am Main, 1932), 127; Rudolph Buchner, "Die deutsche patriotische Dichtung vom Kriegsbeginn 1870," *HZ* 206 (1968): 327–36.

10. Michael Howard, *The Franco-Prussian War: The German Invasion of France*, 2nd ed. (New York, 2001), 59.

11. Bamberger, *Tagebücher*, 135.

12. Gustav Lehmann, *Die Mobilmachung von 1870/71* (Berlin, 1904), 40.

13. Bamberger, *Tagebücher*, 141.

14. Albrecht Graf von Roon, *Denkwürdigkeiten*, 5th ed., 3 vols. (Berlin, 1905), 2:514.

15. David Wetzel, *Duel of Giants* (Madison, WI, 2001), 5–10; Karl Heinz Börner, *Kaiser Wilhelm I* (Cologne, 1987).

16. Quoted in Gordon A. Craig, *From Bismarck to Adenauer: Aspects of German Statecraft* (Baltimore, 1958), 7. The whole tenor of my remarks on Bismarck is drawn from this magnificent vignette.

17. Theodor Fontane, *Briefe an seine Freunde*, 2 vols. (Berlin, 1925), 2:25.

18. *GW*, 2, 142.

19. Ibid., 14/1, no. 582; Craig, *Bismarck*, 10.

20. Roon, *Denkwürdigkeiten*, 2:101.

21. *Fürst Bismarcks Briefe an seine Braut und Gattin*, ed. Fürst Herbert Bismarck (Stuttgart, 1900), 281; Craig, *Bismarck*, 16.

22. Quoted in Siegfried von Kardoff, *Wilhelm von Kardoff* (Berlin, 1909), 130; Craig, *Bismarck*, 19.

23. *GW*, 14/1, no. 747.

24. *Fürst Bismarcks Briefe*, 269; Craig, *Bismarck*, 19–20.

25. Bernhard Fürst von Bülow, *Denkwürdigkeiten*, 4 vols. (Berlin, 1930–31), 4:289.

26. Horst Kohl, *Bismarcks Briefe, 1836–1872* (Bielefeld and Leipzig, 1897), 77 ("Briefe an die Ehefrau," 3 July 1851).

27. Quoted in Herbert Vossler, "Bismarcks Ethos," *HZ* 131 (1951): 274; Craig, *Bismarck*, 21.

28. Craig, *Bismarck*, 13.

29. Hajo Holborn, "Bismarck und Werthern," *Archiv für Politik und Geschichte* 5 (1925–26): 482.

30. Statement at the beginning of 1869 cited by Robert von Keudell, *Fürst und Fürstin Bismarck* (Berlin and Stuttgart, 1901), 419.

31. Bismarck would fully have endorsed Machiavelli here. Cf. *GW*, 13, 468, and *Il Principe*, chap. 21; Craig, *Bismarck*, 24.

32. *GW*, 14, no. 65.

33. Ibid., 8, no. 456; Craig, *Bismarck*, 24.

34. Eberhard Kolb, *Der Weg aus dem Krieg: Bismarcks Politik im Krieg und die Friedensanbahnung 1870–71* (Munich, 1990), 1–50.

35. Wawro, *Franco-Prussian War*, 47.

36. Max Jähns, *Feldmarschall Moltke* (new ed., Berlin, 1894), 171; Gordon A. Craig, *The Politics of the Prussian Army 1645–1945* (Oxford, 1955), 117.

37. Craig, *Politics*, 117; Karl Haenchen, *Revolutionsbriefe 1848: Ungedrucktes aus dem Nachlaß König Friedrich Wilhelms IV. von Preussen* (Leipzig, 1930), 178–79.

38. Arden Bucholz, *Moltke and the German Wars* (New York, 2001), 12–25.

39. Quoted in Gordon A. Craig, *The Battle of Königgrätz: Prussia's Victory over Austria, 1866* (Philadelphia, 1964), 27.

40. Bucholz, *Moltke*, 103–38.

CHAPTER 2. THE POSITION OF THE POWERS

1. See especially the works of Heinrich Lutz, *Österreich-Ungarn und die Gründung des Deutschen Reiches* (Berlin, 1979), 135–72, and "Die aussenpolitischen Tendenzen der Habsburgermonarchie von 1866 bis 1870" (in Eberhard Kolb, ed., *Europa vor dem*

Krieg von 1870 [Munich, 1987], 1–16); Victor-Lucien Tapié, *Autour d'une tentative d'alliance entre la France et l'Autriche, 1867–1870* (Paris, 1971); Heinrich Potthoff, *Die deutsche Politik Beusts von seiner Berufung zum österreichischen Aussenminister Oktober 1866 bis zum Ausbruch des deutsch-französischen Krieges 1870/71* (Berlin, 1968).

2. Metternich (Paris) to Beust, 2 December 1868, in Hermann Oncken, *Die Rheinpolitik Kaiser Napoleons III, von 1863 bis 1870 und der Ursprung des Krieges von 1870/71*, 3 vols. (Stuttgart, 1926), 3, no. 649.

3. Cf. Paul W. Schroeder, "The Lost Intermediaries: The Impact of 1870 on the European System" (in *SSS*, 92–95); Kolb, *Weg*, 1–3.

4. This was revealed in August 1870, and then with the stipulation that the Italians would need three weeks. *OD*, 29, no. 8937.

5. Kolb, *Weg*, 2–5; Potthoff, *Beust*, 262–72; Lutz, *Österreich-Ungarn*, 135–45.

6. Ollivier, *L'Empire*, 11:203–6.

7. Lutz, *Österreich-Ungarn*, 146–49.

8. French note, 1 March 1869, with four draft treaties, in Oncken, *Rheinpolitik*, 3, no. 671.

9. Beust to Metternich, 10 April 1869, ibid., no. 684.

10. Metternich to Beust, 18 April 1869, ibid., no. 685.

11. French draft treaty, 10 May 1869; Metternich to Beust, 20 May 1869, ibid., no. 698.

12. On the Roman question, see above all Norbert Miko, *Das Ende des Kirchenstaates*, 4 vols. (Vienna/Munich, 1962–70); Hubert Bastgen, *Die römische Frage*, 3 vols. (Freiburg, 1917–19); Noel Blakiston, *The Roman Question* (London, 1962); Renato Mori, *Il tramonto del potere temporale, 1866–1870* (Rome, 1967); Georges Dethan, "Napoléon III et l'opinion française devant la question romaine (1860–1870)," *Revue d'histoire diplomatique* 72 (1958): 118–34.

13. Vitzthum (Paris) to Beust, 7 October 1869, in Oncken, *Rheinpolitik*, 3, no. 741. Italics in original.

14. Napoleon III to Francis Joseph, 24 September 1869, *OD*, 25, no. 7674.

15. Beust to Vitzthum, 20 July 1870, in Oncken, *Rheinpolitik*, 3, no. 911, note.

16. Interview, 14 June 1870, Lebrun, *Souvenirs militaires*, 146.

17. Cf. Stéphanie Burgaud, *La politique russe de Bismarck et l'unification allemande: Mythe fondateur et réalités politiques* (Strasbourg, 2010), 231–67; Dietrich Beyrau, *Russische Orientpolitik und die Entstehung des deutschen Kaiserreiches 1866–1870/71* (Wiesbaden, 1974), 106–18; "Russische Interessenzonen und europäisches Gleichgewicht, 1860–1870" (in Kolb, *Europa*, 65–76).

18. Arthur von Brauer, *Im Dienste Bismarcks: Persönliche Erinnerungen*, ed. Helmut Rogge (Berlin, 1936), 101.

19. Reuss to Bismarck, 5 February 1868, *APP*, 6, no. 550.

20. Bismarck to Reuss, 16 February 1868, *GW*, 6a, no. 1064.

21. Burgaud, *Politique*, 346.

22. Ibid.

23. Revertera (Petersburg) to Beust, 14 January 1868, HHSA PA X 58, fol. 567, no. 57D; W. E. Mosse, *The European Powers and the German Question* (London, 1958), 290.

24. Cf. Kolb, *Weg*, 4–5, 17.

25. See Loftus (Berlin) to Granville, 18 July 1870, NA-PRO-FO 64/689; Augustus Loftus, *Diplomatic Reminiscences 1862–1879*, 2nd series (London, 1894), 1:287–88.

26. La Valette to Gramont, 16 July 1870, *OD*, 29, no. 8588; Granville to Lyons (Paris), 16 July 1870, NA-PRO-FO 27/1073; *Bluebook*, 1, 42; Kolb, *Weg*, 27–28.

27. Bismarck to Bernstorff (London), 18 July 1870, *GW*, 6b, no. 1665.

28. Bernstorff to Bismarck, 20 and 21 July 1870, PA, R 4318 o. Fol.; Kurt Rheindorf, *England und der deutsch-französische Krieg 1870/71* (Bonn/Leipzig 1923), 60–61; Viet Valentin, *Bismarcks Reichsgründung im Urteil englischer Diplomaten* (Amsterdam, 1937), 428–31; Kolb, *Weg*, 30.

29. William I to Queen Victoria, 26 July 1870, *The Letters of Queen Victoria*, 2nd series, 1861–1885, ed. George Earl Buckle, 3 vols. (London, 1926–28), 2:51–52.

30. Granville to Bismarck, 30 July 1870, PA, R 4318 o. Fol.; Kolb, *Weg*, 30–31.

31. The draft has been published many times; see, among others, Mosse, *European Powers*, 340–41; Oncken, *Rheinpolitik*, 2:94–95; Kolb, *Weg*, 35–37.

32. Bismarck to Bernstorff, 20 July 1870, *GW*, 6b, no. 1690.

33. Richard Millman, *British Policy and the Coming of the Franco-Prussian War* (Oxford, 1965), 205–6; Horst Lademacher, *Die belgische Neutralität als Problem der europäischen Politik 1830–1914* (Bonn, 1971), 425.

34. Millman, *British Policy*, 207–20; Valentin, *Bismarcks Reichsgründung*, 428–29.

35. Beyrau, *Orientpolitik*, 184–87; Kolb, *Weg*, 17–19; S. V. Obolenskaia, *Franko-Prusskaia voina i obshchestvennoe mnenie Germanii i Rossii* [The Franco-Prussian War and Public Opinion in Russia and Germany] (Moscow, 1977).

36. Burgaud, *Politique*, 242–43, 250, 287, 313.

37. Fr. De Fontenay, *Danish Biographical Dictionary*, 56–98.

38. See his own exaggerated description in Jules Hansen, *Les coulisses de la diplomatie, quinze ans à l'étranger (1864–1879)* (Paris, 1880).

CHAPTER 3. THE LEAGUE OF NEUTRALS

1. Francesco Cataluccio, *La politica estera di E. Visconti Venosta* (Florence, 1940); S. William Halperin, *Diplomat under Stress: Visconti-Venosta and the Crisis of July 1870* (Chicago, 1963), 2–8; Federico Chabod, *Storia della politica estera italiana dal 1870 al 1896*, 2 vols. (Bari, 1951), 1:555, 563, 564–67.

2. Paget to Granville, 18 July 1870, NA-PRO-FO 45/164.

3. Paget to Granville, 16 July 1870, ibid.
4. Ibid.
5. Ibid.
6. Ibid.
7. Granville to Paget, 17 July 1870, NA-PRO-FO 45/164.
8. Halperin, *Diplomat*, 172–73; Kolb, *Weg*, 40–41; Chabod, *Storia*, 1:108–10.
9. Chabod, *Storia*, 1:110.
10. Halperin, *Diplomat*, 173–75.
11. Ibid., 175.
12. Visconti-Venosta to Artom, 15 July 1870, *DDI*, 1/13, no. 154.
13. *L'Opinione*, 21 July 1870.
14. Lutz, *Österreich-Ungarn*, 202–10.
15. Victor Emmanuel to Visconti-Venosta, 9 July 1870, *DDI*, 1/13, no. 41; Vimercati (Paris) to Victor Emmanuel, 10 July 1870, *DDI*, 1/13, no. 66.
16. Chabod, *Storia*, 1:110–12.
17. Paget to Granville, 9 July 1870, NA-PRO-FO 391/23.
18. Victor Emmanuel II to Napoleon III, 21 July 1870, *OD*, 29, no. 8705.
19. *Rendiconti del parlamento italiano: Sessione del 1869–70 (Sessione II della legislatura X: Discussioni della camera dei deputati)*, IV, dal 13 luglio al 25 agosto, 1870, 3420–23.
20. Lutz, *Österreich-Ungarn*, 210–14.
21. István Diószegi, *Österreich-Ungarn und der französisch-preußische Krieg 1870/71* (Budapest, 1974), n. 288.
22. Ibid., 51–52.
23. Ibid., n. 288.
24. Lutz, *Österreich-Ungarn*, 213.
25. Beust to Metternich, 11 July 1870, in Oncken, *Rheinpolitik*, 3, no. 807.
26. Cazaux to Gramont, 15 July 1870, *OD*, 28, no. 8548.
27. Lutz, *Österreich-Ungarn*, 213–14.
28. Ibid., 218–22; L. Ritter von Przibram, *Erinnerungen eines alten Österreichers*, 2 vols. (Stuttgart, 1911), 1:270–71; Em Kónyi, "Graf Beust und Graf Andrássy im Krieg 1870–71" (in *Deutsche Revue* 2 [1890]: 1–28, 145–65, here 14–17); Heinrich von Srbik, *Aus Österreichs Vergangenheit: Vom Prinz Eugen zu Franz Joseph* (Salzburg, 1949), 67–98.
29. Beust to Metternich, 20 July 1870, in Oncken, *Rheinpolitik*, 3, no. 920.
30. See Cadorna to Visconti-Venosta, 9 August 1870, *DDI*, 1/13, no. 463; Visconti-Venosta to Cadorna, 20 August 1870, *DDI*, 1/13, nos. 443, 539; Granville to Brunnow, 31 August 1870, NA-PRO-FO 65/803; *Bluebook*, 4, 27, 36.
31. Visconti-Venosta to Cadorna, 22 July 1870, *DDI*, 1/13/275; Halperin, *Diplomat*, 184–85.

32. Granville to Paget, 18, 19 July 1870, NA-PRO-FO 45/165, fol. 69.

33. Chabot, *Storia* 1:655; Halperin, *Diplomat*, 185.

34. Granville to Cadorna, 17 August 1870, *British and Foreign State Papers, 1870–1871* (London, 1877), 61:682–83; Halperin, *Diplomat*, 187.

35. Buchanan to Granville, 22 August 1870, NA-PRO-FO 65/803, fols. 230ff.

36. Beust to Apponyi (London), 23 August 1870, HHSA PA VIII 75, fol. 147.

37. Metternich to Beust, 19 August 1870, HHSA PA IX 95, fol. 217.

38. Beust to Chotek (Petersburg), 2 August 1870, HHSA PA X 63, fol. 242; Kolb, *Weg*, 93.

39. Albert Sorel, *Histoire diplomatique de la guerre franco-allemande*, 2 vols. (Paris, 1875), 1:255.

40. Beust to Chotek, 9 and 10 August 1870, HHSA PA, X 63, fol. 254; Burgaud, *Politique*, 383–93.

41. Beust to Chotek, 14 August 1870, HHSA PA X 62, fols. 168–74; Werner L. Mosse, *The European Powers and the German Question 1848–71 with Special Reference to England and Russia* (Cambridge, 1958), 318–22; Lutz, *Österreich-Ungarn*, 241–42; Diószegi, *Österreich-Ungarn*, 138–39; Burgaud, *Politique*, 395–97; Kolb, *Weg*, 94.

42. Mosse, *Powers*, 324: Burgaud, *Politique*, 399, 400, 404.

43. Protocol of meeting, HHSA PA IX 95 XL, fols. 687–715; Mosse, *Powers*, 325–28; Lutz, *Österreich-Ungarn*, 243–52; Diószegi, *Österreich-Ungarn*, 138–40; Kolb, *Weg*, 96.

44. Przibram, *Erinnerungen eines alten Österreichers*, 1:270.

45. Kónyi, "Beust und Graf Andrássy 1870–71," 1:14.

46. Metternich to Beust, 23 August 1870, HHSA PA IX 95, fol. 245.

47. Beust to Chotek, 25 August 1870, HHSA PA X 63 (nos. 2, 3, 4), fols. 293–300, 301–6; Kolb, *Weg*, 97.

48. Chotek to Beust, 4 September 1870, HHSA PA X 62, fols. 198–99.

49. Mosse, *Powers*, 327; Burgaud, *Politique*, 399.

50. Mosse, *Powers*, 327–28; Kolb, *Weg*, 97–98; Burgaud, *Politique*, 415, 424, 426.

51. See esp. Beust to Chotek, 15 September 1870, HHSA PA 63, fols. 326–30.

52. See esp. Edvard Radzinsky, *Alexander II: The Last Great Tsar*, translated by Antonina W. Bouis (New York, 2005), 44–48, 104–15.

53. See the portrait painted by Reuss in Reuss to Bismarck, 31 August 1870, PA, R 61 no. 10122, E6–E9; Mosse, *Powers*, 234, n. 5; and Kurt Rheindorf, *Die Schwarze-Meer-(Pontus-)Frage vom Pariser Frieden von 1856 bis zum Abschluss der Londoner Konferenz von 1871* (Berlin, 1925), 50, 72, 81, 86, 90, 143, 158; Burgaud, *Politique*, 400, 401, 405, 410.

54. Kolb, *Weg*, 103–4.

55. Bismarck to Reuss, 10 August 1870, *GW*, 6b, no. 1736.

56. Bismarck to Reuss, 11 August 1870, *GW*, 6b, no. 1737.

57. Reuss to Bismarck, 7 August 1870, PA, R 61 no. 10122, E6–E9.
58. Reuss to Bismarck, 13 August 1870, ibid.
59. Reuss to Bismarck, 14 August 1870, ibid.
60. Reuss to Bismarck, 19 August 1870, ibid.; Kolb, *Weg*, 106–7.
61. Bismarck to Reuss, 22 August 1870, *GW*, 6b, no. 1757.
62. Kolb, *Weg*, 108–9.
63. Bismarck to Schweinitz, 24 August 1870, *GW*, 6b, no. 1758.
64. Kolb, *Weg*, 111–12.

CHAPTER 4. THE END OF NAPOLEON III

1. *Pall Mall Gazette*, 1 August 1870, "From the German Side" (in Wawro, *Franco-Prussian War*, 80).
2. Kolb, *Weg*, 113–14.
3. Rudolf Haym, *Ausgewählter Briefwechsel*, ed. Hans Rosenberg (Stuttgart, 1930), 279.
4. Morier to Granville, 19 July 1870, NA-PRO-FO 30/328.
5. Adolph Wagner, *Briefe, Dokumente, Augenzeugenberichte, 1851–1917*, selected and edited by H. von Rubner (Berlin, 1978), 82–83.
6. Reider to Bray, 25 July 1870, GStAM MA 649; Kolb, *Weg*, 121.
7. Adolph Wagner, *Elsaß und Lothringen und ihre Wiedergewinnung für Deutschland* (Leipzig, 1870), 6.
8. Gordon A. Craig, *German History, 1866–1945* (Oxford, 1978), 29–30.
9. Bismarck to the Foreign Office, 15 August 1870, *GW*, 6b, no. 1747.
10. Bismarck to Thile, 25 August 1870, *GW*, 6b, no. 1764; circular to Thile, same day, *GW*, 6b, no. 1766.
11. See Buchanan (Petersburg) to Granville, 5 September 1870, NA-PRO-FO 65/804, no. 337; Paul Knaplund, *Gladstone's Foreign Policy* (New York, 1935), 270–73; Kolb, *Weg*, 152.
12. Draft of statement, Abeken to Bernstorff, PA, R 4318 o. Fol.
13. Cf. Allan Mitchell, *Bismarck and the French Nation, 1848–1890* (New York, 1971), 56–57, 59.
14. Kolb, *Weg*, 156.
15. Draft of statement to Reuss, 11 August 1870, *GW*, 6b, no. 1737.
16. I am grateful to Professor Paul W. Schroeder for pointing all this out to me.
17. Wawro, *Franco-Prussian War*, 186–210; Howard, *Franco-Prussian War*, 183–203.
18. *Tagebücher des Generalfeldmarschalls Graf von Blumenthal aus den Jahren 1866 und 1870/1871*, ed. Albrecht Graf von Blumenthal (Stuttgart, Berlin, Cotta, 1902), 91.

19. Wawro, *Franco-Prussian War*, 219.

20. Philip H. Sheridan, *Personal Memories of P. H. Sheridan*, 2 vols. (New York, 1888), 2:402–3; Wawro, *Franco-Prussian War*, 224.

21. Wawro, *Franco-Prussian War*, 224.

22. Sheridan, *Memoirs*, 2:404–5; Wawro, *Franco-Prussian War*, 226.

23. Wawro, *Franco-Prussian War*, 226.

24. Howard, *Franco-Prussian War*, 221.

25. Ibid., 222.

26. Ibid.

27. Wawro, *Franco-Prussian War*, 228.

28. *GW*, 6b, nos. 1773–74; Howard, *Franco-Prussian War*, 222.

29. Wawro, *Franco-Prussian War*, 228–29.

30. Moritz Busch, *Tagebuchblätter*, 3 vols. (Leipzig, 1899), 1:165.

31. Bismarck to Herbert Bismarck, 7 September 1870; Wilhelm Busch, *Das deutsche grosse Hauptquartier und die Bekämpfung von Paris im Feldzuge 1870–71* (Stuttgart and Berlin, 1905), 10; Howard, *Franco-Prussian War*, 229.

32. Julian Schmidt, *Bilder aus dem geistigen Leben unserer Zeit*, vol. 2, *Neue Folge* (Leipzig, 1871), 454.

33. Rudolf von Jhering, *Briefe an seine Freunde* (Leipzig, 1913), 249–50.

34. Lothar Gall, "Zur Frage der Annexion von Elsaß und Lothringen 1870," *HZ* 206 (1968): 265–326; Kolb, *Weg*, 133–44.

35. Morier to Granville, 2 September 1870, NA-PRO-FO 30/328.

36. Cf. Jacques Desmarest, *La Défense Nationale: 1870–71* (Paris, 1949), 76–83; J. Tchernoff, *Histoire politique contemporaine: Le parti républicain au coup d'état et sous le Second Empire d'après des documents et des souvenirs inédits* (Paris, 1906), 609–12.

37. See especially J. P. T. Bury, *Gambetta and the National Defence: A Republican Dictatorship in France* (London, 1936), 31–45, 65–95.

38. Howard, *Franco-Prussian War*, 234; prefect reports from Chambery, Mende, Quimper, Périgueux, Tulle, for 24–30 September 1870, in *DO*, vol. 1.

39. Howard, *Franco-Prussian War*, 225.

40. Cf. Bury, *Gambetta*, 77–95.

41. *DT*, 2:408–25, 456–73; Howard, *Franco-Prussian War*, 237.

42. See Bury, *Gambetta*, 89–100; and esp. Jules Favre, *Gouvernement de la Défense Nationale*, 3 vols. (Paris, 1871–75), 1:103–52.

43. Except where otherwise noted, this sketch of Trochu is drawn from Stéphane Rials, *De Trochu à Thiers, 1870–1873* (Paris, 1985); Jean Brunet-Moret, *Le Général Trochu* (Paris, 1958); and Vital Cartier, *Un méconnu: Le Général Trochu* (Paris, 1914).

44. Except where otherwise noted, this sketch of Gambetta is drawn from J. P. T. Bury, *Gambetta and the National Defence* (London, 1936); and Jean-Marie Mayeur, *Léon Gambetta: La patrie et la république* (Paris, 2008).

45. Desmarest, *Défense National*, 64.

46. Except where otherwise noted, this sketch of Favre is drawn from Pierre Antoine Perrod, *Jules Favre: Avocat de la liberté* (Lyon, 1988); and Maurice Reclus, *Jules Favre 1809–1880: Essai de biographie historique et morale d'après des documents inédits* (Paris, 1912).

47. Except where otherwise noted, this sketch of Thiers is drawn from Henri Malo, *Thiers 1797–1877* (Paris, 1932); Georges Valance, *Thiers: Bourgeois et révolutionnaire* (Paris, 2007); and J. P. T. Bury, *Thiers 1797–1877: A Political Life* (London, 1986).

CHAPTER 5. FERRIÈRES

1. See Bismarck to Foreign Office, 2 September 1870, *GW*, 6b, no. 1774; Bismarck to Bernstorff, 9 September 1870, 10 September 1870, *GW*, 6b, nos. 1788, 1790; Bismarck to Thile, 12 September 1870, *GW*, 6b, no. 1808.

2. Sorel, *Histoire*, 1:285–86; Favre, *Gouvernement*, 1:222–23; Metternich to Beust, 6 September 1870, HHSA PA IX 96, fol. 289.

3. Cf. Howard, *Franco-Prussian War*, 234.

4. See, e.g., Favre, *Gouvernement*, 1:385; Sorel, *Histoire*, 1:298; Joseph Reinach, ed., *Dépêches, circulaires, décrets, proclamations et discours de Léon Gambetta*, 2 vols. (Paris, 1891), 1:121. See also AMAE-CP, 1871/72, 511–14; HHSA PA 19, 215–19, fol. 392.

5. Sorel, *Histoire*, 1:349–51; Favre, *Gouvernement*, 1:112–13. Also on Favre's mind were developments in Russia. On 8 September 1870, Reuss had telegraphed to Bismarck that Favre, through his contact with Gabriac, the chargé d'affaires, had concluded that "the Tsar of Russia may propose to the King [William I] a peace: Integrity of France, payment [by France] of war costs; refusal by Prussia, war to the utmost. But the Tsar refuses to share with me any information reported to him." Kolb, *Weg*, 228.

6. Favre, *Gouvernement*, 1:385.

7. Ibid., 387; Sorel, *Histoire*, 1:298–99; Kolb, *Weg*, 231.

8. Cf. Kolb, *Weg*, 227–28.

9. Bismarck to representatives abroad, 11 September 1870, PA, R 8422, o. Fol.

10. Gustave Rothan, *Souvenirs diplomatiques: L'Allemagne et l'Italie 1870–71*, 2 vols. (Paris, 1884–85), 1:79.

11. Granville to Lyons, 7 September 1870, NA-PRO-FO 27/1793.

12. Buchanan to Granville, 15 September 1870, no. 21, NA-PRO-FO 65/804.

13. Kolb, *Weg*, 234.

14. Sorel, *Histoire*, 1:349; Favre, *Gouvernement*, 1:132–33.

15. Kolb, *Weg*, 238–39; Favre, *Gouvernement*, 1:164–65; and esp. Sorel, *Histoire*,

1:349–63, who, drawing on material from unnamed but reliable sources, gives a vivid account of the dialogue that took place.

16. Favre, *Gouvernement*, 1:165.

17. Favre to Gabriac (Petersburg), 13 September 1870, AMAE-CP Russie, vol. 244, fol. 283.

18. Cf. Sorel, *Histoire*, 1:363; Kolb, *Weg*, 242–43.

19. Kolb, *Weg*, 246–47.

20. Sorel, *Histoire*, 1:353–54.

21. Favre appears to have coined this phrase. Bismarck to Diplomatic Missions, 27 September 1870, *GW*, 6b, no. 1835.

22. Favre, *Gouvernement*, 1:166.

23. Ibid., 187.

24. Bismarck to AA, 21 September 1870, PA, R 25, no. 1077; Bismarck to Bernstorff and AA, 24 September 1870, PA, R 4318 o. Fol.

25. Christiansen, *Paris Babylon*, 179.

26. Verdy du Vernois, *Im Grossen Hauptquartier 1870/71: Persönliche Erinnerungen* (Berlin, 1895), 120.

27. Roon, *Denkwürdigkeiten*, 3:214.

28. Blumenthal, *Tagebücher*, 99.

29. Kolb, *Weg*, 246–47.

30. Ibid., 248.

31. Reclus, *Favre*, 368.

32. Ibid., 369–70.

33. See the views of Garnier-Pagès, "Tout le monde sait quels sont les principes et les idées qui auraient pu nous sauver" (in *DT*, 1:440).

34. Christiansen, *Paris Babylon*, 175.

35. Favre, *Gouvernement*, 1:276–77; E. B. Washburne, *Recollections of a Minister to France, 1869–1877*, 2 vols. (New York, 1889), 1:154–55.

36. Amaury Prosper Dréo, *Procès-verbaux des séances du conseil 1870–71* (Paris, 1903), 196–97; Reclus, *Favre*, 380; Kolb, *Weg*, 251–52.

37. Christiansen, *Paris Babylon*, 180.

38. Howard, *Franco-Prussian War*, 233.

39. *DO*, 1:404.

40. *DO*, 1:428.

41. Reinach, *Dépêches*, 1:41.

42. *DO*, 1:382.

43. Hazel Benjamin, "Official Propaganda and the French Press during the Franco-Prussian War," *JMH* 4, no. 2 (1932): 214–30; *DT*, 2:408–25, 456–73.

44. Dréo, *Procès-verbaux*, 128–29; Favre, *Gouvernement*, 1:205–6; Kolb, *Weg*, 244–45.

45. Monet-Brunet, *Trochu*, 229–50.

46. General Thoumas, *Paris, Tours, Bordeaux* (Paris, 1893), 79; Howard, *Franco-Prussian War*, 238.

47. *DO*, 2:255; Howard, *Franco-Prussian War*, 238.

48. *DO*, 1:403.

49. Dréo, *Procès-verbaux*, 154–55.

50. *DT*, 5 (2): 203.

51. Reinach, *Dépêches*, 1:41–45.

CHAPTER 6. BISMARCK, BAZAINE, AND THIERS

1. Wawro, *Franco-Prussian War*, 194–96.

2. François Achille Bazaine, *Épisodes de la guerre de 1870 et le blocus de Metz* (Madrid, 1883), 178; Howard, *Franco-Prussian War*, 269.

3. Howard, *Franco-Prussian War*, 269.

4. Augustin Filon, *Souvenirs sur l'Impératrice Eugénie* (Paris, 1920), 202–3; Anneliese Klein-Wuttig, *Politik und Kriegführung in den deutschen Einigungskriegen, 1864, 1866, und 1870/71* (Berlin, 1934), 105–7; Maurice Baumont, *L'échiquier de Metz: Empire ou république 1870* (Paris, 1971), 102–87; Kolb, *Weg*, 261; and, above all, Regnier's own *Quel est votre nom?* (Brussels, 1871).

5. Christiansen, *Paris Babylon*, 157–58.

6. Regnier, *Nom*, 22–23.

7. Ludwig Bamberger, "Vor fünfundzwanzig Jahren," in *Gesammelte Schriften*, 5 vols. (1894–98), vol. 1 (Berlin, 1898), 417–52.

8. Bazaine, *L'Armée du Rhin depuis le 12 août jusqu'au 29 octobre 1870* (Paris, 1872), 125–26; *DT*, 4:242.

9. *MMK*, 322–24; *Procès Bazaine* (Paris, 1873), 187; Paul Bronsart von Schellendorff, *Geheimes Kriegstagebuch 1870–1871*, ed. Peter Rassow (Bonn, 1954), 116.

10. *GW*, 6b, no. 1874; Kolb, *Weg*, 261; Craig, *Prussian Army*, 207.

11. Bazaine, *Épisodes*, 194.

12. Bazaine, *L'armée du Rhin*, 178–80; *Épisodes*, 219–20; Filon, *Souvenirs*, 213–15.

13. Kolb, *Weg*, 269–71.

14. Bazaine, *Épisodes*, 220–21.

15. There are some discrepancies between Boyer's account as quoted here and *DT*, 4:246–49.

16. Bazaine, *L'Armée*, 180–82; Baumont, *L'échiquier*, 261–63; Kolb, *Weg*, 268.

17. *DT*, 4:212, 283–85; Bazaine, *Épisodes*, 217–18.

18. Bernstorff to Bismarck, 27 October 1870, PA, R 4318 o. Fol; *Im Kampfe für Preussens Ehre: Aus dem Nachlaß des Grafen Albrecht v. Bernstorff*, ed. Karl Ringhoffer (Berlin, 1906), 630–32.

19. *DT*, 4:268; Howard, *Franco-Prussian War*, 280.

20. Howard, *Franco-Prussian War*, 280.

21. *GW*, 6b, no. 1886.

22. Bismarck to Bernstorff, 15 October 1870, *GW*, 6b, no. 1869.

23. Howard, *Franco-Prussian War*, 280–81.

24. Malo, *Thiers*, 466–96; Friedrich Hirth, "Ungedruckte Berichte von Adolphe Thiers aus dem Jahre 1870," *PJbb* 183 (1921): 159–86.

25. Favre, *Gouvernement*, 1:415–16.

26. J. Holland Rose, "The Mission of M. Thiers to the Neutral Powers of Europe in 1870," *Transactions of the Royal Historical Society* 3, no. 11 (1917): 35–60, here 41. Thiers's reports from London are in Favre, *Gouvernement*, 1:134–39.

27. Rose, "Mission," 38–39.

28. Adolphe Thiers, *Notes et souvenirs, 1870–1873* (Paris, 1903), 20; Rose, "Mission," 42–43.

29. Chaudordy to Favre, 24 September 1870; Jean-Baptiste Chaudordy, *La France à la suite de la guerre 1870–71* (Paris, 1887), 123; Sorel, *Histoire*, 2:43.

30. Chaudordy, *France*, 123–24; Rose, "Mission," 43.

31. Schweinitz, *Denkwürdigkeiten*, 277.

32. Sergei Goriainov, *Le Bosphore et les Dardanelles* (Paris, 1910), 304.

33. Rose, "Mission," 44–48; Thiers to Chaudordy, 10 October 1870, BN NAF 20, 164–66; Hirth, "Berichte," 173–75; Thiers, *Notes et souvenirs*, 33–37; Joseph Jules de Gabriac, *Souvenirs diplomatiques de la Russie et d'Allemagne, 1870–1872* (Paris, 1896), 15ff.

34. François Charles-Roux, *Alexandre II, Gortchakoff, et Napoléon III* (Paris, 1913), 501, 503.

35. Bismarck welcomed the prospect of a deal with Thiers. When Brassier, representative of the NGC in Florence, wired him that Thiers desired to meet him, Bismarck wired back: "A visit by M. Thiers would be welcome to me." Bismarck to Brassier, 15 October 1870, *GW*, 6b, no. 1867; Kolb, *Weg*, 278.

36. Thiers, *Notes et souvenirs*, 63–67; Favre, *Gouvernement*, 1:317–19.

37. Christiansen, *Paris Babylon*, 205.

38. Jules Ferry later declared, "La population parisienne nous était, de haut en bas de l'échelle, absolument hostile." *DT*, 1:397–98; Favre, *Gouvernement*, 1:337.

39. Favre, *Gouvernement*, 1:385–87; Howard, *Franco-Prussian War*, 337–39; Roger L. Williams, *The French Revolution of 1870–1871* (New York, 1969), 100–103.

40. Thiers, *Notes et souvenirs*, 81–82; Favre, *Gouvernement*, 2:14–15.

41. Kolb, *Weg*, 283.

42. Bronsart, *Geheimes Kriegstagebuch*, 160–62; Busch, *Tagebuchblätter*, 1:376–77.

43. Thiers, *Notes et souvenirs*, 95; Favre, *Gouvernement*, 2:22–23.

44. Bronsart, *Kriegstagebuch*, 162–64.

45. Thiers, *Notes et souvenirs*, 96.

46. Ibid., 98–99.

47. *DT*, 1:26.

48. See Moltke's memo of 29 October 1870, *MMK*, 346–48.

49. Bronsart, *Kriegstagebuch*, 159.

50. Christiansen, *Paris Babylon*, 207.

51. Robert I. Giesberg, *The Treaty of Frankfurt* (Philadelphia, 1966), 62.

52. Ibid.

CHAPTER 7. BISMARCK'S ANXIETIES

1. See, for instance, his dispatches to the king in Busch, *Kriegstagebücher*, 1:333–35; memo, 14 December 1870, PA 14 December 1870, *GW*, 6b, no. 1975.

2. Howard, *Franco-Prussian War*, 285–98; Wawro, *Franco-Prussian War*, 266–68; Kolb, *Weg*, 305–6.

3. Charles de Freycinet, *La guerre en province pendant le siège de Paris, 1870–1871* (Paris, 1871), 103; *DT*, 3:61.

4. Friedrich III, *Kriegstagebuch*, ed. H. O. Meisner (Berlin, 1926), 78–80.

5. Favre, *Gouvernement*, 1:163.

6. Reinach, *Dépêches*, 1:201.

7. Ibid., 203.

8. According to Bismarck, he first learned that he was to be excluded from military deliberations while he was riding toward the front, but this assertion is not wholly reliable. *GW*, 15:312.

9. Bismarck to Moltke, 22 October 1870, *GW*, 6b, no. 1885.

10. Busch, *Tagebuchblätter*, 1:332.

11. Wawro, *Franco-Prussian War*, 280–82.

12. Klein-Wuttig, *Politik*, 93; Albrecht von Stosch, *Denkwürdigkeiten des Generals und Admirals Albrecht von Stosch*, ed. Ulrich von Stosch (Stuttgart, 1904), 196; Hans von Haeften, "Bismarck und Moltke," *PJbb* 177 (1919): 85–124, here 89.

13. Bismarck, Immediatbericht, 28 November 1870, *GW*, 6b, no. 1933; Klein-Wuttig, *Politik*, 128–30; Busch, *Tagebuchblätter*, 1:451.

14. Bronsart, *Kriegstagebuch*, 281; Haeften, "Bismarck und Moltke," 96–99; Klein-Wuttig, *Politik*, 132–35.

15. Rudolf Stadelmann, *Moltke und der Staat* (Krefeld, 1950), 235.

16. Bismarck, *Briefe an seine Gattin*, 54.

17. Hermann Oncken, ed., *Grossherzog Friedrich I. von Baden und die deutsche Politik von 1854–1871*, 2 vols. (Stuttgart, 1927), 2:167.

18. Helmuth von Moltke, *Essays, Speeches, and Memoirs of Field Marshal Count Helmuth von Moltke* (New York, 1893), 227.

19. Wilhelm Busch, *Das deutsche grosse Hauptquartier und die Bekämpfung von Paris im Feldzuge 1870–1871* (Berlin and Stuttgart, 1905), 22–36; Bronsart, *Kriegstagebuch*, 200–201.

20. Stadelmann, *Moltke*, 245.

21. Jähns, *Feldmarschall Moltke*, 534; Craig, *Prussian Army*, 209.

22. Haeften, "Bismarck und Moltke," 89–91; Klein-Wuttig, *Politik*, 141–45.

23. Howard, *Franco-Prussian War*, 283.

24. Reinach, *Dépêches*, 2:54.

25. Fedor von Rauch, *Briefe aus dem grossen Hauptquartier der Feldzüge 1866 und 1870/71 an die Gattin* (Berlin, 1911), 210; Howard, *Franco-Prussian War*, 379.

26. Georg Heinrich Rindfleisch, *Feldbriefe, 1870–71* (Göttingen, 1905), 101; Howard, *Franco-Prussian War*, 380.

27. Christiansen, *Paris Babylon*, 229.

28. Bismarck, Immediatbericht, 5 December 1870, *GW*, 6b, no. 1950.

29. Friedrich III, *Kriegstagebuch*, 319.

30. Klein-Wuttig, *Politik*, 356; Howard, *Franco-Prussian War*, 352–57; Kolb, *Weg*, 306.

31. Blumenthal, *Tagebücher*, 164.

32. Bismarck, Immediatbericht, 18 November 1870, *GW*, 6b, no. 1920.

33. Helmut von Moltke, *Militärische Korrespondenz: Aus den Dienstschriften des Krieges 1870–71* (Berlin, 1896), 424; Bronsart, *Kriegstagebuch*, 208–9; Kolb, *Weg*, 307.

34. Klein-Wuttig, *Politik*, 140–41.

35. Bronsart, *Kriegstagebuch*, 227; Howard, *Franco-Prussian War*, 356, n. 4.

36. Blumenthal, *Tagebücher*, 190.

37. Moltke to William I, 30 November 1870, *MMK*, 417; Howard, *Franco-Prussian War*, 355.

38. Roon, *Denkwürdigkeiten*, 3:244–56; Howard, *Franco-Prussian War*, 355.

39. Wawro, *Franco-Prussian War*, 290.

40. Ibid.

41. Oncken, *Friedrich I*, 294–311; Haeften, "Bismarck und Moltke," 99–101.

42. The views of the General Staff on the question of the bombardment of Paris wholeheartedly accorded with those of their chief. Carl Wilhelm von Blume, *Die Beschiessung von Paris und die Ursachen ihrer Verzögerung* (Berlin, 1899); Howard, *Franco-Prussian War*, 457–58.

43. Friedrich III, *Kriegstagebuch*, 483–84; A. O. Meyer, "Bismarck und Moltke," in *Stufen und Wandlungen*, ed. Kurt von Raumer and Theodor Schieder (Stuttgart, 1943), 332–33; Howard, *Franco-Prussian War*, 355–56.

44. Bismarck, Immediatbericht, 9 January 1871, *GW*, 6b, no. 1999.

45. Klein-Wuttig, *Politik*, 152–53; Haeften, "Bismarck und Moltke," 98–100.

46. Draft of Moltke's letters in Stadelmann, *Moltke und der Staat*, 503–8, appendix 8; Howard, *Franco-Prussian War*, 438.

47. Craig, *Prussian Army*, 214.

48. Stosch, *Denkwürdigkeiten*, 227.

49. Alexander II to William I, 31 October 1870; Gorchakov to Bismarck, 1 November 1870 with a copy of Gorchakov's circular of 31 October 1870, *GP*, 2:4–6; Kolb, *Weg*, 297.

50. On this, see Rheindorf, *(Pontus-)Frage*, 75–98; W. E. Mosse, "Public Opinion and Foreign Policy: The British Public and the War Scare of 1870," *Historical Journal* 6 (1963): 38–58; Werner E. Mosse, *The Rise and Fall of the Crimean System* (London, 1963), 220–25; Barbara Jelavich, *The Ottoman Empire, the Great Powers and the Straits Question, 1870–1887* (Bloomington, 1973), 25–50.

51. Rheindorf, *(Pontus-)Frage*, 94–97; Beyrau, *Russische Orientpolitik*, 231–37; Burgaud, *Politique*, 406–13.

52. See Chotek's meeting with Tsar Alexander II and Gorchakov, discussed in the second half of chapter 3.

53. Bismarck to Reuss, 7 November 1870, *GW*, 6b, no. 1919, preface.

54. Bismarck to Reuss, 8 November 1870, *GW*, 6b, no. 1919.

55. Jonathan Parry, *The Rise and Fall of Liberal Government in Victorian Britain* (Cambridge, 1993), 221–73.

56. Reuss to Bismarck, 9 November 1870, PA, R 12150 o. Fol.

57. Beyrau, *Russische Orientpolitik*, 238–45; Hélène Carrère d'Encausse, *Alexandre II: Le printemps de la Russie* (Paris, 2008), 282–92; Burgaud, *Politique*, 419–23.

58. Rheindorf, *(Pontus-)Frage*, 75–86; Beyrau, *Russische Orientpolitik*, 230–35; Goriainov, *Le Bosphore*, 158–60.

59. Bismarck to Reuss, 7 November 1870, *GW*, 6b, no. 1919.

60. Rheindorf, *(Pontus-)Frage*, 97–98; Goriainov, *Le Bosphore*, 163–65; Lutz, *Österreich-Ungarn*, 352–64.

61. Favre, *Gouvernement*, 2:242–44.

62. Rheindorf, *England*, 185–86; Mosse, "Public Opinion and Foreign Policy," 38–40; Granville to Lyons, 28 November 1870; T. W. L. Newton, *Life of Lyons*, 2 vols. (London, 1913), 1:340.

63. Howard, *Franco-Prussian War*, 434.

64. Christiansen, *Paris Babylon*, 259.

65. *GW*, 6b, no. 2006; Favre, *Gouvernement*, 2:304–6.

66. Kolb, *Weg*, 318.

67. Bismarck to Reuss, 5 December 1870, *GW*, 6b, no. 1951.

68. Napoleon III to Bismarck, 23 November 1870, *GW*, 6b, no. 1952; Louis Girard, Antoine Prost, and Rémi Gosset, *Les conseillers généraux* (Paris, 1967), 265.

69. Busch, *Tagebuchblätter*, 1:396–97. Just how the members of the *Corps législatif* were to mobilize sentiment for peace remained unclear. Napoleon had expressed himself on the subject in his letter to Eugénie of 19 November 1870 (*Revue des deux mondes* 100, 7e pér., vol. 59 [1930]: 19); Kolb, *Weg*, 312, n. 60.

70. Castlenau to Bismarck, 23 December 1870; Carl von Monts, *Napoleon III auf Wilhelmshöhe 1870/71* (Berlin, 1909), 142–43.

71. Monts, *Napoleon III*, 142–42; Joachim Kühn, "Bismarck und Bonapartismus, 1870/71," *PJbb* 169 (1916): 49–100, here 81–92.

72. Kolb, *Weg*, 313–14.

73. Bernstorff to Bismarck, 7 December 1870, *GW*, 6b, no. 1956.

74. Bismarck to Bernstorff, 25 December 1870, *GW*, 6b, no. 1989; Kuhn, "Bismarck und Bonapartismus," 84–85.

75. Bernstorff to Bismarck, 3 January 1871, PA, R 12149 o. Fol.

76. Bernstorff to Bismarck, 11 January 1871, ibid.

77. Bismarck to Bernstorff, ibid.

78. Bernstorff to Bismarck, 12 January 1871, ibid.; Kolb, *Weg*, 325.

79. Kolb, *Weg*, 325.

80. Ibid., 326.

81. Ibid., 326.

CHAPTER 8. ARMISTICE

1. Christiansen, *Paris Babylon*, 254–55.

2. Dréo, *Procès-verbaux*, 544.

3. Reinach, *Dépêches*, 1:49.

4. Gambetta to Favre, 31 October 1870, *DO*, 2:287–88.

5. Reinach, *Dépêches*, 2:54.

6. Louis Jules Trochu, *Œuvres posthumes*, 2 vols. (Tours, 1896), 1:327; Auguste Alexandre Ducrot, *Défense de Paris*, 4 vols. (Paris, 1875–78), 1:301–21; Howard, *Franco-Prussian War*, 333.

7. Wawro, *Franco-Prussian War*, 283.

8. Maurice, comte d'Hérisson, *Journal d'un officier d'ordonnance: Juillet 1870–février 1871* (Paris, 1885), 319.

9. Christiansen, *Paris Babylon*, 258.

10. Favre, *Gouvernement*, 2:351–52; Brunet-Moret, *Le général Trochu*, 268–69.

11. Howard, *Franco-Prussian War*, 368–69.

12. Christiansen, *Paris Babylon*, 260.

13. *DT*, 1:354; Favre, *Gouvernement*, 2:366.

14. Favre, *Gouvernement*, 2:371; Dréo, *Procès-verbaux*, 576.

15. Dréo, *Procès-verbaux*, 575–76.

16. Favre, *Gouvernement*, 2:362–417.

17. Ibid., 381–82.

18. Ibid., 383–84.

19. Ibid., 386–89.

20. Ibid., 391; Dréo, *Procès-verbaux*, 583–84.

21. Dréo, *Procès-verbaux*, 587.

22. Ibid., 591–98.

23. Kolb, *Weg*, 341.

24. Busch, *Tagebuchblätter*, 2:94; Bronsart, *Kriegstagebuch*, 312–14; Kolb, *Weg*, 343.

25. Reclus, *Favre*, 434–37.

26. Louis Eichthal, *Le general Bourbaki par un de ses anciens officiers d'ordonnance* (Paris, 1885), 345–54; Howard, *Franco-Prussian War*, 429.

27. *DT*, 3:340; Wawro, *Franco-Prussian War*, 295–97.

28. Reclus, *Favre*, 437–39; Dréo, *Procès-verbaux*, 576.

29. *DT*, 3:444–48.

30. Dréo, *Procès-verbaux*, 580–91, 602–5, 609–14.

31. Wawro, *Franco-Prussian War*, 297.

32. Ibid., 298–300.

33. Moltke, *Dienstschriften*, 357–58.

34. According to Frederick I of Baden, *Grossherzog Friedrich I. von Baden und die deutsche Politik von 1854–1871: Briefwechsel, Denkschriften, Tagebücher*, ed. Herman Oncken, 2 vols. (Stuttgart, Leipzig, Berlin, 1927), 2:346.

35. Christiansen, *Paris Babylon*, 264–65.

36. Anne Hogenhuis-Seliverstoff, *Juliette Adam, 1836–1936: L'instigatrice* (Paris, 2001), 3–28, 55–75.

37. Juliette Adam, *Mes illusions et nos souffrances pendant le siège de Paris*, 6th ed. (Paris, 1906), 97; Christiansen, *Paris Babylon*, 265.

38. Bronsart, *Geheimes Kriegstagebuch*, 317–18; Moltke, *Dienstschriften*, 359–62; Frederick I of Baden, *Briefwechsel*, 2:349–50.

39. Christiansen, *Paris Babylon*, 267.

40. Ibid.

41. Reinach, *Dépêches*, 1:56.

42. Dréo, *Procès-verbaux*, 619.

43. Favre, *Gouvernement*, 3:17–19.

44. Bronsart, *Geheimes Kriegstagebuch*, 318–22; Friedrich III, *Kriegstagebuch*, 362–63.

45. Kühn, "Bismarck und der Bonapartismus," 84–92.

46. Hogenhuis-Seliverstoff, *Adam*, 29–33; Favre, *Gouvernement*, 2:405–13.

47. Cf. Kolb, *Weg*, 352.

48. *DT*, 2:489; Frank H. Brabant, *The Beginning of the Third Republic in France* (London, 1940), 31–33.

49. Stosch, *Denkwürdigkeiten*, 228.

50. Bismarck to Favre, 3 February 1871, in Favre, *Gouvernement*, 3:21–22.

51. Dréo, *Procès-verbaux*, 650–57; Bury, *Gambetta and the National Defence*, 255–64.

52. Reinach, *Dépêches*, 1:56–57.

53. Brabant, *Beginning*, 48–49.

54. Reinach, *Dépêches*, 1:56–57. Favre, *Gouvernement*, 34–36; Bury, *Gambetta*, 261–62.

55. Adam, *Mes illusions*, 118–19; *DT*, 1:555.

56. Giesberg, *Treaty of Frankfurt*; Favre, *Gouvernement*, 3:24; Brabant, *Beginning*, 59–60.

57. Brabant, *Beginning*, 61–67; R. R. Locke, "A New Look at Conservative Preparations for the French Elections of 1871," *French Historical Studies* 5 (1968): 351–58.

58. Locke, "Look," 357–58; Giesberg, *Treaty of Frankfurt*, 101–2; Brabant, *Beginning*, 70–72.

59. Brabant, *Beginning*, 72; see also R. R. Locke, *French Legitimists and the Politics of Moral Order in the Early Third Republic* (Princeton, 1974), 5–27.

60. Favre, *Gouvernement*, 3:78–79; Malo, *Thiers*, 440–42.

61. France, *Annales de l'assemblée nationale: Compte-rendu in extenso des séances* (Paris, 1871–), 1:4; Giesberg, *Treaty of Frankfurt*, 103.

62. Giesberg, *Treaty of Frankfurt*, 100.

63. *Annales*, 1: vol. 64; Favre, *Gouvernement*, 2:520.

64. Thiers, *Notes et souvenirs*, 109–10; Favre, *Gouvernement*, 3:74–79; Howard, *Franco-Prussian War*, 446.

65. Thiers, *Notes et souvenirs*, 117.

66. Ibid., 103; Giesberg, *Treaty of Frankfurt*, 107.

67. Busch, *Tagebuchblätter*, 1:95–98.

68. Oncken, *Friedrich I*, 2:303; Richard Hartshorne, "The Franco-German Boundary of 1871," *World Politics* 2 (1950): 209–50, here 229–31.

69. Klein-Wuttig, *Politik*, 158; Stadelmann, *Moltke und der Staat*, 223; Thiers, *Notes et souvenirs*, 123.

70. Alfred Graf von Waldersee, *Denkwürdigkeiten*, ed. H. O. Meissner, 3 vols. (Stuttgart, 1922–25), 1:162.

71. Favre, *Gouvernement*, 3:89–107.

72. Sorel, *Histoire*, 2:233; Heinrich Abeken, *Ein schlichtes Leben in bewegter Zeit* (4th ed., Berlin, 1910), 243.

73. Thiers, *Notes et souvenirs*, 123.

74. Ibid., 124; Sorel, *Histoire*, 2:237; Giesberg, *Treaty of Frankfurt*, 111.

75. *NFA*, 3, vol. 1, no. 1.

76. Howard, *Franco-Prussian War*, 448; Favre, *Gouvernement*, 3:42; Thiers, *Notes et souvenirs*, 125–26.

77. Text in Hans Goldschmidt, *Bismarck und die Friedensunterhändler, 1871* (Berlin/Leipzig, 1929), 12–16; Favre, *Gouvernement*, 3:517–25; Howard, *Franco-Prussian War*, 449.

78. Cf. Howard, *Franco-Prussian War*, 449.

79. Stadelmann, *Moltke und der Staat*, 507–9; Oncken, *Friedrich I*, 358–60.

80. Giesberg, *Treaty of Frankfurt*, 119–22.

81. Waldersee, *Denkwürdigkeiten*, 1:127; Howard, *Franco-Prussian War*, 450.

82. Waldersee, *Denkwürdigkeiten*, 1:163; Louis Schneider, *Aus dem Leben Kaiser Wilhelms, 1849–1873*, 3 vols. (Berlin, 1888), 3:200.

CONCLUSION

1. Parliament, *Hansard's Parliamentary Debates*, Ser. III, vol. 204, February–March 1871, speech of 9 February 1871, 81–82.

2. See esp. Lothar Gall, "Das Problem Elsaß-Lothringen," in *Reichsgründung 1870/71*, ed. Theodor Schieder and Ernst Deuerlein (Stuttgart, 1970), 366–85; Colin Heywood, *The Development of the French Economy, 1750–1914* (Cambridge, 1995), 23

3. Mosse, *European Powers*, 338–42.

4. Bismarck to Bernstorff, 21 August 1870, *GW*, 6b, no. 1755.

5. Mitchell, *The German Influence in France*, 21–40.

6. Paul W. Schroeder, "The Lost Intermediaries: The Impact of 1870 on the European States System" (in Schroeder, *SSS*, 77–95).

7. I am grateful to Paul W. Schroeder for pointing this out to me.

8. Eberhard Kolb, *Der schwierige Weg zum Frieden: Das Problem der Kriegsbeendigung 1870/71* (Munich, 1985), 9, 16.

9. Ibid., 17; Kolb, "Kriegsführung und Politik 1870/71," in Schieder and Deuerlein, *Rechsgründung*, 95–118, here 100–118.

10. Wawro, *Franco-Prussian War*, 280.

11. Ibid., 278–80, 290–92, 304–5.

12. Cf. W. L. Langer, *European Alliances and Alignments, 1871–1890*, 2nd ed. (New York, 1935), 85–105; Klaus Hildebrand, ed., *Das Deutsche Reich im Urteil der grossen Mächte und europäischen Nachbarn (1871–1945)* (Munich, 1995), 3–31.

13. Craig, *Prussian Army*, 204–19; Kolb, *Weg*, 304–26, 341–57, 348–49; Klein-Wuttig, *Politik*, 94–127; Stadelmann, *Moltke*, 179–96.

14. Cf. Ernst Engelberg, *Bismarck: Urpreusse und Reichsgründer* (Berlin, 1985), 675–85.

15. Kolb, *Schwierige Weg*, 13–14.

16. Ibid., 17, 22–23.

17. Kolb, *Weg*, 309–10; cf. Herbert Geuss, *Bismarck und Napoleon III: Ein Beitrag zur Geschichte der preußisch-französischen Beziehungen 1851–1871* (Cologne/Graz, 1959), 306.

18. Kolb, *Schwierige Weg*, 19–20.

19. On the Commune see above all Kolb, "Der Pariser Commune-Aufstand und die Beendigung des deutsch-französischen Krieges," *HZ* 215 (1972): 265–98.

20. Paul W. Schroeder, "International Politics, Peace, and War, 1815–1914," in *The Nineteenth Century: Europe, 1789–1914*, ed. T. C. W. Blanning (Oxford, 2000), 158–209, here 183.

Bibliographical Essay

The purpose of this essay, like the one in the companion volume to which it is a successor, is to acknowledge my many teachers and to record my many obligations, I hope with some degree of accuracy. The essay, like the volume it serves, may stand apart from its predecessor, but, at the same time, it is inextricably connected with it. Inevitably, I used in *A Duel of Giants* (*DG*) many of the books I used again here, and this put me into a dilemma: whether to repeat the full evaluation I gave in the first volume, making this essay too long and partially redundant, or to supply only a cross-reference, thereby compelling the reader to shuffle back and forth from one book to another. I therefore decided to adopt a compromise that I trust will be acceptable: whenever a title discussed in any detail in *DG* reappears here, I have confined myself to giving essential bibliographical information, together with a short commentary (though in some cases I found longer ones to be necessary), and then added in parenthesis a cross-reference to the first appearance in the first volume.

The bibliography is divided into three sections, the same arrangement as before. Part 1 focuses on the background, mainly the outstanding personalities that appear in the narrative. Part 2 deals with the primary sources on diplomacy of the Franco-Prussian War itself and is divided into three sections: materials in the archives of the powers; the outstanding series published from these archives; and the private papers of the major actors, themselves arranged as rulers, prime and foreign ministers, diplomats, and others. Each section is arranged by country, ordered as befits a work of diplomatic history, according to the French alphabet, that is, Germany (including Prussia), Austria-Hungary, France, Great Britain, Italy, and Russia. The final section deals with the outstanding works of secondary literature on the Franco-Prussian War itself.

I need hardly emphasize that this essay, like its earlier companion, is subjective and incomplete; ranging as it does over a vast subject, for years of interest to scholars and replete with controversy, it could hardly be anything else. As was the case earlier, I have in the main cited titles that supplied me with ideas, drove me to ask questions, or fired me to dissent. As to information on cities of publication, I have adopted the following formula: unless otherwise indicated, all books with German titles have been published in Berlin; all those with French, in Paris; all those with English, in London. Where a book has been translated into English, I usually give both the English and the original version.

PART 1. BACKGROUND
Personalities

GERMANY. Surveying the literature on him in 2001, I wrote (*DG*, 200): "There is no outstanding biography of William I in English." To the best of my knowledge, this remains true today. I have already singled out for praise *Kaiser Wilhelm I*, by Karl Heinz Börner (Cologne, 1984), an authoritative study of its subject. The book by Erich Marks (original 1897 but many subsequent editions) with the same title is a work of great length and great learning, illuminated by flashes of insight. Börner's essay "Wilhelm I: Vom Kartätschenprinz zum deutschen Kaiser," in *Gestalten der Bismarckzeit*, ed. Gustav Seeber (1978), is an instructive contribution, packed with valuable and stimulating ideas on William's attitude toward the formation of the German empire. The last volume of *Aus dem Leben Kaiser Wilhelms, 1849–1873*, by Louis Schneider, 3 vols. (1888), remains informative for all its relative antiquity. Mention should also be made of *Wilhelm I: Kaiserfrage und Kölner Dom*, by Karl Hempe (Stuttgart, 1936), and of Günter Richter's essay "Kaiser Wilhelm I," in *Drei deutsche Kaiser*, ed. Wilhelm Treue (Freiburg, 1987) (all discussed in *DG*, 200–202). *Wilhelm der Erste: Sein Leben und seine Zeit*, by Paul Wiegler (Hellerau, 1927), has some points of interest, though the cautious critic has submerged the creative scholar.

Books on Bismarck, of course, exist in profusion, and I can mention only a few. The most recent, *Bismarck: A Life*, by Jonathan Steinberg (New York, 2011), also happens to be one of the best. It reached me only when this manuscript was complete; the book is a model of unassuming scholarship and understanding. Of equal importance is the recent biography by the great French historian Jean-Paul Bled (2011). His book has rare distinction as a work of scholarship, and it also merits high praise technically as an attempt to write diplomatic history without pretentiousness or dullness.

The works up to 1966 are listed in the *Bismarck Bibliographie* by Karl Erich Born (Cologne, 1966). It gives 6,138 titles. *Das Bismarck-Problem in der Geschichtsschreibung nach 1945*, by Lothar Gall (Cologne, 1971), rather than refining accepted views, has defined the views that have become accepted in recent years. Extensive biographies of Bismarck to which I have alluded, such as Otto Pflanze's authoritative three-volume study (Princeton, 1990) (German translation, 2 vols. [Munich, 1997]); Lothar Gall's magisterial life (English translation [1986]), a book of incomparable understanding; Ernst Engelberg's two-volume treatise (1985, 1990), a Marxist account, sometimes relentlessly dramatic; Johannes Willms's polemic (Munich, 1997); and Rainer Schmidt's competent and shrewd account (Stuttgart, 2004) are skillful analyses that deserve to be consulted. All, especially Gall, have insightful information on the diplomacy of the Franco-Prussian War. Gordon A. Craig's incisive portrait in *From Bismarck to Adenauer: Aspects of German Statecraft* (Baltimore, 1958) breaks fresh ground in short space; the life by A. J. P. Taylor (New York, 1955), though controversial, is fun to read (all in *DG*, 201–2). The biography by Eberhard Kolb (Munich, 2009) is concise, witty, and persuasive.

Of the older literature, too, there is a vast sea. Erich Marcks (Stuttgart, 1909), a work of scholarship and penetration; Max Lenz (Leipzig, 1911), for a long time the standard German life; Erich Brandenburg (Hamburg, 1914), with an appendix volume published in 1916 (Leipzig); and Paul Matter, 3 vols. (1905–8), the great French biography, remain indispensable. Of the more general works, those by Leonhard von Muralt (Göttingen, 1955); Otto Becker, edited and supplemented by Alexander Scharff (1958); Arnold Oscar Meyer (Stuttgart, 1949), original edition of 1944 destroyed in Berlin, which the author described "as my contribution to the national war effort"; and Erich Eyck, 3 vols. (Zürich, 1941–44), are beautiful examples of historical composition (all in *DG*, 202).

The new character on the German side in these pages is, of course, Helmuth von Moltke, and, as one might suspect, there is an abundance of lives, unfortunately not many in English. As was the case with Bismarck, what follows is only a suggestion of the more important works available. *Moltke and the German Wars, 1864–1871*, by Arden Bucholz (New York, 2001), is the place to start—a book of the highest quality, packed with erudition, enlivened with anecdotes, and a delight to read. The first chapter of Bucholz's excellent earlier work titled *Moltke, Schlieffen and Prussian War Planning* (New York, 1991) sheds considerable light on Moltke's early career. However, the book by Eberhard Kessel (Stuttgart, 1957), though old, remains the standard life—an admirable study in military history, though weak on politics; it is an updated version of the work published by the same author in 1935. *Moltke: Vom Kabinettskrieg zum Volkskrieg: Eine Werkauswahl*, ed. Stig Förster (Bonn, 1992), is a selection of Moltke's works published over the years; it expands upon a summary of Moltke's own writings that may be found in *Strategy: Its Theory and Application; The Wars for German Unification* (Westport, CT, 1971). Though the book is not specifically addressed to Moltke, there is an excellent account of his achievements in *Command in War* by Martin van Creveld (Cambridge, MA, 1985). Creveld's revaluation of Moltke's motives and methods, especially during the time of his conflict with Bismarck in the wars of 1866 and 1870, is especially acute and enlightening but is no match for the analysis of Moltke's strategy given by Dennis Showalter in *Railroads and Technology* (Hamden, CT, 1976), a book that will be read with pleasure as long as anyone cares about military history or, for that matter, about history at all. Hajo Holborn, "The Prusso-German School: Moltke and the Rise of the General Staff," in *Makers of Modern Strategy*, ed. Peter Paret et al. (Princeton, 1986), is a reprint of the same article from the first edition of the book that appeared in 1943; it covers its subject competently, clearly, and judiciously. Rudolf Stadelmann, *Moltke und der Staat* (Krefeld, 1950), is a book that still holds its own and provides a penetrating analysis of Moltke's political views as they appeared in his Aufmarsch plans. The older works by Max Jähns (new edition, Berlin, 1894); Wilhelm Bigge, 2 vols. (Munich, 1901); Karl Haenchen (Leipzig, 1930); and F. E. Whitton (London, 1921) are commendable expositions. Bradley J. Meyer, "The Operational Art: The Elder Moltke's Campaign for the Franco-Prussian War," in *The Operational Art: Developments in the Theories of War*, ed. B. J. C.

McKercher and Michael A. Hennessy (Westport, CT, 1996), is an analysis of considerable value.

FRANCE. What I said in *DG*, 200—that the need for a comprehensive biography of Napoleon III remains great—is less true now than it was then. Over the past ten years, there has been an outpouring of books on this subject in French. Again, I give only a sample of this literature. *Napoléon III, l'homme, le politique: Actes du colloque organisé par la Fondation Napoléon, Collège de France, amphithéâtre Marguerite de Navarre, 19–20 mai 2008,* ed. Pierre Milza (2008), is the point of departure, an almost encyclopedic work, not easy to read but essential as a work of reference. *Napoléon III: Visionnaire de l'Europe des nations,* by Gaël Nofri (2010), is an enchanting book, instructive for the serious historian, equally entertaining for the general reader. *Napoléon III: L'empereur du peuple,* by Raphaël Dargent (2009), brings its subject and his times back to life, though the author romanticizes the French working class. The lives by Michel de Decker (2008) and Pierre Milza (2004) are very good indeed; they analyze political and economic matters very clearly and are beautifully written and impeccably impartial. Napoleon III has at last found a good life in English. The work of Fenton Bresler (1999) is a delightful biography, just right for its subject; careful, discursive, and scholarly at the same time. *Napoleon III and His Regime: An Extravaganza,* by David Baguley (Baton Rouge, LA, 2000), is as much a work of literature as one of history; the author is a superb storyteller; his book is tinged with infectious zest and can be read with much profit and considerable pleasure. *Napoleon III and the Second Empire,* by Roger Price (1997), is a book of deep research by an outstanding scholar, written in a lively style, but in the end we are little wiser than we were at the beginning. Compelling as these titles are, we must not ignore some older ones. Those by W. H. C. Smith (1972); F. A. Simpson, 3rd ed. (1951); J. P. T. Bury (1964); and especially Heinrich Euler (1961) are outstanding narratives that provide indispensable introductions to Napoleon's difficulties in the first days of the Franco-Prussian War (all in *DG*, 202–3).

Eugénie has received her share of attention. The life by Desmond Seward (Stroud, 2004) is a most thorough and admirable book, a work that will take a permanent place among political biographies. The lives by Robert Sencourt (New York, 1931) and Maurice Paléologue (1928) are competent but rather unbalanced. Better is the book by Harold Kurtz (1964), and especially *Distaff Diplomacy*, by Nancy Nicholas Barker (Austin, 1967), though these romanticize their subject and are too effusive in their praise. Explanations can be found for Eugénie, and excuses. It remains true that no scrupulous person would have acted as she did. Hers was a patriotism of survival (all in *DG*, 2002).

Emile Ollivier and the Liberal Empire of Napoleon III, by Theodore Zeldin (Oxford, 1963) (*DG*, 203) remains unsurpassed. Christiane Ndiaye's *Emile Ollivier* (Quebec, 2003) contains a series of biographical studies that are awkward and narrow in scope.

Le Duc de Gramont, by Constantin de Grunwald (1950) (*DG*, 203), does not go very deep. Gramont, like Ollivier, is in need of a modern life.

There is a spate of literature on Gambetta and Thiers, though a dearth on Favre and Trochu. To start with Gambetta: Jean-Marie Mayeur, *Léon Gambetta: La patrie et la République* (2008), is an essay resonating with zest and charm, a wise improvement on conventional biography, fun to read and useful into the bargain. The life by Pierre Barral (Toulouse, 2008) is shorter, more sweeping, but competent, and up-to-date. Pierre Antonmattei, *Léon Gambetta: Héraut de la République* (1999), is a most valuable treatise, based on exhaustive research, though written to extol the man the author admires. *Gambetta and the National Defence* (1970); *Gambetta and the Making of the Third Republic* (1973); and *Gambetta's Final Years* (1986), by J. P. T. Bury, are volumes by the leading authority on the subject; they are strong in their dissection of character and unrivalled in their simplification of complex issues. The first is most relevant to our theme—an admirably clear account that focuses on the rivalries between the Provisional Government and the Delegation. Still of interest is *Gambetta et l'Alsace-Lorraine*, by Henri Galli (1911), an exhaustive and splendid book that deserves a place among the major secondary works of the period.

Jules Favre: Avocat de la liberté, by Pierre Antoine Perrod (Lyon, 1988), is a work of impeccable scholarship, but it has not eclipsed the older life by Maurice Reclus (1912), a vivid and dramatic study that makes for very good reading.

De Trochu à Thiers, 1870–1873, by Stéphane Rials (1985), is a most valuable addition to the literature addressed to its subject, a historical contribution second to none. *Le Général Trochu* by Jean Brunet-Moret (1933) is a useful contribution to explaining the man. Vital Cartier, *Un méconnu: Le Général Trochu* (Paris, 1914) is an older engaging life, but the judgments often suggest that Trochu holds the pen.

There are some excellent books on Thiers. Primacy of place must go to the biography by Henri Malo (1932). Meticulous scholarship, deep understanding, and an easy style leavened with wit combine to place this book high in the canon of works on this subject. It is beautifully printed and contains sixteen handsome plates. *Thiers: Bourgeois et révolutionnaire*, by Georges Valance (2007), is a sustained work of mature historical analysis. Equally outstanding is the biography by Pierre Guiral (1986); it is a careful scholarly account, with few personal touches, but vivid and important all the same; it has, as well, the inestimable value of being well documented. *Monsieur Thiers*, by René de La Croix, le duc de Castries (1983), is the work of a narrator, not a historian, a lively story, replete with anecdotes but too ingenious in places. *Monsieur Thiers: D'une république à l'autre* (1997) assembles contributions by distinguished scholars who, under the auspices of the Académie des Sciences, Lettres et Arts de Marseille, met on 14 November 1997 at that city to mark the bicentenary of Thiers's birth. It is impeccably edited and often original and insightful, but many of the pieces have the inevitable defects of conference papers. The best of the essays is that by Arnaud Lacan (29–53), a first-rate analysis of Thiers's economic philosophy. For the English reader, there is *Thiers, 1797–1877: A Political Life*, by J. P. T. Bury and R. P. Tombs (1986), very good indeed, precisely what one would expect from these authors; the book analyzes political and social issues clearly and is extremely well written and impeccably impartial. Less satisfactory is the biography by René Albrecht-Carrié (Boston, 1977), scholarly in its way, but the personality does not come alive. "Louis Adolphe Thiers, Liberator of French Territory, 1871–73," by George Wallace Kyte, a PhD dissertation completed at Berkeley in 1943, has a promising title but disappointing contents.

PART 2. PRIMARY SOURCES
Archives

GERMANY (including PRUSSIA). Among the primary sources used in preparation of this volume, the documents that repose in the Politisches

Archiv des Auswärtigen Amtes (AA) in Berlin naturally took an outstanding place. The selection of documents is generous and discriminating, the indexing so complete that the use of the series for a study such as the present one presents few problems. In my various visits to the AA, a handsome building not far from the great Berlin boulevard Unter den Linden, I was always courteously received and almost always permitted to use a digital camera to photograph any document for which I asked.

In addition to these sources, the author had recourse to the official state archives of Bavaria, Württemberg, and Baden. I was able to consult these files on several occasions for clarification of specific points of inquiry.

AUSTRIA-HUNGARY. The vast holdings of the former Austro-Hungarian Foreign Office repose in the Haus-, Hof- und Staatsarchiv in Vienna, in the entrance to which two statues of Maria Theresa and Francis Joseph smile down approvingly on the arriving researcher. Of these records, too, the Politisches Archiv division most of all, I was able to make extensive use. Parts III (dealing with Prussia), IX (France), and XII (Russia) are all packed with lucid and invaluable information, though inevitably overlong. I found them, given their relatively detached view of Franco-Prussian relations, not to mention their importance for relations between Vienna and Berlin, to be of high value for the purposes of this study.

FRANCE. The comparable files of the Archives du Ministère des Affaires Étrangères (AMAE) at the Quai d'Orsay are of even greater importance. But they are now housed in a drab tower in La Courneuve, about two and a half hours by train from Paris—far removed from their original home on the banks of the spectacular Seine. Of special importance are the volumes of the Correspondance Politique, in which there may be found official records—instructions, dispatches, and telegrams—exchanged between the foreign office and the French diplomatic missions abroad; in addition, there sometimes have been added a number of private letters (lettres particulaires) addressed to the heads of these missions by senior figures of the French foreign office. The summary record of their pertinent contents is arranged chronologically by country. Among the files examined, this writer found the extensive reports on the press in all countries, but particularly in Russia, to be of immense value. These included (normally in French translation but sometimes, in the case of French-language items, in the form of newspaper clippings) the texts—or excerpts thereof—of editorials and articles on the activities between the two belligerents from the leading Russian newspapers of the day, and, since the periodicals in question today are difficult, if not impossible, to find and, for a number of reasons, not easy to photograph when found, these materials are of outstanding historical value.

There are, it should be noted, a number of personal papers that may have a bearing on the events recounted in this volume. These papers appear in the files of the Mémoirs et Documents section of the AMAE, but I was not in a position to remain in Paris for the long period of time required for their study. I regret my inability to do so.

DENMARK. The relevant record here is a series of edited volumes by Åge [or Aage] Friis, *Det nordslesvigske spørgsmaal 1864–1879: Aktstykker og Breve til Belysning af den danske Regerings Politik* (Copenhagen, 1921–48). This series contains records relating to Napoleon III's attempt to achieve an amphibious landing in the Baltic and to the dealings of various Danish operatives abroad, of whom Julius Hansen is most outstanding. The author had only occasional recourse to this material through use of the Internet.

GREAT BRITAIN. The official records may be supplemented by a Bluebook correspondence titled *Correspondence Respecting the Negotiations Preliminary to the War between France and Prussia*, but the contents are slim and on the whole disappointing. However, the official files are available to scholars at the National Archives at Kew Gardens. The office is an hour's train ride from London, and, on a nice spring morning, one can view the beautiful trees and hills of the countryside before delving into the records of the diplomatic correspondence. But, once one is inside, the going gets tougher. The manner in which the records are catalogued and made available to scholars is cumbersome in comparison with continental practices, though with patience most inquiries will eventually yield their fruit. This is the case with Foreign Office 68/688 Prussia (and the North German Confederation); with

27/1789–1792 and 1797–1802 France; with 65/164 Italy; and with 68/804–805 Russia, where there reposes the correspondence, respectively, of Loftus, Lyons, Paget, and Buchanan with Granville. The Granville–Buchanan correspondence is particularly revealing, throwing light on the crisis that developed between Great Britain and Russia from October 1870 to January 1871 over the Black Sea. It also shows the talent, possessed in abundance, of the British and Russian ministers, for rubbing each other the wrong way. Unlike his predecessor, Lord Clarendon, who died in June 1870 and whose private papers can be found in the Bodleian Library at Oxford, Granville had no comparable collection, but, since he was sulky and indolent and had a crushingly dull personality, this is not surprising. Finally, mention should be made of The Confidential Print "Respecting the War between France and Germany," a very helpful record indeed, though the material within its covers is excerpted from the official correspondence and does not constitute the whole of the record.

ITALY. Here mention should first be made of the materials in the Archivio Storico Diplomatico del Ministero degli Affari Esteri in Rome. They were transferred to the Eternal City when Italy's capital moved from Florence in 1871. About half an hour by taxi from the magnificent Spanish Steps, these small but attractive rooms house, in the words of the online description and official brochure, "over 60,000,000 documents addressed to the relations of the Powers of Europe with the Kingdom of Italy." Of outstanding importance is the Archivio di Gabinetto (1861–87), busta 219: guerra franco-prussiana trattative segrete 8 luglio–14 settembre 1870, where one can examine the correspondence between Visconti-Venosta and his ministers abroad. Equally significant is no. 586 (confidential), Serie Politica (1867–87), Prussia (1867–70), carton 1328. In these records one can also examine the correspondence in the private diaries of the members of the Lanza cabinet, particularly as they related to the role Italy was to play in the formation of the League of Neutrals. Here again, as in Paris and Berlin, it is possible for the interested scholar to supplement the use of the official files by recourse to published diplomatic correspondence, most outstandingly the *Documenti diplomatici italiani*, discussed in the section "Official Publications."

RUSSIA. The archives of the Russian Federation have been catalogued in a huge collection known as Gosudarstvennyi arkhiv Rossiiskoi Federatsii (GARF), which has been divided into two periods: pre–and post–Soviet Union. These records are available to the interested scholar in Moscow in the Archiva vnesnej politiki Rossijskoj Federacii (Foreign Policy Archive of the Russian Federation). Many of these documents, now numbering some five million, no doubt can shed considerable light on crucial questions relating to the period under investigation.

In addition to the official archival documents, mention should also be made of several fine collections and manuscripts available in the Manuscript Division of the Russian State Library (so renamed in 1992 from the Lenin State Library) in Moscow and in the Library of the Institute of Russian Literature—Pushkin House, in Saint Petersburg. Unfortunately, the distance and the time, to say nothing of the expense, involved in traveling to Moscow prevented me from exploring these sources.

Official Publications

GERMANY (including PRUSSIA). *Die auswärtige Politik Preussens, 1858–1871*, ed. Erich Brandenburg et al. (1932–39), is a magnificent anthology. The last four volumes are particularly relevant to the subject at hand and give lucky dips from the British and Russian archives, as well. The author was a meticulous scholar, justly celebrated for his work on the Reichsgründung, and he also published a valuable edition of the letters of William I. The problem with this great compilation is its size; the volumes are so immense that they cannot be held without muscular exhaustion. Another defect: they contain none of Bismarck's correspondence, leaving the scholar no choice but to shuffle back and forth between this source and the collected volumes of Bismarck's works (discussed further in *DG*, 210).

The first two volumes of *Die grosse Politik der europäischen Kabinette*, ed. Johannes Lepsius, Albrecht Mendelssohn Bartholdy, and Friedrich Thimme (1922), have been superseded by GW-NFA, discussed in the section "Prime and Foreign Ministers."

Russland 1852–1871: Aus den Berichten der bayerischen Gesandtschaft in

St. Petersburg, ed. Barbara Jelavich (Wiesbaden, 1963), is a slight but invaluable collection by a historian of great distinction that somehow managed to escape my attention in *DG*. The documents are in chronological order, and there is a good table of contents.

AUSTRIA-HUNGARY. The outstanding source remains Hermann Oncken, *Die Rheinpolitik Kaiser Napoleons III. von 1863 bis 1870 und der Ursprung des Krieges von 1870/71*, 3 vols. (Stuttgart, 1926). It is of commanding importance for the Triple Alliance negotiations of 1868–69 and shows clearly why these failed. The introductory essay is a scathing indictment of French policy by the editor that has been translated into English as *Napoleon III and the Rhine* (1928) (*DG*, 211).

DENMARK. *Det nordslesvigske spørgsmaal 1864–1879*, ed. Åge [Aage] Friis, 6 vols. (Copenhagen, 1921–38), surveys the holdings of the Danish foreign ministry; the author/editor was a historian of the first rank, very critical of Bismarck. The last five volumes are particularly relevant to the subject at hand. There is a reduced collection in French, *L'Europe, le Danemark et le Slesvig du Nord: Actes et lettres provenant d'archives étrangères pour servir à l'histoire de la politique extérieure du Danemark après la Paix de Vienne, 1864–1879* (Copenhagen, 1939–43), that, while helpful, by no means replaces the original. *Europa, Danmark, og Nordslesvig [1864–79]*, ed. Åge Friis and Povl Bagge, 4 vols. (Copenhagen, 1939–59), updates the first volume.

FRANCE. *Les origines diplomatiques de la guerre de 1870–1871*, 29 vols. (1910–32), is the major work of the period (*DG*, 211). Though most useful for the July crisis, large portions of vols. 21–24 (1928–29), vol. 28 (1931), and the last sixty-three pages of the appendix to vol. 29 (1932) contain a wealth of information on the negotiations for the Triple Alliance. The last volume opens with the flurry of diplomatic activity that preceded the French declaration of war on 19 July 1870 and carries the story down to 4 August 1870. Of particular importance is the light shed by this volume on the French war aims and on the conflict between Gramont and the ambassadors of South Germany (123–439). Clear, pithy, an invaluable analysis of not only journalistic attitudes but also political and military trends, the volume is also replete with fascinating observations on individual personalities; it may, like its predecessors, stand as a model of its kind, indispensable as a work of scholarly reference.

The records found in *Documents diplomatiques français, 1871–1914*, 41 vols. (1929–59), begin on 10 May 1871, the very date on which this volume ends.

GREAT BRITAIN. The British government knew the importance of parliamentary support and, with a view to acquiring it, presented samplings from the official record in the form of Bluebooks. There are six on the war of 1870–71. The last two—five and six (1–3 [1871])—throw some light on the withdrawal of the British ambassador, Lord Lyons, to Tours and on the question posed by the German demands on France for an indemnity, but they are no substitute for the material contained in the original records. *Foundations of British Foreign Policy*, ed. H. W. V. Temperley and Lillian Penson (Cambridge, 1938) (*DG*, 214), gives a random selection of documents from our period but is otherwise of little use.

ITALY. Note was made in the section on archives of the collection of documents titled *I documenti diplomatici italiani*, which trace the history of that country from its founding down to the armistice of 1943. The first series gives the correspondence between 1861 and 1870. Vol. 13 (1963) covers the period from 5 July to 20 September 1870. It is invaluable for the light it throws on the French attempts to renew the September convention, on Visconti-Venosta's efforts to form the League of Neutrals, and on the machinations of Victor Emmanuel II. The documents are arranged in chronological order, and the editing is a model of conscientious efficiency.

RUSSIA. The Russian material for this period has not been published by the tsarist, Soviet, or Russian governments, but a few important documents have seen publication in the Russian historical documentary series *Krasnyi arkhiv* (*DG*, 212) and in secondary treatises of one sort or another, described in the next section.

Published Private Papers
Rulers

GERMANY (including PRUSSIA). The published collections of the papers of William I are, almost without exception, dull and uninteresting. *Correspondence of William I and Bismarck*, 2 vols., ed. and translated by J. A. Ford (1903); *Kaiser Wilhelms I Briefe an Politiker und Staatsmänner*, ed. Johannes Schultze (1930); and *Kaiser Wilhelms des Grossen Briefe, Reden und Schriften*, 2 vols, ed. Ernst Berner (1906), have some points of interest. William's speeches from the throne for 1870 appear in vol. 15 (1921) and those for 1871 in vol. 16 (1922) of *Das Staatsarchiv*, ed. Ludwig Aegidi and Alfred Klauhold, 16 vols. (1861–1922). *Kaiser Wilhelm und die Begründung des Reiches*, ed. Ottokar Lorenz (1902), gives his correspondence with his relatives (all in *DG*, 213). *Briefe Kaiser Wilhelms I. nebst Denkschriften und anderen Aufzeichnungen in Auswahl*, ed. Erich Brandenburg (Leipzig, 1911), is a collection of his letters and jottings by one of the great scholars of the Reichsgründung.

Augusta, Empress of Germany, by Clara Tschudi, translated by E. M. Cope (1900), has some points of interest on the relations between the empress and Bismarck—but many of the stories are embellished ones, originating from Bismarck's memoirs; the translation from the Norwegian is choppy.

Briefe der Kaiserin Friedrich, ed. Sir Frederick Ponsonby and translated by Anton Mayer (1936), has some lively material on matters relating to the crown princess. There is an earlier English edition (1928) that is less complete. Finally, while on the subject of diaries, letters, and correspondence of the German rulers, mention must be made of the *Kriegstagebuch* by Emperor Friedrich III, ed. H. O. Meisner (1926), which is even more important for wartime diplomacy than it is for the July crisis. At the time of the war, Frederick III was crown prince; he tried to mediate in the fight between Bismarck and Moltke, and his papers contain a number of passages on this subject that are either directly revealing or representative of what was being said about both men in William I's entourage. There is an excellent English translation by Francis A. Welby (1902) (all in *DG*, 213).

Grossherzog Friedrich I. von Baden und die deutsche Politik von 1854–

1871: Briefwechsel, Denkschriften, Tagebücher, ed. Hermann Oncken, 2 vols. (1927); *Aus dem Leben des Königs Albert von Sachsen*, ed. Paul Hassel, 2 vols. (1898–1900); *Aus meinem Leben und aus meiner Zeit*, by Ernest II of Saxe-Coburg, 3 vols. (1887–89), are three older works that can be read with profit (all in *DG*, 213).

Karl Alexander Müller's "Bismarck und Ludwig II im September 1870" (in *HZ* 3 [1913]: 89–132), though old, is thorough and accurate. Even better and more specialized is *König Ludwig II. und Bismarcks Ringen um Bayern 1870/71*, by Hans Rall (Munich, 1973), a discriminating and subtle study of its subject, based on the Bavarian, Prussian, and British archives.

AUSTRIA-HUNGARY. Most of the letters of Francis Joseph have little of either personal or political interest. The ones that do are reproduced in the life by John Van der Kiste (Gloucester, 2005), a sort of intellectual biography, sensible and stimulating. If it errs, it is in not attempting to modify traditional views according to the evidence of more recent historians. *Francis Joseph*, by Steven Beller (London, 1996), is less satisfactory; the emperor does not appear. *Kaiser Franz Josef ganz privat: "Sie haben's gut, Sie können ins Kaffeehaus gehen!,"* by Gabriele Praschl-Bichler (Vienna, 2005), is a solid account, a most exciting popular story of the world as the emperor saw it, though there's nothing new or terribly important in it. For politics, romance, and court intrigue, there are *Franz Josef I. in seinen Briefen*, ed. Otto Ernst (Vienna, 1924); *Briefe Kaiser Franz Josephs I. an seine Mutter, 1838–1872*, ed. Franz Schnürer (Stuttgart, 1930); *Briefe Kaiser Franz Josephs an Kaisern Elizabeth, 1859–1898*, ed. Georg Nostitz-Rieneck, 2 vols. (Vienna, 1966); and *Briefe Kaiser Franz Josephs an Frau Katharina Schratt*, ed. Jean de Bourgoing (Vienna, 1949) (all in *DG*, 213–14). *Die politische Korrespondenz der Päpste mit den österreichischen Kaizern, 1801–1918*, ed. Friedrich Engel-Janosi, Richard Blass, and Erika Weinzierl (Vienna, 1964), is an effective, accurate, and compact compilation.

Engel-Janosi has also produced a book and an article that give much of Francis Joseph's correspondence and can be read with profit: vol. 1 of *Österreich und der Vatikan, 1846–1918* (Graz, Vienna, Cologne, 1958) and "Austria in the Summer of 1870" (in *Journal of Central European Affairs* 5 [1945–46]: 335–53).

FRANCE. My comment (in *DG*, 214) "that Napoleon III wrote few letters and fewer still survive" was not a correct one. In fact, *Napoleon III: Ein Selbstbildnis in ungedruckten und zerstreuten Briefen und Aufzeichnungen*, ed. Johannes Kühn (Arenenburg, 1993), contains almost nine hundred of his letters; they are fascinatingly readable, a triumph of restraint and artistry and a model for every would-be editor. I am grateful to Professor Maik Ohnezeit for pointing out this error (*Der Deutsch-Französische Krieg 1870/71: Vorgeschichte, Verlauf, Folgen*, ed. Jans Ganschow, Olaf Haselhorst, and Maik Ohnezeit [Graz, 2009], 26n., itself a work of outstanding quality [discussed in the section "The Diplomacy of the Franco-Prussian War"]) and wish to take this occasion to apologize for its occurrence. *Napoléon III: Actes et paroles; Guide*, by Alain Carteret (2008), is an up-to-date compilation; it is full of fascinating points and contains valuable information even for the expert. *Victoria et Napoléon III: Histoire d'une amitié*, by Antoine d'Arjuzon (Biarritz, 2007), contains a selection of correspondence of both monarchs. It also merits high praise technically as an attempt to assemble diplomatic documents without dullness.

Eugénie wrote more than her husband. *Souvenirs d'une demoiselle d'honneur auprès de l'impératrice Eugénie, 1868–1871*, by Marie-Louyse des Garets (Clermont-Ferrand, 2003), has some interesting penetrations but is rather thin. The older works are more numerous. Some examples: *Papiers et correspondance de la famille impériale*, 2 vols. (1871); *Lettres familières de l'impératrice Eugénie*, 2 vols., ed. Duke of Alba (1935); the *Memoirs of the Empress Eugenie*, ed. Maurice Comte Fleury, 2 vols. (New York, 1920); Count Egon Caesar Corti, "Les idées de l'impératrice Eugénie sur le redressement de la carte de l'Europe," (in *Revue des idées napoléoniennes* 19, no. 2 [July–December 1922]: 147–60) (all in *DG*, 214). *Souvenirs sur l'impératrice Eugénie*, by Augustin Filon (1920), published after the author's death, is a work of great length and great learning that reveals the darker side of its subject; the gossip is convincing, the portions relating to political events more doubtful.

Memoirs of the Prince Imperial, 1856–1879, translated by Augustin Filon (1913), is less helpful. "Les alliances de l'Empire en 1869 et 1870," by Napoleon III's cousin, Prince Jérôme, which appeared in the *Revue des deux mondes* [48, 3e pér.] 26 (1878): 489–500, is fatuous, inane, and unreliable.

It is difficult to classify Trochu; though a military man, he was president of the Government of National Defense (and governor of Paris) from 4 September 1870 to 21 January 1871 and therefore qualifies as a ruler. In any case, his *Œuvres posthumes*, 2 vols. (Tours, 1896), contains much invaluable information, clear on the military side, weak on politics.

GREAT BRITAIN. Here mention should first be made of the splendid three volumes of the second series of *The Letters of Queen Victoria*, ed. George Earle Buckle (1926–28) (*DG*, 214). Vol. 3 contains the correspondence relating to the wartime diplomacy, and it provides a good deal of other useful information, as well, though it is important to remember that, Victoria being Victoria, the prime ministers who wrote to her were more concerned with telling her what she wanted to hear than what was on their minds. *Darling Child: Private Correspondence of Queen Victoria and the Crown Princess of Prussia, 1871–1878*, ed. Roger Fulford (1976), throws an occasional flicker of minor light onto the palace intrigues during the last months of the war; it is agreeable that the pieces are arranged chronologically, but the index is less than satisfactory.

ITALY. *Vittorio Emanuele II*, by Giuseppe Massari (Milan, 1901); *Pio IX et Vittorio Emanuele II dal loro carteggio privato*, ed. Pietro Pirri, 5 vols. (1944–61); and *Lettere di Vittorio Emanuele II*, ed. Francesco Cognasso, 2 vols. (1966), are meticulous works of high scholarship (all *DG*, 215). *Du mouvement législatif en Italie sous le premier roi Victor Emanuel II (1859–1878) avec notes comparatives*, by Innocenzo Fanti (Imola, 1880), is old, sad, and drab.

RUSSIA. *Alexandre II: Le printemps de la Russie*, by Hélène Carrère d'Encausse (2008), is a masterly study; it exploits fully the Russian sources and is particularly strong on foreign policy; *Alexander II: The Last Great Tsar*, by Edvard Radzinsky and translated by Antonina W. Boius (New York, 2005), has an excellent bibliography; it is sound in its scholarship and sensible in its judgments, though not very readable, as it is a word for word transcription from the Russian. *Tsar of Freedom*, by Stephen Graham (Hamden, CT, 1968), is inconclusive and generally disappointing. *Aleksandr II*, by S. S.

Tatishchev, 2 vols. (Saint Petersburg, 1903), has some telling points on the tsar's relations with William I (*DG*, 215). An updated single volume appeared under the same title in 2006. "Alexander II: A Revisionist View," by Alfred J. Rieber (in *JMH* 43 [1971]: 42–58), is a most important contribution by an accomplished master, tying together domestic and international history with interesting reports on Russian politics and politicians.

OTHERS. Information on the problems of Austrians with the Russians in Romania and the Chotek mission can be found in *Aus dem Leben König Karls von Rumänien*, by Mite Kremnitz, 4 vols. (Stuttgart, 1894–1900) (*DG*, 215).

Prime and Foreign Ministers

GERMANY (including PRUSSIA). The essential source for Bismarck (foreign minister, 1862–67; federal chancellor, 1867–71; imperial chancellor, 1871–90) remains *GW* (Friedrichsruh edition, 15 vols. and 4 supplementary vols. [1924–35]). Since I last wrote, however, an ambitious undertaking has been launched by the Otto von Bismarck Foundation that will revise substantially what was produced by the previous *GW* editors (Hermann von Petersdorff, Friedrich Thimme, Werner Frauendienst, Willy Andreas, and Wolfgang Windelband). I am delighted to summarize the scope of this undertaking, to comment briefly on the results thus far produced, and to thank the director of the Foundation, Professor Dr. Ulrich Lappenküper, for allowing me to tap his special knowledge of the project.

The new edition of Bismarck's works bears the title *Neue Friedrichsruher Ausgabe* (*NFA*); its principal editors—all Bismarckian scholars of the first rank—are Konrad Canis, Lothar Gall, Klaus Hildebrand, and Eberhard Kolb. This project was commenced in 2002 (though conceived in 1998), and it is organized into three categories: materials covering (1) the years 1854–62; (2) 1862–71; (3) 1871–98. In each of these periods the correspondence is ordered as (a) written works; (b) speeches; (c) interviews/talks. The most valuable of the materials are unquestionably the written works (primarily political writings and the letters), which will be merged this time and not, as was the case before, treated as the subjects of separate volumes.

The first volume to appear, the private letters and official correspondence dealing with the period 1871–73 (ed. Andrea Hopp) (Paderborn, 2004), is an accomplishment of the first order; it gives a uniquely intimate view of the motives and background of German foreign policy for this period. The first 100 documents (of 506) are addressed to the events of the agitated winter and spring of 1871—the preliminaries of peace, the Commune, and the final settlement of 10 May of that year. Of outstanding quality, in particular, is the table of contents, which makes the information eminently readable through its method of presentation. Four other volumes have appeared in the series: vol. 2, *Schriften, 1874–1876*, ed. Rainer Bendick (2005); vol. 3, *1877–1878*, ed. Michael Epkenhans and Erik Lommatzsch, and vol. 4, *1879–1881*, ed. Andrea Hopp (both 2008); and vol. 5, *1882–1883* (2010), by Ulrich Lappen-küper. Not only do these volumes contain material hitherto unpublished— largely, though by no means exclusively, drawn from the original files of the diplomatic correspondence available at Politisches Archiv in Berlin—but they also make for dynamic and compelling reading, not least because of the range and clarity of their organization, the forceful commentaries of the edi- tors in summarizing the contents of the material in their respective works, and the vivid language in which those commentaries are expressed.

However, for the period July–December 1870 we must rely on the volumes in the older *GW*. I have already described the arrangement of this collection (*DG*, 215) and see no point in reproducing here what I said there. However, I must be allowed to mention, if only because of its outstanding importance as source material, a work to which I did not have access when I first wrote, and that is *Bismarcks spanische "Diversion" 1870 und der preußisch-deutsche Reichsgründungskrieg*, which comprises three volumes: vol. 1, *Der Weg zum spanischen Thronangebot: Spätjahr 1866–4. April 1870*; vol. 2, *Aus der Krise der kleindeutschen Nationalpolitk in die preußisch-französische Julikrise 1870, 5. April 1870–12. Juli 1870*; and vol. 3, *Spanische "Diversion," "Emser Depesche" und Reichsgründungslegende bis zum Ende der Weimarer Repub- lik, 12. Juli 1870–1. September 1932*, ed. Josef Becker with the collaboration of Michael Schmid (Paderborn, 2003–7)—a fascinating anthology of docu- ments on the subject from the aftermath of the Austro-Prussian War to the end of the Weimar Republic that combines technical mastery with superb gift of exposition. The introduction, in particular, is a beautiful example of histori- cal composition. Though I disagree with the motives the editor ascribes to

269

Bismarck in the July crisis—see the exchange between Becker and myself in *CEH* 41 (2008): 93–121—I stand by what I said in reviewing the first two volumes of it in *CEH* 37 (2004): "a work of art . . . and one that fills a gap of high importance in the literature addressed to this subject" (612, 606). Becker has recently updated his arguments in a book-length article titled "'Provozierter Defensivkrieg' 1870, 'Emser Legenden' und 'Sybel-Syndrom' in der Bismarck-Historiographie: Vom Votum der Quellen zum 'Veto der Quellen'; Aus Anlaß von 'vermischten Beiträgen' in den FBPG und der HZ über eine Edition zur unmittelbaren Vor- und Nachgeschichte des Reichs-gründungskriegs 1870–71" (in *FBPS* 21, no. 1 [2011]: 5–72). While primarily a response to the critics of the arguments in the three-volume work just cited and thus focusing on developments of a somewhat earlier date, this article contains valuable information on events of the period during and after the war with relation to which the existing secondary literature was not always helpful. As for Bismarck's correspondence relating to the diplomacy of the Franco-Prussian War—that is, the period from 19 July 1870 to 10 May 1871, the outstanding source for this period is the material printed (alas, in the Fraktur typescript) in vol. 6b (1931) of *Politische Schriften: 1869–1871*. The volume has been meticulously edited, with long introductions to the impor-tant pieces, by Friedrich Thimme. For the *Gespräche*, the relevant work is vol. 7, to the founding of the German Reich, ed. Willy Andreas (1924); the *Reden*, vol. 11, 1869–1878, ed. Wilhelm Schüssler (1929); for the personal letters, *Briefe*, vol. 14, pt. 2, 1862–98, ed. Wolfgang Windelband and Werner Frauendienst (1933). Bismarck's speeches can be found in full only in the fourteen volumes edited by Horst Kohl (1892–95). There are many collec-tions of his letters: *Fürst Bismarcks Briefe an seine Braut und Gattin*, ed. Fürst Herbert von Bismarck (Stuttgart, 1900); those to William I, referred to in the section "Published Private Papers" (*DG*, 212) in the latter's correspon-dence; those to his sister Malwine von Arnim, ed. Horst Kohl (Leipzig, 1915); to his son, ed. Wolfgang Windelband (1922); those to Leopold von Gerlach, ed. Horst Kohl (1896); and those to Alexander von Schleinitz (foreign minis-ter, 1858–61), ed. Horst Kohl (Stuttgart, 1905) (all described in detail in *DG*, 216). The great Bismarckian scholar Heinrich von Poschinger also produced three large volumes of source material of the highest order: *Also sprach Bis-marck*, 3 vols. (Vienna, 1910–11). The second volume, which deals with the years 1870–78, is the most important from the perspective of this study; *Neue Tischgespräche und Interviews* (1895), a painstaking and accurate chronicle of Bismarck's conversations with leading politicians, parliamentarians, and military figures, some of which take place in the period of the war of 1870, with an excellent English translation by Syndey Whitman (1900); and *Fürst Bismarck und die Diplomaten, 1852–1890* (Hamburg, 1900), a meticulous account for which no words of praise are too strong.

Bismarck's *Gedanken und Erinnerungen* have gone through many editions, but the most famous is still the original (Stuttgart, 1898). The memoirs are, as has long been recognized, highly unreliable. Bismarck selected, suppressed, and arranged evidence on no principle other than the need to present himself in the most favorable light. He was grievously wrong about many things. He bore his antagonism to almost every one of his contemporaries, with the notable exception of William I, at the worst possible time, when the feelings of many Germans against perceived enemies everywhere had been aroused to a white heat of intensity and their capacity for tolerance was at its lowest ebb. Still, as a work of literature, Bismarck's memoirs have few, if any, equals. They are indeed the only collection of their kind that can be recommended as bedside reading for the layman. The last edition of *GW*, vol. 15 (1932), includes material not included in the original volumes. The editors of *NFA* are in the throes of preparing a new edition of the memoirs that is slated to appear as a single volume in a fourth section of the work after the first three sections have been completed. Of the many translations of the memoirs into English, by far the best is *Reflections and Reminiscences*, ed. Theodore S. Hamerow (New York, 1968).

Of the ministers in the South German states, *Denkwürdigkeiten*, by Chlodwig Hohenlohe-Schillingsfürst, 2 vols. (Stuttgart, 1906) (*DG*, 216), is helpful on relations between Berlin and Munich but not as valuable for the wartime period as the last volume (4 [1908]) of his *Aus meinem Leben*. The actions of Hohenlohe-Schillingsfürst's opponent may be followed in *Denkwürdigkeiten*, by Otto Count Bray-Steinburg (Leipzig, 1901); it contains some interesting penetrations but is otherwise a drab chronicle. On Hesse-Kassel, *Die Tagebücher des Freiherrn Reinhard von Dalwick zu Lichtenfels aus den Jahren 1860–71*, ed. Wilhelm Schüssler (Stuttgart, 1920), is complacent, assertive, and verbose.

AUSTRIA-HUNGARY. Beust's memoirs, *Aus drei Viertel-Jahrhunderten*, 2 vols. (Stuttgart, 1887) (*DG*, 216) are very interesting, though not very reliable. On the other hand, the work *Graf Julius Andrássy*, by Edouard Wertheimer, 3 vols. (Stuttgart, 1910–13), is of outstanding importance, a work of great energy and scholarship; it is particularly useful for the debates over the Chotek mission. *Bismarck und Andrássy: Ungarn in der deutschen Machtpolitik in der 2. Hälfte des 19. Jahrhunderts*, by István Diószegi (Vienna, 1999; translated from the Hungarian by Albrecht Friedrich), is an indispensable book for understanding the complex relationship between the two men, written with much learning though with little sparkle.

FRANCE. I have already given a detailed summary of the material on Ollivier (*DG*, 208, 217), and, since he was on the scene for less than three weeks in the period covered by this volume, I will not repeat that summary here. His final miscellany, *Lettres de l'exil, 1870–1874* (1921) (*DG*, 217) is a polemic addressed to the policies of his successors.

Gramont defended himself passionately though unconvincingly in *La France et la Prusse* (1872) (*DG*, 217).

Un ministère de la guerre de vingt-quatre jours, by Charles Palikao (1871), contains the impressions (none of them very reliable) of the last prime minister of the Second Empire.

Favre did much better: his *Gouvernement de la Défense Nationale*, 3 vols. (1871–75), occasionally romanticizes the revolution and exaggerates his role in the shaping of events; on the other hand, it is a work of literature as well as of history, at once scholarly, delightful to read, and highly enlightening.

Chaudordy defended his policies in a book titled *La France à la suite de la guerre de 1870–71* (1887). Its structure is weak, but it does contain useful information, effective portraits of individuals, and reliable judgments.

GREAT BRITAIN. The material on Gladstone is, of course, vast, though not always very good. Unquestionably, the place to start is *The Gladstone Diaries*, 14 vols., ed. M. R. D. Foot (1968–94). It displays great scholarship, literary mastery, and clear, personal convictions, though some of the latter are not always convincing. Gladstone's own *Gleanings of Past Years*, 7 vols. (1879–98), are a most fascinating account of the world—as Gladstone saw it. Vol. 3

(1879) covers the years 1843–78; it is able and stimulating but not always persuasive. Also of importance is Gladstone's (anonymous) article "Germany, France, and England" (in *The Edinburgh Review*, 18 October 1870), full of eloquently formulated, if controversial, points. There is a devastating analysis of this piece in the essay "Gladstone as Bismarck" by Paul W. Schroeder (in *SSS*, 97–119). Another provocative essay is that of Francis Loewenheim, "The Old Prussian and the People's William," in *From the Berlin Museum to the Berlin Wall*, ed. David Wetzel (Westport, CT, 1996), 61–85. Gladstone's correspondence with Granville between 1868 and 1876 has been brilliantly edited by Agatha Ramm (Cambridge, 1998), with a supplementary essay by H. C. G. Matthew; this is a reprint of a two-volume work that was originally published in 1952. Two perceptive recent works are *Reading Gladstone*, by Ruth Clayton Windscheffel (New York, 2008), and *Gladstone: God and Politics*, by Richard Shannon (2007), the former weak on foreign policy, the latter thorough, accurate, and imaginative. The lives of H. C. G. Matthew (1995); Roy Jenkins (1997); Eugenio Biagini (New York, 2000); and Peter Stansky (Boston, 1979) are all well written, but they are too serious, always a mistake except in the greatest biographies. Of the older works, *Gladstone*, by Philip Magnus (1954), combines meticulous scholarship, deep understanding, and an easy style leavened with wit. *The Queen and Mr. Gladstone*, by Philip Guedalla (New York, 1934), is an exciting book distinguished by a sobriety of style and mastery of sources. *Gladstone's Foreign Policy*, by Paul Knaplund (New York, 1935), is a long book, full of entertainment, but its conclusions give a one-sided and misleading picture of events. Even more is this true of the work *Bismarck, Gladstone and the Concert of Europe*, by W. N. Medlicott (1956); it sees Gladstone as the apostle of the rule of law and Bismarck as the apotheosis of manipulated alliances and antagonisms. The article by Schroeder referred to earlier is a splendid corrective to this interpretation. *Gladstone, Disraeli and Later Victorian Politics*, by Paul Adelman (Harlow, 1983), has a good bibliography, if little else. *The Politics of British Foreign Policy in the Era of Disraeli and Gladstone*, by Marvin Swartz (1985), is a finely written dramatic story but contains few new items.

Granville's biography by Edmond Fitzmaurice, 2 vols. (1905), is inadequate and dull, a life sentence on a treadmill; there is not a breath of life in it from start to finish (*DG*, 217).

ITALY. Italian memoirs are sporadic but often good. A good example is the last two volumes of the *Carteggi di Bettino Ricasoli* (prime minister, 1861–62, 1887–95), ed. Mario Nobili et al., 29 vols. (Bologna, 1939–2011). Marco Minghetti (prime minister, 1863–64) provides some important details on the Roman question in *La convenzione di settembre* (Bologna, 1899). The last two volumes of the *Carte di Giovanni Lanza*, ed. Cesare Maria de Vecchi di Val Cismon, 11 vols. (Turin, 1935–43), contain useful material on the Triple Alliance negotiations. *La politica estera di E. Visconti-Venosta*, by Francesco Cataluccio (Florence, 1940), is a most admirable work in political history, essential reading for the League of Neutrals (all in *DG*, 218).

RUSSIA. There are two important books on Gorchakov. I have already mentioned (in *DG*, 218) the biography by S. N. Semanov (Moscow, 1962), short and perceptive, despite its unabashedly Marxist bias. Much better is the biography titled *Kant'sler A. M. Gorchakov* (Moscow, 1998), ed. by E. M. Primakov, a fine piece of scholarship, as well as an admirable work of synthesis. It is especially good on his career as chancellor, though weak on his earlier life.

Diplomats

GERMANY (including PRUSSIA). There are two important works of Hans Lothar von Schweinitz, ambassador to Vienna: *Denkwürdigkeiten*, 2 vols. (1927), and *Briefwechsel* (1928). Johann von Bernstorff (ambassador to Great Britain) appears in *Im Kampfe für Preussens Ehre*, by Karl Ringhoffer (1906); it was published posthumously and caused a great stir when it did (all in *DG*, 218). *Botschafter Paul Graf von Hatzfeldt*, ed. Gerhard Ebel, 2 vols. (Boppard am Rhein, 1976), is packed with valuable information on a figure who played a leading role in the negotiations for an armistice and was later ambassador to Great Britain. Hatzfeldt's *Briefe an seine Frau* (Leipzig, 1907) presents the letters written to his wife from the German headquarters during the war and is of value for the differences between Bismarck and the military men. Hajo Holborn, "Bismarck und Werthern" (in *Archiv für Politik und Geschichte* 5 [1925–26]: 469–507), gives excerpts of the correspondence between Bismarck and his minister in Munich before, during, and after the war.

AUSTRIA-HUNGARY. Henry Salomon, *L'Ambassade de Richard de Metternich* (1931), is a mountain of dusty stuff (*DG*, 219). *Denkwürdigkeiten*, by Karl Friedrich Vitzthum von Eckstädt (Stuttgart, 1886), is a compelling history of Austro-French relations during this period, valuable on the negotiations for the Triple Alliance by a seasoned diplomat who was also a close confidant of Beust's.

FRANCE. Some fine books here. *La France et la Russie en 1870*, ed. Émile-Félix Maurice, Count Fleury (1902), is a compelling exposition based on the French and Russian records. Written long after the event and having the nature of a treatise on Franco-Russian relations of the period as well as a memoir, this book is unique in its quality as a picture of that relationship, as seen from the French embassy in the Russian capital. Gustave Rothan, a gossip and intriguer, wrote a curious book on our period, half history, half recollection: *L'Allemagne et l'Italie* (1885) (*DG*, 219). Jules Ferry's "Lettres à Gambetta" (in *Revue de Paris* 6 [1904]), contains a few revelations. The author was prefect of the department of the Seine and would become president of the Third Republic. *Dépêches, circulaires, décrets, proclamations et discours de Léon Gambetta*, ed. Joseph Reinach, 2 vols. (1886–91), is a most penetrating source book, giving Gambetta's pronouncements from Tours and Bordeaux. They are telling oratory; they contain some of the finest passages in the French language, and they were Gambetta's greatest performance, an example for ages to come. Thiers's *Notes et souvenirs . . . 1870–1873* (1903) combines sobriety of style with clear stimulating judgments. There is a good English translation by F. M. Atkinson (1915). "La correspondance inédite de M. Thiers pendant la guerre de 1870–71," which appeared in *Revue des deux mondes* [88, 6e pér.] 33 (1916): 758–81; 34 (1916): 51–78, is a competent and reliable compilation with material that is not contained in the *Notes*. "Ungedruckte Berichte von Adolphe Thiers aus dem Jahre 1870," ed. Friedrich Hirth (in *PJbb* 183 [1921]: 159–86), is even more helpful. Victor Edmond Vital Regnier's *Quel est votre nom? N. ou M.? Une étrange histoire devoilée* (Brussels, 1870) (English translation, 1872) details anonymously but quite competently the activities of the clandestine Bonapartist agent.

Souvenirs diplomatiques de Russie et d'Allemagne, by Joseph Gabriac

(1896), contains glimpses of insight. Jean-Gilbert-Victor Fialin Persigny revealed something, though not much, of himself in his *Mémoires* (1896). *Persigny, un ministre de Napoléon III, 1808–1872*, by Honoré Farat (1957), goes much deeper; there are long excerpts from his papers, and his personality comes through, as well. *Un diplomate à Londres: Lettres et notes, 1871–1877*, by Charles Gavard (1895) (English translation, 1897), is a not very satisfactory posthumous compilation by the chief secretary, then minister plenipotentiary, at the French embassy during the war.

DENMARK. *Les coulisses de la diplomatie*, by Jules Hansen (1880), covers the years 1864–79 and gives the colorful but unreliable impressions of a journalist who was really functioning as an agent of the French foreign office.

GREAT BRITAIN. The biographies of the British ambassadors are numerous, but almost all are long, dull, and uncritical. There is one important exception. *Memoirs and Letters of the Right Hon. Sir Robert Morier*, ed. Rosslyn Wemyss (his daughter), 2 vols. (1911), is a vigorous and clear exposition. Morier was secretary of the British legation at Darmstadt and one of the most impressive and interesting figures in the history of British diplomacy of this period, a consummate insider whose knowledge of German affairs rivaled Bismarck's. Of the other ambassadors there is nothing much of significance. Lord Lyons (France) received a superficial life by T. W. L. Newton, 2 vols. (1913); *The Diplomatic Reminiscences of Lord Augustus Loftus*, 4 vols. (1892–94), is vain, dry, and meandering (both in *DG*, 219). On the other hand, Archibald Forbes, *My Experiences of the War between France and Germany*, 2 vols. (1871), is a painstaking and accurate chronicle by a British journalist who was also a diplomat.

ITALY. *Ricordi diplomatici (1870)*, excerpted from *Nuova antologia* 56, ser. 3. (1 March 1895), gives the impressions of Constantino Nigra during the last days of the July crisis; there is an excellent French translation: "Souvenirs diplomatiques, 1870" (in *BURS* [1895]) (*DG*, 219–20). Even better are the *Carteggi politici inediti di Francesco Crispi*, ed. T. Palamenghi-Crispi (Rome, 1912). It is anything but unbiased—really a blistering critique of Victor Emmanuel II and, to a lesser extent, Visconti-Venosta, but, since Crispi had good connections with a number of those who had taken an active part in Italian diplomacy of 1870–71, the book cannot be ignored. Crispi would later be prime minister of his country (1887–91, 1893–96). There are excellent English (1914) and German (1921) translations.

RUSSIA. *Saburov Memoirs*, ed. J. Y. Simpson (New York, 1929), has some points of interest on the Triple Alliance negotiations (*DG*, 220).

UNITED STATES. Among the many messages sent to Berlin after the formal proclamation of the new empire in 1871, few were more laudatory than that of President Ulysses S. Grant of the United States, who congratulated the Germans on having completed their long-desired unification. Grant's message was a reflection of American opinion, strongly anti-French and pro-Prussian, during the war. The Americans who lent their hands to Bismarck left vivid accounts of their undertakings. *Recollections of a Minister to France, 1968–1877*, by E. B. Washburne, 2 vols. (New York, 1887), is an engrossing reconstruction of diplomatic details, perhaps at times too hard on the members of the Government of National Defense. P. H. Sheridan, *Personal Memoirs*, 2 vols. (New York, 1888), is of equal rank and shows that the author was as well suited to be a negotiator as a fighter.

Other Witnesses

If the material for the previous two sections of this bibliography is rich, it is overwhelming for this one, and for this reason, if for no other, I must confine myself to items of central importance. For the military, the place to start is *Bibliographie générale de la Guerre de 1870–1871*, by Barthélemy-Edmond Palat (who used the pseudonym Pierre Lehautcourt) (1896); it lists more than six thousand titles and remains indispensable more than one hundred years after it was published. Equally indispensable is the classic work *Geschichte der Kriegskunst im Rahmen der politischen Geschichte*, by Hans Delbrück, completed by Emil Daniels, 4 parts in 7 vols. (1900–1936). Delbrück was Germany's most distinguished military historian, and he had an enormous influence on later writers. The work covers, of course, a longer period than ours, but it is written with such care, competence, and scholarly acumen that one can avoid it only at one's peril. Vol. 6, by Emil Daniels (1929), deals with the war of 1870; it was published as part of part 4, which explores the modern period of military history (since 1792), and was the only work of importance to appear after 1914 until Michael Howard's classic, published some thirty years later.

GERMANY (including PRUSSIA). The official history is the primary source: *Der deutsch-französische Krieg, 1870/71*, 2 pts. in 5 vols. (1872–81) (English translation by F. C. H. Clarke, 2 pts. in 5 vols. [1874–84]). It was, of course, closely controlled by the General Staff. Nearly all volumes are accompanied by maps in separate portfolios. Of the generals, Helmut von Moltke, of course, stands at the top of the list. His *Militärische Werke*, 4 pts. in 14 vols. with supplements (1892–1912), is incontestably the most important record for source material on him. Section 1, pt. 3, of this work, *Militärische Korrespondenz: Aus den Dienstschriften des Krieges 1870–71* (1896), is, for our purposes, the fundamental document. The essential material in this volume lies in the exchanges between Moltke and Bismarck. Moltke's own *Geschichte des deutsch-französischen Krieges von 1870–1871* (1895) is a mixture of official history—based on contemporary records—and personal memories. The work is, of course, slanted in Moltke's favor, sometimes deliberately, often not. There is an excellent English translation (New York, 1892) and a less satisfactory French one (1891). *Moltke in der Vorbereitung und Durchführung der Operationen*, published by the Großer Generalstab as Heft 36 in the series *Kriegsgeschichtliche Einzelschriften* (1905), details his rise to the position of chief military adviser to the king. It sees Bismarck's resentment of that rise as the source of the difficulties between the two men (54–55)—a myth that was shot to pieces long ago by Gordon A. Craig, in *The Politics of the Prussian Army 1640–1945* (Oxford, 1955) (*DG*, 235). The General Staff also compiled Moltke's *Taktisch-strategische Aufsätze aus den Jahren 1857–1871* (1900) as section 2, part 2, of his *Militärische Werke*, an important, stimulating, and forcefully written work, though with the expected anti-Bismarck slant. Some of Moltke's ruminations on war strategy, devolving mainly from his correspondence, were published in an English translation by Michael Bell in 1971 in a work titled *Strategy: Its Theory and Application; The Wars for German Unification, 1866–1871*.

Members of Moltke's staff have also had a free run. Under his direct supervision there worked three heads of section: Colonel Paul Bronsart von Schellendorff for movements, Colonel Karl Herman Bernhard von Brandenstein for rail transport and supplies, and Colonel Julius von Verdy du Vernois for intelligence. The latter has left two penetrating accounts: *Studien über den Krieg auf Grundlage des deutsch-französischen Krieges 1870–71*, 3 vols. (1891–1909), a detailed guide; and *Im Grossen Hauptquartier 1870–71* (1895), a scathing attack on Bismarck; parts of the latter appeared in the *Deutsche Rundschau* in 1874 and 1895 (see the preface). There is a mediocre English translation of the latter book (New York, 1968, first published in London, 1897). Bronsart, who would later become minister of war, 1883–89, produced the *Geheimes Kriegstagebuch, 1870–1871*, ed. Peter Rassow (Bonn, 1954), important and stimulating, if overdramatized. There is nothing by Brandenstein. The *Tagebücher des Generalfeldmarschalls Graf von Blumenthal aus den Jahren 1866 und 1870/71*, ed. Albrecht Graf von Blumenthal (Stuttgart, 1902), contains much information. Blumenthal was chief of staff of the Third Army and did not always see eye to eye with Moltke. Their disputes over the battle of Orléans are revealed in riveting fashion here. As with the books by Vernois and Bronsart, there is an English translation (1903), precise and reliable. *Denkwürdigkeiten*, by Albrecht von Stosch, ed. Ulrich von Stosch (Stuttgart, 1904), contains the letters and diaries of an able general intern; those of Alfred Graf von Waldersee, 3 vols., ed. H. O. Meisner (Stuttgart, 1922–25), give the impressions of the young military attaché in Paris who one day would have Moltke's job. *General der Infanterie Graf von Werder*, by Ernst Schmidt (Oldenburg, 1912), is an essay of unalloyed hero worship by the commander of the Baden and Württemberg divisions of the German army.

Albrecht Graf von Roon, *Denkwürdigkeiten*, 5th ed., 3 vols. (1905), is a work of great penetration and erudition, running over with incisive and important observations. Especially valuable are its impressions of the atmosphere at Versailles during the agitated winter of 1870–71 when the rivalry between Moltke and Bismarck reached its apogee.

Many lesser military figures or writers on military matters wrote immediately after the war; the list that follows hardly scratches the surface. *Die Mobilmachung von 1870/71*, by Gustav Lehmann (1904), is the official history—a first-rate work, scholarly and eminently readable; *Das grosse Hauptquartier und die deutschen Operationen im Feldzuge 1870 bis zur Schlacht von Sedan*, by Eduard Friederich (1898), provides a vivid portrait of the speed of operations in July and August; *Kriegsgeschichtliche Beispiele des Festungskrieges aus dem deutsch-französischen Kriege von 1870/71*, 12 pts. in 3 vols. (1899–1909), by Herman Frobenius, is more interesting for atmosphere than for facts; and this is even more true of *Das Deutsche Grosse Hauptquartier und die Bekämpfung von Paris im Feldzuge 1870–71*, by Wilhelm Busch (Stuttgart, 1905). *Briefe aus dem Deutsch-Französischen Kriege*, by Julius von Hartmann (Kassel, 1893), provides some points of illumination; *Die Schlacht von Wörth*, by August Alexander Keim (1891), gives the details of an early Prussian victory, though with no recounting of its political ramifications; *Der Krieg um die Rheingrenze 1870*, by Friedrich Wilhelm Rüstow, 2 vols. (Zurich, 1870–71), is a contemporary but penetrating account by a Swiss journalist. *Briefe aus dem grossen Hauptquartier der Feldzüge 1866 und 1870/71 an die Gattin*, by Fedor von Rauch (Berlin, 1911), throws a vivid light on the hero-worshipping of Moltke by his officers. *Feldbriefe, 1870–71*, by Georg Heinrich Rindfleisch (Göttingen, 1905), has some points of interest. *Die Beschiessung von Paris und die Ursachen ihrer Verzögerung*, by Carl Wilhelm von Blume (Berlin, 1899), is a relentlessly dramatic presentation, though marked by minor errors.

In passing, note may be taken of the magnificent nineteen-volume *Gesamtausgabe* by Carl Bleitreu (Bad Langensalza, 2009–10). Originally published between 1898 and 1910 by Verlag Carl Krabbe in Stuttgart, this fictionalized history, in Fraktur, of the war contains more than two hundred drawings by artist Christian Speyer (also from Stuttgart). Viewing these drawings is an experience in itself, a never-ending feast of places, faces, and atmospheres the overall impact of which is overwhelming and unforgettable.

Many of Bismarck's aides were avid writers, and many produced works of high quality, concealing nothing and writing in respectful and slightly awed tones. I have given extensive commentaries on these earlier (*DG*, 220–21), and here I will attempt to be briefer. *Denkwürdigkeiten*, by Bernhard Fürst von Bülow, 4 vols. (1930–31), contains the impressions of the secretary of state in the new Reich; the style is drab and aloof, leaving the story to speak for itself. *Im Dienste Bismarcks: Persönliche Erinngerungen*, by Arthur von

Brauer, ed. Helmut Rogge (1936), is a lively and important book by the Russian expert in its foreign ministry. *Ein schlichtes Leben in bewegter Zeit*, by Heinrich Abeken (4th ed., 1910; first published, 1898), with an English translation, *Bismarck's Pen: The Life of Heinrich von Abeken*, edited from his letters and journals by his wife (1911); *Tagebuchblätter*, by Moritz Busch, 3 vols. (Leipzig, 1898–99), with a superb English translation, *Bismarck: Some Secret Pages of His History*, 3 vols. (1898); *Fürst und Fürstin Bismarck*, by Robert von Keudell (1901); *Aus dem Leben Theodor von Bernhardis* (9 vols., 1898–1906), vol. 8, "Zwischen zwei Kriegen" (1901), covering the period 1867–1869, helpful for the Triple Alliance negotiations but, for the purposes of this volume, overtaken by the material in vol. 9, "In Spanien und Portugal," dealing with 1869–71 (1906); "Hermann von Thile und Bismarck," by Johann Sass (in *PJbb* 217 [1929]: 257–79); *Lebenslauf*, by Württemberg journalist Julius Fröbel, 2 vols. (Stuttgart, 1890–91); *Die Bedeutung des preussischen Innenministers Friedrich Albrecht Graf zu Eulenburg für die Entwicklung Preussens zum Rechtsstaat*, by Gerhard Lange (1993); *Lebenserinnerungen*, by Julius von Eckardt (Leipzig, 1910)—all these are vivid, absorbing, and easy to read and explain the events in which their respective subjects were involved. Abeken has, it should be noted, finally received a biography by Wolfgang Frischbier (Paderborn, 2008), a work of the highest caliber, based on an abundance of invaluable source materials, not all of which are (or were, at least, when the present study was prepared) readily available to the interested scholar.

Mention should also be made of two important books unflattering to Bismarck: Ludwig Bamberger, *Bismarcks grosses Spiel: Die geheimen Tagebücher Ludwig Bambergers*, ed. Ernst Feder (Frankfurt am Main, 1932) (a foreshadowing of which appeared in Bamberger, "Vor fünfundzwanzig Jahren," in *Gesammelte Schriften*, 5 vols. [1894–98], vol. 1 [1898], 417–52); and the *Memoiren zur Zeitgeschichte* of the Saxon diplomat (though Prussian born) Oskar Meding, 3 vols. (Leipzig, 1881–84).

There is an abundance of material on those writers who wrote about the war and the issues to which it gave rise. Again, what follows is only a dip into this vast sea. *Erinnerungen*, by Hans Viktor Unruh, ed. Heinrich von Poschinger (Stuttgart, 1895), contains the impressions of a Prussian politician who served as a member of the North German Confederation and, later, of the

Reichstag. *Briefe, Dokumente, Augenzeugenberichte*, by Adolph Wagner, ed. Heinrich Rubner (1978), is a splendid compilation of works by an economist and prominent Kathedersozialist (academic socialist). *Denkwürdigkeiten*, by Wilhelm Stieber, ed. Leopold Auerbach (1884), contains the recollections of Bismarck's chief officer for intelligence; in 1978, a new version of his memoirs appeared under the title *Spion des Kanzlers* (Stuttgart, 1978) (English translation by Jan Van Heurck, *The Chancellor's Spy* [New York, 1979]); it is based on sources of the most dubious validity (the original is said to have been lost in 1945) and should not be substituted for the 1884 memoirs. *Briefwechsel*, by Johann Gustav Droysen, ed. Reinhart Hübner (1929), is informative, though rather clumsily organized. The author was the most outstanding of the great family of German historians and wrote a classic history of Alexander the Great. Hübner also wrote a biography, *Albrecht von Roon* (Hamburg, 1933), that is thin and superficial.

Of the countless number of contemporary accounts justifying the German war aims, most outstandingly the demand for the annexation of Alsace-Lorraine, I call attention only to the works of a few: Wolfgang Menzel, a distinguished literary historian and critic; W. H. Eras, a journalist and politician; Ludwig Pietsch, painter, bon vivant, writer, an adviser to the crown prince during the war; Berthold Auerbach, a brilliant poet and author who was also a Jew—all these are pugnacious polemics with many acute observations. All except Auerbach (Stuttgart) were published in Berlin in 1871. No mention of the contemporaries and their activities would be complete without a word about the colorful, if controversial, historian who was very much on the scene and who, even more than the figures listed, was on the pro-German side of the fence. The reference here is to Heinrich von Treitschke, whose "Was fordern wir von Frankreich?" (in *PJbb* 26 [1870]: 367–409) (English translation, "What We Demand from France" [1870]), combines hatred for the defeated foe, anti-Semitism, and unvarnished imperialism. Treitschke's correspondence during this period can be found in his *Briefe*, ed. Max Cornicelius, 3 vols. (Leipzig, 1912–20). His papers contain a number of passages on wartime developments and are either directly revealing or representative of what was being thought and said among the educated classes in Germany during this time.

AUSTRIA-HUNGARY. *Erinnerungen eines alten Österreichers*, by Ludwig von Przibram, 2 vols. (Stuttgart, 1910–12), is a book on the Austrian press bureau, entertaining when read in small doses but boring after a time (*DG*, 222); *Dreissig Jahre aus dem Leben eines Journalisten*, by Hugo Pollak, 3 vols. (Vienna, 1894–98), is good on atmosphere but of little importance as a work of history.

FRANCE. *Le Second Empire vu par un diplomate belge*, by Eugène Napoléon Beyens, 2 vols. (Lille, 1924–26), records the views of the Belgian ambassador to the Second Empire; *Souvenirs militaires*, by Barthélémy Lebrun (1895) is important, if not altogether reliable, for the negotiations for the Triple Alliance (both in *DG*, 222). *La France nouvelle* by Lucien Anatole Prévost-Paradol (1868) is a work of great energy and scholarship, indispensable for understanding the political atmosphere of Paris in the last days of the Second Empire. J. Tchernoff, *Histoire politique contemporaine: Le parti républican au coup d'état et sous le Second Empire d'après des documents et des souvenirs inédits* (1906), accumulates vast material and presents it with clarity.

On the political side, by far the most valuable work is the *Enquête parlementaire sur les Actes du Gouvernement de la defense nationale* (Versailles, 1872–75), the fruit of the commission of inquiry set up by the National Assembly; it is a compilation of meticulous scholarship that no historian of the period can afford to ignore. It contains six volumes that are divided into three sections.

(A) Dépêches Télégraphiques—a collection of those telegrams that seemed to the commission most interesting from a political, administrative, or military point of view, made up of the vast correspondence of those officials who had the right to communicate with each other free of charge. The sources upon which the commission drew were, however, not complete. Some of the archives of the post offices were destroyed in the course of the war; other documents were removed or mislaid by the French at moments of fear or hurried evacuation. Thus, very few of the dispatches could be traced, and here there is a much fuller telegraphic record of the doings of the Delegation after 9 December than before that date, for the archives of the post office at Tours disappeared, whereas those at Bordeaux remained intact. But, despite these gaps, it is possible to discern the general lines of policy followed by the government in the provinces, and these two volumes are invaluable for a study of republican administrators, for an estimate of the reactions of civil and military officials to the outstanding measures the government sought to undertake and, most important, for the methods of Gambetta himself and of the men (often his rivals) with whom he had to deal.

(B) Dépositions—the evidence of witnesses interrogated by the Commission. The value of these depositions naturally varies considerably. Some of the witnesses supported their evidence with notes and documents; others relied solely upon their memories; some were questioned much sooner than others; some preferred to answer questions briefly, whereas others (like Trochu and Gambetta) gave long, continuous narratives that generally tended to be apologetic explanations of their own conduct; some were freely communicative, others reticent and inclined to regard this commission of notables as a decidedly hostile institution.

(C) Rapports—the reports detailing the various special aspects of the national defense, like foreign policy, the defense of Paris, and the Army of the East. The tone of these reports tends to vary according to the prejudices of the rapporteur, and none of them was prejudiced in favor of the government whose efforts they purported to serve.

All in all, however, the documents in this great collection throw a vivid light on the activities of the Government of National Defense between 4 September 1870 and 12 February 1871 and constitute a priceless addition to the available source material on the subject.

Amaury Prosper Dréo, *Procès-verbaux des séances du conseil 1870–71* (Paris, 1903), contains the private notes by Dréo for the benefit of his father-in-law, Louis Garnier-Pagès, Gambetta's friend and partner in the Government of National Defense. They are scanty, but they are the only record of what happened at the sessions of a council that kept no official minutes, and they are nonetheless valuable because they are unofficial.

For the military, the official history is in *La guerre de 1870/71*, published by the Revue d'histoire rédigée à Section historique de l'État-major de l'armée, 37 vols. with supplements (1901–13). This magnificent work includes no fewer than eleven separate studies of various phases of the war from the first days of the fighting to the siege of Paris, and each of them has maps and *documents annexes*. The most valuable of the series is unquestionably the one dealing with *Les operations autour de Metz*, 3 vols. in 6 (1903–5). It is a very rare item, available only in a few major libraries; the paper, especially that of the first volume, is of very poor quality and is almost impossible to read. Nevertheless, the book displays a wonderful level of accuracy, clarity, and scholarship and vividly depicts Bazaine's frustrations with the manifold undertakings with which he was preoccupied. Equally important are the works of Barthélemy-Edmond Palat written under his pseudonym Pierre Lehautcourt and titled respectively *L'Histoire de la Guerre de 1870–1871*, 7 vols. (1901–8) and *La Défense Nationale*, 8 vols. in 7 (1893–98); altogether these volumes rank among the most perfect works ever published on military strategy at a high level written by a master of research and a master of narrative. The field commanders come off less well: Louis Léon Faidherbe, *Campagne de l'Armée du Nord en 1870–71* (1871), has flashes of insight but is otherwise uninspiring. The same is true of the memoirs of François Du Barail, 3 vols. (various eds., 1896, first published, 1893–95), Victor Bizot (Lyons, 1914), General Charles Antoine Thoumas (1893), and Camille Clément La Roncière Le Noury (1872), though this last focuses on the otherwise neglected role of the French navy. *Campagne de 1870–1871: La deuxième armée de la Loire*, by A. E. Chanzy (3rd ed., 1871), is a long narrative and with technical details, inevitably heavy going, and in any case, it runs the case against the armistice too hard. *Défense de Paris*, by Auguste Alexandre Ducrot, 4 vols. (1875–78), though old, is a contribution that rewards careful reading; the book is long; it spares no detail, but it will fascinate every reader who enjoys the world of military maneuver.

Bazaine wrote two volumes: *L'armée du Rhin depuis le 12 août jusqu'au 29 octobre 1870* (1872) and *Épisodes de la guerre de 1870 et le blocus de Metz* (Madrid, 1883), at once very good and very bad; he has a wonderful gift for analyzing battles but has the fault of including the irrelevant as well as the essential. The charges against Bazaine are detailed in *Procès Bazaine* (1873), straightforward, sober, persuasive. Bazaine has received many biographies, but only two are worth mentioning: Robert Christophe (2nd ed., 1947), fascinatingly readable, and Maurice Baumont (1978), insightful but lopsided.

Souvenirs, by General Louis Jarras (1892), contains the valuable reflections of the officer who became Bazaine's chief of staff; they were edited by his wife. *Froeschwiller* (near Wörth), by Henri Bonnal (1899), is an admirable study of one of the early battles of the war. Bonnal also wrote a longer and more detailed account, *L'esprit de la guerre moderne: La manoeuvre de St. Privat, 18 juillet–18 août 1870*, 3 vols. (1904–12), documenting the unbelievable confusion that prevailed in the ranks of the French army. *La vérité sur les désastres de l'Armée de l'Est et sur le désarmement de la Garde nationale* (1883) is a thorough, spirited—and, on the whole, not unpersuasive—defense of Favre by Julie Favre, his widow. The writer has every gift, presenting political decisions, scientific technicalities, and bureaucratic entanglements with equal grace. *La guerre en province pendant le siège de Paris, 1870–1871*, by Charles de Freycinet (1871), is a competent, though hardly searching, survey. *Le général Bourbaki par un de ses anciens officiers d'ordonnance*, by Louis d'Eichthal (1885), has some points of interest.

Ce qui est arrivé à la France en 1870: Fragments inédites, by Arthur de Gobineau, first published in *Europe, revue mensuelle*, no. 9 (1 October 1923): 5–26, new ed. edited by A. B. Duff (1970), recounts the impressions of the famous French racist; as with all his books, the verdict precedes the analysis. *Nouveau journal d'un officier d'ordonnance*, by Maurice Comte d'Hérisson (1889), is an informative and competent account of Bazaine's aide de camp and Favre's factotum in the negotiations that led to the armistice.

There is a pronounced spate of memoir literature emanating from persons who were concerned, in one way or another, with the problems of the war. *Allemands et Français*, by Gabriel Monod (1872), is the clear brief outline of a pastor and theologian, all the more remarkable because his mother happened to be from Alsace. More intemperate is *Mon journal pendant la guerre (1870–1871)*, by Comte Joseph d'Haussonville (1905), a politician and diplomat who operated in Belgium. *Actualités et souvenirs politiques*, by Baron Jérôme David (1874), is the dramatic, exciting, but superficial work of a man who at heart was a monarchist.

On the destruction of the Empire after Sedan: *La journée du 4 septembre au Corps Législatif*, by Ernest Dréolle (1871), is a ponderous tome; *L'Hôtel de Ville de Paris au 4 septembre et pendant le siège*, by Étienne Arago (1874), is a lively account by a playwright and politician; the author has a wonderful gift for getting himself into a tangle without apparently intending to do so. *Souvenirs du quatre septembre*, by Jules Simon (1874), is much superior to both; it presents a clear, compelling narrative and makes some useful comments; his general speculations are less rewarding. *Souvenirs, 1848–1878*, by

Charles de Freycinet (1912), is an important contribution to historical knowledge by a remarkable figure who was Gambetta's assistant in the ministry of war; the author presents himself as an engineer, a man of facts and figures who could analyze with great refinement the complicated play of forces in French political life but who was singularly unable, like Gambetta himself, to master, particularly in these years, the less familiar subtleties of international relations. *Napoleon III auf Wilhelmshöhe*, by Carl von Monts (1909), can be used with some profit, though not much. The book presents Napoleon III as a bull in a china shop, smashing all the crockery, including his own. Finally, while on the subject of memoirs, diaries, and correspondence, we must mention the various papers of Juliette Adam, the chief of which for our purposes is *Mes illusions et nos souffrances pendant le siège de Paris* (6th ed., 1906). Adam was a well-known author, the chief republican hostess of the time, and an uncommonly acute and intelligent observer whose book is invaluable for the light it sheds upon republican politics and personalities. Anne Hogenhuis-Seliverstoff draws on these and other materials to produce a biography titled *Juliette Adam, 1836–1936: L'instigatrice* (2001), a work of a wholly superior order, packed with valuable ideas and stimulating information.

GREAT BRITAIN. James Howard Harris Malmesbury's *Memoirs of an Ex-minister* (3rd ed., 1885) contains the unreliable jottings of a former prime minister who was sympathetic to Napoleon; the text is discursive, rambling, and uninteresting, like its subject. *Daily News Correspondence of the War between Germany and France 1870–1* (1871) has some points of interest (both in *DG*, 223).

There is an enormous amount of material on Benjamin Disraeli (prime minister, 1867–68, leader of the opposition during the war). Only a handful need be mentioned. A good bibliography is *Benjamin Disraeli: A List of Writings by Him, and Writings about Him, with Notes*, by R. W. Stewart (Metuchen, NJ, 1972). There is much of interest for our purposes in the last part of the biography by W. F. Monypenny and G. E. Buckle, 2 vols. (new ed., 1929; first published in 6 vols., 1910–20). The lives by Adam Kirsch (2008) and Christopher Hibbert (2006) are competent but much less substantial than those of Stanley Weintraub (1993) and Robert Blake (1967), which reproduce large portions of his papers—all these published in New

York. Occasionally, each author slips too much from biography into general history and sometimes exaggerates the importance of what were really coterie affairs. Broadly speaking, they hold the balance right. *Disraeli's Reminiscences*, ed. Helen M. Swartz and Marvin Swartz (1975), contains the random jottings Disraeli made in the 1860s and 1870s. There is a rich perfume in these jottings. A few are genuine reminiscences. Most are casual anecdotes. Few other prime ministers could have written them, and none would have had the impudence to do so.

ITALY. *Memorie* (edizione diplomatica dall'autografo definitivo, Turin, 1907) and, above all, *Scritti e discorsi politici e militari*, 3 vols. (Bologna, 1934–37), by Giuseppe Garibaldi, are excellent volumes. The latter show how Italy escaped from alliance with France and traces the preparations for the Italian occupation of Rome (*DG*, 223).

RUSSIA. Mikhail Nikolaevich Annenkov, *Der Krieg im Jahre 1870: Bemerkungen und Betrachtungen eines russischen Officiers* (1871), the German translation of a book first published in Russian (Saint Petersburg, 1871), is a valuable contemporary source.

PART 3. SECONDARY WORKS
Guides and Sources

Two important guides are Widolf Wedlich, "Der deutsch-französische Krieg 1870/71: Literaturbericht und Auswahlbibliographie mit Anhang 'Die Presse der Jahre 1870–71'" (in *JBZ* 42 [1970]: 395–458); and *La Guerre de 1870/71 et ses conséquences*, ed. Philippe Levillain and Rainer Riemenschneider (Bonn, 1990), a collection of penetrating essays; each one is well written and has solid learning behind it (both in *DG*, 223). *Franco-German War of 1870: Source Book* (Leavenworth, KS, 1922) is a less satisfactory compilation by the army services school; as might be expected, its cited titles are those dealing only with the military side of the war, while international politics is ignored altogether.

On the French side, *Foreign Policy of the Second Empire*, by William E.

Echard (New York, 1988), is a clear and compelling outline by a great authority on the subject (*DG*, 224). Echard has also edited the *Historical Dictionary of the French Second Empire, 1852–1870* (Westport, CT, 1985), a most useful resource and guide that includes comprehensive coverage of political, military, and social history; there is a brief bibliography for each entry, especially good on the events of July–August 1870. *Historical Dictionary of the Third French Republic, 1870–1940*, ed. Patrick H. Hutton, 2 vols. (New York, 1986), is a valuable anthology that consists of twenty-four stimulating interpretive essays and numerous entries on military affairs and international relations.

Countries

GERMANY (including PRUSSIA). Otto Becker, *Bismarcks Ringen um Deutschlands Gestaltung*, ed. and rev. by Alexander Scharff (Heidelberg, 1958), is a credible and ambitious book, admirably planned and admirably executed. Herbert Geuss, *Bismarck und Napoleon III: Ein Beitrag zur Geschichte der preußisch-französischen Beziehungen 1815–1871* (Cologne, 1959), presents a competent picture of Prussian policy during the war. *Deutschlands Weg zur Grossmacht: Studien zum Verhältnis von Wirtschaft und Staat während der Reichsgründungszeit 1848–1881*, by Helmut Böhme (Cologne, 1966), manages to achieve the remarkable feat of discovering that Germany could have been unified without Bismarck. Many works appeared in 1970–71 that were addressed to the founding of the Second Empire. Of these, *Reichsgründung 1870/71*, ed. Theodor Schieder and Ernest Deuerlein (Stuttgart, 1970), is easily the best, a collection of immensely learned pieces. Some examples: "Kriegführung und Politik," by Eberhard Kolb, 95–119; "Bismarck: Seine Helfer und seine Gegner," by Walter Bußmann, 119–47; and especially "Die Reichsgründung in der deutschen Geschichtsschreibung," by Elisabeth Fehrenbach, 259–90—all enlightening and engrossing, scholarly and persuasive in their judgments. Fritz Stern, *Gold and Iron: Bismarck, Bleichröder, and the Building of the German Empire* (New York, 1977), is an incredibly learned study, written by a historian of faultless grasp who is also a beautiful writer (all discussed in greater detail in *DG*, 225).

AUSTRIA-HUNGARY. Most books given in *DG*, 225–26, are relevant here. *Österreich-Ungarn und der französisch-preussische Krieg 1870–1871*, by István Diószegi (Budapest, 1974), is a contribution to knowledge of the first rank, though Heinrich Lutz, *Österreich-Ungarn und die Gründung des Deutschen Reiches* (Frankfurt, 1979), has pointed out a number of factual blemishes (215–19). *Die deutsche Politik Beusts von seiner Berufung zum österreichischen Aussenminister Oktober 1866 bis zum Ausbruch des deutschfranzösischen Krieges 1870/71*, by Heinrich Potthoff (Bonn, 1968), is an able and stimulating essay, though narrow in scope. *Autour d'une tentative d'alliance entre la France et l'Autriche, 1867–1870*, by Victor-Lucien Tapié (Vienna, 1971), is a thin, though elegant and informed, essay. E. Kónyi, "Graf Beust und Graf Andrássy im Krieg 1870–71" (in *Deutsche Revue* 2 [1890]: 1–28, 145–65), contains a valuable selection of the correspondence between the two dominant figures at the Habsburg court. *Prime Minister Gyula Andrássy's Influence on Habsburg Foreign Policy during the Franco-German War of 1870–1871*, by János Decsy (Boulder, CO, 1979), is academic writing at its drabbest; reading it is like trying to eat a steak-and-kidney pie that has never been near the oven. The meat, though excellent in quality, is highly indigestible.

FRANCE. *Histoire du Second Empire*, by Pierre de la Gorce, 7 vols. (1904–8), remains the classic work (*DG*, 226). The last volume embraces the period covered by this study. E. Malcolm Carroll, *French Public Opinion and Foreign Affairs, 1870–1914* (New York, 1931), excerpts large selections of French editorial opinion on international politics, but, by doing so, it raises the usual question as to whether such pieces shape opinion or express it. This is even truer of the article "Official Propaganda and the French Press during the Franco-Prussian War," by Hazel C. Benjamin (in *JMH* 4 [1932]: 214–30). *Bismarck and the French Nation, 1848–1890*, by Allan Mitchell (New York, 1971) is very enjoyable and a first-rate contribution to the subject. Equally authoritative but more sweeping and high-level is *Relations franco-allemandes, 1815–1975*, by Raymond Poidevin and Jacques Bariéty (1977) (*DG*, 227), which surpasses *France under the Republic: The Development of Modern France*, by D. W. Brogan (1940). *The Political System of*

Napoleon III, by Theodore Zeldin (1958), remains the classic account of the empire's administrative tactics. *The Fall of the Third Napoleon*, by Theodore Aronson (1970), is agreeable light reading (*DG*, 203).

GREAT BRITAIN. *The Foreign Policy of Victorian England*, by Kenneth Bourne (Oxford, 1970), is a long essay displaying conventional assumptions about British foreign policy, accompanied by a judicious selection of representative documents. The standpoint is what might be called British respectable. The author clings firmly to the principle of writing nothing that would give offense to any one likely to dine at the high table of any Cambridge or Oxford college. *The Nineteenth Century, 1814–80*, by P. M. Hayes (1975), is a competent survey. *Cambridge History of British Foreign Policy*, ed. Sir A. W. Ward and G. P. Gooch, 3 vols. (Cambridge, 1922–23, reprinted 1970), is moving and surprisingly frank; the second volume, dealing with the period in which our subject falls, is an admirable undertaking, full of interest. Richard Millman, *British Policy and the Coming of the Franco-Prussian War* (Oxford, 1965), though devoted to the period prior to the war's outbreak, is important for background on the question of Belgian neutrality. Jonathan Parry, *The Rise and Fall of Liberal Government in Victorian Britain* (Cambridge, 1993), is a book of the highest distinction; the author deals with his subject in a dispassionate manner and is especially good on political themes. *British Naval Policy in the Gladstone-Disraeli Era, 1866–1880*, by John F. Beeler (Stanford, 1997), is a competent and compelling study, though the reader may regret the pedestrian style. Viet Valentin, *Bismarcks Reichsgründung im Urteil englischer Diplomaten* (Amsterdam, 1937), is a painstaking and accurate chronicle. Klaus Hildebrand's two pieces, "Grossbritannien und die deutsche Reichsgründung" (in *HZ*, new ser., Beiheft 6 [1980]: 9–62) and "Die deutsche Reichsgründung im Urteil der britischen Politik" (in *F* 5 [1977]: 399–424), have themes of great importance (both in *DG*, 227), as do *England und der deutsch-französische Krieg 1870/71*, by Kurt Rheindorf (Bonn, 1923), and Helmut Reinalter, "Norddeutscher Kaiser oder Kaiser von Deutschland?" (in *ZBLG* 39 [1976]: 847–82). "L'opinion britannique et les affaires françaises de 1870," by Patrick Bury (in *Revue d'histoire diplomatique* 84 [1970]: 337–51), is a concise examination of the topic.

ITALY. The outstanding book remains *Storia della politica estera italiana dal 1870 al 1896*, by Federico Chabod, 2 vols. (Bari, 1965), a book beyond praise and beyond cavil. There is a wonderful one-volume English translation by William McCuaig (Princeton, 1996). Two authoritative articles by Rudolf Lill are indispensable: "Italiens Aussenpolitik, 1866–1871" (in *EK*, 93–102) and "Aus den italienisch-deutschen Beziehungen, 1869–1876" (in *QuFiAB* 46 [1966]: 399–454), the latter a model of art and charm. *Das Ende des Kirchenstaates*, by Norbert Miko, 4 vols. (Vienna, 1961–69), exhausts the subject; the last volume is particularly relevant for the diplomacy of the war. *La situazione europea e la politica italiana dal 1867 al 1870*, by Carlo di Nola (Roma, 1956), is a competent book but without the glow of personalities. *Diplomat under Stress: Visconti Venosta and the Crisis of July 1870*, by S. William Halperin (Chicago, 1963), is a competent volume that gives plenty of facts. Maurice Eddleston, *Italian Neutrality in the Franco-Prussian War* (1935), is a good example of how history should not be written. It is an anthology of quotations from the archives rather than an analysis, and the reader may complain that he has been given all the crumbs from the cake but no plums. The two last chapters of *Victor Emanuel, Cavour and the Risorgimento*, by Denis Mack Smith (1971), have much of interest for our purposes (all in *DG*, 227–28). *Das Deutschlandbild in der italienischen Presse 1870–71*, by Wolfgang Suchanek (Bonn, 1975), is a well-researched doctoral thesis but is poorly constructed—a series of essays, rather than a chronological account.

RUSSIA. *Russische Orientpolitik und die Entstehung des deutschen Kaiserreiches 1866–1870/71*, by Dietrich Beyrau (Wiesbaden, 1974), is a splendid achievement, and the same is true of his articles "Russische Interessenzonen und europäisches Gleichgewicht 1860–1970" (in *EK*, 65–76) and "Russland zur Zeit der Reichsgründung" (in *ER*, 63–137) (both in *DG*, 228). Beyrau's arguments have been modified and in some cases overtaken by Stéphanie Burgaud in *La politique russe de Bismarck et l'unification allemande: Mythe fondateur et réalités politiques* (Strasbourg, 2010), a magnificent contribution. The details have the fascination provided by the analysis of a game of chess; not only is the book well written and skillfully arranged, but also its understanding makes it a book in a thousand even if the detailed narrative does not always sustain the motives ascribed to Bismarck by the author.

Barbara Jelavich, *St. Petersburg and Moscow: Tsarist and Soviet Foreign Policy, 1814–1974* (Bloomington, IN, 1974), is narrower in scope than its title would suggest, but its observations—especially on Russian relations with Bismarck—are deep, careful, and scholarly, though they sometimes contradict Burgaud's views.

OTHERS. "Bayern und Deutschland nach dem Prager Frieden," by Hans W. Schlaich, in *Gesellschaft und Herrschaft: Forschungen zu sozial-und landesgeschichtlichen Problemen vornehmlich in Bayern: eine Festgabe für Karl Bosl zum 60. Geburtstag*, ed. Richard van Dülmen (Munich, 1969), 301–38, is a clear and compelling essay; Wolf D. Gruner, "Bayern, Preussen, und die süddeutschen Staaten" (in *ZBLG* 37 [1974]: 799–827), is a first-rate contribution to historical knowledge; "Zwischen Bismarck und Napoleon: Das Problem der belgischen Neutralität von 1866–1870," by Horst Lademacher, is distinguished by its criticism of Napoleon's Belgian policy. "Die Schweiz und die Wende von 1870/71," by Peter Stadler, is witty, as well as informative and competent (these last two in *EK*, 103–12, 113–18; all in *DG*, 229). Still, none of these can match "The Lost Intermediaries: The Impact of 1870 on the European States System," by Paul W. Schroeder (in *SSS*, 76–95). This essay, like his others mentioned in this bibliography, is a model of insight and erudition written with a delightful mixture of scholarship and wit; it sets a standard that few other historians can approach. *Le Luxembourg dans la guerre de 1870*, by Christian Calmes (Luxemburg, 1970), is a sensible, stimulating book and a stern warning against generalizations.

UNITED STATES. *American Opinion of German Unification, 1848–71*, by John Gerow Gazley (New York, 1926), is an important, wide-ranging study with material on Burnside and Sheridan.

The Diplomacy of the Franco-Prussian War
General

Le XIXe siècle [pt. I]: 1815 à 1871 (1954), vol. 5 of *Histoire des relations internationales* (8 vols., 1953–58), ed. Pierre Renouvin, is much more than a diplomatic history that deserves to be translated into English; *The Struggle for Mastery in Europe*, by A. J. P. Taylor (Oxford, 1954), is a classic work, sometimes contradictory; Alfred Stern, *Geschichte Europas seit den Verträgen von 1815 bis zum Frankfurter Frieden von 1871* (1913–24), is old but still of value. *From Vienna to Versailles*, by L. C. B. Seaman (New York, 1963), is an interpretive essay, always stimulating if not always convincing; *The Chancelleries of Europe*, by Alan Palmer (1983), is a good, popular account (all in *DG*, 229–30). *European Alliances and Alignments, 1871–1890*, by William L. Langer (New York, 1931), though old, is a work of the highest distinction; the first chapter, dealing with the problems Bismarck confronted after the war, is of particular value for our theme. This is even truer of the work by Klaus Hildebrand titled *Das vergangene Reich: Deutsche Aussenpolitik von Bismarck bis Hitler, 1871–1945* (Stuttgart, 1995), a first-rate piece of history, not exciting or sensational but level-headed, sane, and, above all, realistic. *Europa in den Augen Bismarcks: Bismarcks Vorstellung von der Politik der europäischen Mächte und vom europäischen Staatensystem*, by Dominik Haffer (Paderborn, 2010), deals with the period from the Crimean War to unification; it goes competently and devoutly over the subject, and, although it does not add much new information, it is excellently composed and contains an exhaustive bibliography.

In addition, there are a number of valuable studies I examined for this book that I did not mention earlier. Outstanding among these is *Great Power Diplomacy, 1814–1914*, by Norman Rich (New York, 1992); magnificent on every count, it combines technical mastery with a superb gift of exposition and is especially strong on the period of German unification. Dennis Showalter, *The Wars of German Unification* (Oxford, 2004), has no rival and is unlikely ever to have any. *The Great Powers and the European States System, 1814–1914*, by F. R. Bridge and Roger Bullen (2nd ed., 2005), is a book packed with information and controversial ideas; F. H. Hinsley, *Power and the Pursuit of Peace: Theory and Practice in the History of Relations between States* (2nd ed., 2005), is a work of great learning illuminated by flashes of insight but is unduly dependent on published English sources. In addition, mention should be made of two seminal articles by Paul W. Schroeder: "Alliances 1815–1945: Weapons of Power and Tools of Management," combining dazzling scholarship and art; and "The Nineteenth Century System: Balance of Power or Political Equilibrium," an exercise in diplomatic history as well as political science that explores its subject with rigorous detachment and discards many traditional and accepted views (both in *SSS*, 195–222, 223–41). Schroeder's book-length essay "International Politics, Peace and War, 1815–1914" (in *The Nineteenth Century*, ed. T. C. W. Blanning [Oxford, 2000], 158–209) is even better; the legends come crashing down one after another. Finally, anyone interested in archival research would do well to consult the *New Guide to the Diplomatic Archives of Western Europe*, by Daniel H. Thomas and Lynn M. Case (Philadelphia, 1975), a series of valuable essays by distinguished historians, giving helpful information on history, holdings, access, classification, and regulations, though some, particularly on the German records, are in need of updating.

Specialized, Arranged More or Less Chronologically

When it comes to secondary literature in book form, primacy of place must go to the magnificent two-volume work by the great French scholar Albert Sorel, *Histoire diplomatique de la guerre franco-allemande* (1875). The second half of the first volume and the entire second volume are devoted to the period treated by this study. Sorel surveys the great decisions and events with Olympian vision and detachment; though written by a contemporary who wound up on the losing side, the book is uniformly fair to every party from Gambetta to Bismarck, and it can be read for entertainment, as well as for instruction. Of the more recent works, there is none that can rival *Der Weg aus dem Krieg: Bismarcks Politik im Krieg und die Friedensanbahnung, 1870/71*, by Eberhard Kolb (Munich, 1989), an incomparable book, by far the best book written on the diplomacy of the subject since Sorel—a work sound in its scholarship, brilliant in its organization, and compelling in its style. No discussion of the outstanding books on the war would be complete without the mention of the magisterial work of François Roth that, though not specifically addressed to the diplomacy of the Franco-Prussian War, sheds considerable light on that subject: *La Guerre de 1870* (1990). This book is of particular importance for the impact of the war on national memories of the two countries involved, a subject on which there is great need for further research. Of the other general histories: *Diplomatie und Kriegspolitik vor und nach der Reichsgründung*, by Ernst Engelberg (1971), is informative on some issues but anchored to Marxist dogma and does not begin to compare to Kolb or Roth. *Der deutsch-französische Krieg 1870/71: Vorgeschichte, Verlauf, Folgen*, ed. Jan Ganschow, Olaf Haselhorst, and Maik Ohnezeit (Graz, 2009), is powerfully argued and well documented; the first and last sections are particularly strong.

There are three books of importance on the mood in France during and after the French declaration of war: *La Guerre de 1870*, by Henri Welschinger, 2 vols. (1910), is compelling and very critical of the major actors on the French side—see the review by F. A. Simpson in *EHR* 101 (January 1911): 194–97. *La France et la Prusse devant l'histoire*, by Arsène Legrelle, 2 vols. (4th ed., 1874), is a summary of the position of the French authorities that is occasionally enlivened by anecdotes from less solemn sources. The best book on the background of the war is *Der Kriegsausbruch, 1870*, by Eberhard Kolb (Göttingen, 1970), a model of brief exposition (all in *DG*, 231–32). *Paris Babylon: The Story of the Paris Commune*, by Rupert Christiansen (New York, 1995), is an engrossing story of the city not only during the Commune but also during the siege, one that can be read with joy and profit; the author has the gifts of a novelist. The same can be said of the account of Alistair Horne, *The Fall of Paris: The Siege and the Commune 1870–71* (1965), a popular account, perhaps too hard on the city's inhabitants, but the narrative is a delight to read, as dry and sparkling as champagne. *Histoire de la diplomatie du Gouvernement de la défense nationale*, by Jules Valfrey, 3 vols. (1871–72), has some points of merit but has been surpassed by the work of Sorel, already cited in this section.

There are a number of books and articles on the Roman question in addition to the fourth volume of the work of Miko, cited earlier. *Die römische Frage*, ed. Hubert Bastgen, 3 vols. (Freiburg, 1917–19), is a sound piece of scholarship, a laborious compilation of the major documents, and persistently dull. *The Roman Question: Extracts from the Despatches of Odo Russell from Rome, 1858–1870*, ed. Noel Blakiston (1962), is a foray into a thick jungle; the editor has been overwhelmed by his material and vindicates the dictum that the historian must first discover his evidence and then throw three-quarters of it away. *Il tramonto del potere temporale, 1866–1870*, by Renato Mori (Rome, 1967), is much better; it goes deeply into the controversial issues and displays a firm mastery of the sources. Georges Dethan, "Napoléon III et l'opinion française devant la question romaine (1860–1870)" (in *Revue d'histoire diplomatique* 72 [1958]: 118–32), is an able and stimulating essay.

RUSSIAN REACTION TO THE OUTBREAK OF THE WAR. In addition to the work by Stéphanie Burgaud, already cited, *The European Powers and the German Question, 1848–71, with Special Reference to England and Russia*, by W. E. Mosse (Cambridge, 1958), is a competent study, very instructive, though top-heavy with detail. François Charles-Roux, *Alexandre II, Gortchakoff, et Napoléon III* (1913), though old, remains a book of outstanding distinction, in which grace and learning sit easily together. There are many quotations from Russian and French sources. *Russia and the Formation of the Romanian National State, 1821–1878*, by Barbara Jelavich (Cambridge, 1984), is a work of major importance, showing that Russia's European policy and its Romanian policy did not always correspond. "Russian Military Strength on the Eve of the Franco-Prussian War," by William C. Askew (in *Slavonic and East European Review* 30, no. 74 [December 1951]: 185–205), is an exposition of a very high order but is overshadowed by *Franko-Prusskaia voina i obshchestvennoe mnenie Germanii i Rossii* (The Franco-Prussian War and Public Opinion in Germany and Russia), by Svetlana Valerianovna Obolenskaia (Moscow, 1977), a book rich in material from new sources and with a grasp of the issues at stake.

BELGIAN NEUTRALITY. *Die belgische Neutralität als Problem der europäischen Politik, 1830–1914*, by Horst Lademacher (Bonn, 1971), despite its awkward construction, is a major exercise in diplomatic history, exploring the question with rigorous detachment. "Great Britain and the Belgian Railways Dispute of 1869," by Gordon A. Craig (in *AHR* 50 [1945]: 738–61), is a compelling exposition of bewitching charm; as always, the author writes with his inimitable pungency. The article on the same subject by Daniel H. Thomas (in *The Historian* 26 [1964]: 228–43) is less impressive.

THE GERMAN PRESS. Four contributions by Eberhard Naujoks are fundamental: *Bismarcks auswärtige Pressepolitik und die Reichsgründung (1865–1871)* (Wiesbaden, 1968), authoritative but very long and rather dull in presentation; "Bismarck und die Organisation der Regierungspresse" (in

HZ 205, no. 11 [1967]: 46–80), admirably clear on his relationship with the Berlin newspapers; "Ein Jahrzehnt Forschung über Bismarcks Pressepolitik" (in *F* 7 [1979]: 508–26), comprehensive but also balanced and sensible; and "Die Elsaß-Lothringer als ‚preußische Minderheit' 1870–1914" (in *Expansion und Integration: Zur Eingliederung neugewonnener Gebiete in den preußischen Staat*, ed. Peter Baumgart [Cologne, 1984], 449–73), insightful and stimulating. Naujoks manages to be a truly honest historian who does not make a parade of his honesty.

IMPACT OF SEDAN. *Politik und Kriegführung in den deutschen Einigungskriegen 1864, 1866 und 1870/71*, by Anneliese Klein-Wuttig (1934), is old, but it is well organized and well written and contains many substantial and stimulating judgments. *Bonapartism after Sedan*, by John Rothney (Ithaca, NY, 1969), has some errors of details but is otherwise an important contribution. "Kriegführung und Politik 1870/71," by Eberhard Kolb (in *Reichsgründung*, ed. Schieder and Deuerlein, 95–118), is an article that could hardly be better done; it makes for good reading as well as exciting history. *Les conseillers généraux en 1870*, by Louis Girard, Antoine Prost, and Rémi Gossez (1967), is an effective, compact book that reproduces telling portions of the diaries of the French officials. It is particularly strong on the period after Sedan. *The German Influence in France after 1870*, by Allan Mitchell (Chapel Hill, NC, 1979), is a solid political study, but the great weight the author places on the later recollections of the founders of the Republic raises doubts. *La crise allemande de la pensée francaise, 1870–1914*, by Claude Digeon (1959), is a book that will be much to the taste of people who like to read books about books.

ALSACE-LORRAINE, BACKGROUND. *Die deutsch-französische Tragödie, 1848–1864: Politische Beziehungen und psychologisches Verhältnis*, by Rudolf Buchner (Wiesbaden, 1965), is stimulating, if somewhat ponderous. Its conclusions have been admirably modified and updated by Hans Fenske, "Das Elsaß in der deutschen öffentlichen Meinung von 1820 bis 1866" (in *ZGORh* 119 [1971]: 233–80), and "Eine westliche Grenzfrage? Das Rheinland, Elsaß und Lothringen in der öffentlichen Meinung 1851–1866" (in *Aspects des relations franco-allemandes à l'époque du Second Empire 1851–*

1866, ed. Raymond Poidevin and Heinz-Otto Sieburg [Metz, 1982], 137–60); both contributions are brilliant in their presentation and display the author's high ability to reduce an enormous subject to manageable proportions.

In the course of the 1960s, *HZ* provided the forum in which writers of great authority argued the issues. Walther Lipgens, "Bismarck, die öffentliche Meinung und die Annexion von Elsaß und Lothringen 1870" (in *HZ* 199 [1964]: 31–112), is a contribution of high scholarship, but his argument that Bismarck was bent on annexation from the outset and that he used the press to arouse otherwise uninterested German public opinion on the subject of acquisition is unconvincing. "Zur Frage der Annexion von Elsaß und Lothringen 1870," by Lothar Gall (in *HZ* 206 [1968]: 265–326), is much fairer in its judgments; displaying a mastery of the sources, it shows, without question, that Bismarck's decision was one at which he arrived independently and without the pressure of external forces. All the same, "Die deutsche patriotische Dichtung vom Kriegsbeginn 1870 über Frankreich und die elsässische Frage," by Rudolf Buchner (in *HZ* 206 [1968]: 327–36), is a reminder (albeit a short and terse one) that, in the political atmosphere that developed after the first German victories, this pressure was by no means absent. "Bismarck und das Aufkommen der Annexionsforderung," by Eberhard Kolb (in *HZ* 209 [1969]: 318–56), is a spirited argument that these provinces were strategically essential; the author writes on the basis of extensive, indeed almost exhaustive, research in the official records. Kolb's equally spirited "Ökonomische Interessen und politischer Entscheidungsprozeß: Zur Aktivität deutscher Wirtschaftskreise und zur Rolle wirtschaftlicher Erwägungen in der Frage von Annexion und Grenzziehung 1870/71" (in *VSWG* 60 [1973]: 343–85) is an unsurpassed example of how economic history should be written and shows how the elegant writer can work its conclusions into a new synthesis.

Josef Becker, "Baden, Bismarck, und die Annexion von Elsaß und Lothringen" (in *ZGORh* 115 [1967]: 167–204), is a compelling and searching exposition. An expanded version of the same article appears in *Oberrheinische Studien* 2 (Karlsruhe, 1973), 133–73; it is full of descriptions of the subject and is based on fine work in state archives.

La Lorraine annexée: Étude sur la présidence de Lorraine dans l'Empire allemand, 1870–1918, by François Roth (Nancy, 1976), is a study of the highest order, though it is a pity that a work of such distinction lists so few references. The author has forcefully updated his conclusions in successive works, all published in Nancy: 1981, 1984, and 1985. "Unfähigkeit zur Verfassungsreform: Das 'Reichsland' Elsaß-Lothringen von 1870–1918," by Hans Ulrich-Wehler (in Wehler, *Krisenherde des Kaiserreichs 1871–1918: Studien zur deutschen Sozial- und Verfassungsgeschichte*, 2nd ed. [Göttingen, 1979], 23–69), is a first-rate essay that exploits fully the available sources, though some of its judgments lack proportion.

"Das lothringische Erzgebiet als Kriegsziel der deutschen Großbourgeoisie im deutsch-französischen Krieg 1870/71: Materialien über die sozialökonomischen Hintergründe der Annexion Elsaß-Lothringens," by Hans Wolter (in *ZfG* 19 [1971]: 34–64), is a Marxist account that adds little.

NEGOTIATIONS WITH BAZAINE. *Bazaine, coupable ou victime?: À la lumière de documents nouveaux*, by Edmond Ruby and Jean Regnault (1960), is a fair outline of the case; the first half, which deals with the problem of the French dilemma after Sedan, is particularly revealing, the second half less so. Maurice Baumont, *L'échiquier de Metz, empire ou république, 1870* (1971), is the fullest account, but the author is unduly dependent on the papers of the Duc d'Aumale, the leading prosecutor at Bazaine's trial. Baumont's biography of Bazaine (1978) is an improvement on previous lives but adjusts events to his theories rather than adjusting his theories to events. Jean Cahen-Salvador, *Le procès du Maréchal Bazaine* (Lausanne, 1946), has some points of interest. François Semur, *L'affaire Bazaine: Un maréchal devant ses juges* (Turquant, 2009), is a delightful book in which we learn not only a great deal about Bazaine but much about human life in general.

NEGOTIATIONS, FALL 1870. "The Mission of M. Thiers to the Neutral Powers of Europe," by J. Holland Rose (in *Transactions of the Royal Historical Society*, ser. 3, vol. 11 [1917]: 35–60), is an old though competent account written with a pleasant style. *Thiers und Bismarck*, by Georg Küntzel (Bonn, 1905), is not much more than a crude summary. *The French Revolution of 1870–1871*, by Roger L. Williams (New York, 1969), is a book of the first importance, with much material on the uprising of 31 October by a leading historian of the Second Empire. Heinrich Meier-Welcker, "Der Kampf mit der Republik" (in *Entscheidung 1870: Der deutsch-französische Krieg*, ed. Wolfgang von Groote und Ursula von Gersdorff [Stuttgart, 1970], 105–64), is a good essay with its own atmosphere. "Les opérations financières de la France pendant la guerre de 1870–71," by Just Haristoy (in *Revue de science et de législation financières* 12 [1914]: 389–434), provides a full description of the issues and is based on fine work in the private papers and official archives.

BISMARCK AND MOLTKE. Mention has been made earlier of *The Politics of the Prussian Army 1640–1945*, by Gordon A. Craig; it deserves to be listed here, as well. This magisterial volume shows the depth of the resentment between the two men. More detailed and equally magisterial is *The Franco-Prussian War*, by Michael Howard (1961; 2nd ed., New York, 2001); the second edition contains a new preface by the author. Howard's is a superb story, and his book is as much a work of literature as it is a history. No less impressive is the book by the same title and on the same subject by Geoffrey Wawro (New York, 2003), which excels on every count—a book that will be read with profit as long as anyone cares about the history of the Franco-Prussian War or, for that matter, about history itself. Stephen Badsey, *The Franco-Prussian War* (Oxford, 2003), is a compact survey, though it does not begin to approach the standard set by Howard and Wawro. "Der Kriegsrat zu Herny am 14. August 1870" (in *MGM* 9 [1971]: 5–13), though short, is another indispensable contribution to the literature addressed to this subject by Eberhard Kolb; it shows that the soldiers were planning from the start to exclude Bismarck from the war deliberations. "Bismarck und Moltke vor dem Fall von Paris und beim Friedenschluß," by Arnold O. Meyer, in *Stufen und Wandlungen der deutschen Einheit*, ed. Kurt von Raumer and Theodor Schieder (Stuttgart, 1943), 329–41, is an excellent and provocative article, free from mistakes of fact, though not from some errors of judgments. Three articles in *PJbb* are outstanding contributions of wide grasp and understanding: "Bismarck und Moltke," by Oberst von Haeften (in *PJbb* 177 [1919]: 85–124); "Roon und Moltke vor Paris," by Emile Daniels (in *PJbb* 121 [1905]: 1–25, 220–41), which, despite its title, has much material on Bismarck; and Daniels's "Die Behandlung der französischen Kriegsgefangenen von 1870" (in *PJbb* 120 [1905]: 34–78), a most penetrating account and a model of art and charm.

BLACK SEA CRISIS. Some important works here with an old one by Kurt Rheindorf still at the top of the list: *Die Schwarze-Meer-(Pontus-)Frage vom Pariser Frieden von 1856 bis zum Abschluss der Londoner Konferenz von 1871* (1925), a first-rate production that illustrates clearly the outstanding aspects of Bismarck's policy. "The British Public and the War Scare of November 1870" (in *Historical Journal* 6 [1963]: 38–58) and *The Rise and Fall of the Crimean System, 1855–1871*, by W. E. Mosse (1963), are carefully researched and clearly written contributions but take Disraeli too seriously. *The Ottoman Empire, the Great Powers, and the Straits Question, 1870–1887*, by Barbara Jelavich (Bloomington, IN, 1973), is incomparably the best and most important account of this crucial subject. *Le Bosphore et les Dardanelles*, by Serge Goriainov (1910), provides a mountain of important details, including material from the Russian archives to which the author had access—but it has been overtaken by the work of Burgaud, cited earlier. There are two doctoral dissertations on this subject that I have not been able to read: *Die Schwarze-Meer Konferenz von 1871*, by Heinrich Mertz (Tübingen, 1927), and *Bismarck und Südosteuropa vom Krimkrieg bis zur Pontuskonferenz*, by Claus Bormann (Hamburg, 1967).

PRELIMINARIES OF PEACE. *Die Pariser Presse und die deutsche Frage: Unter Berücksichtigung der französischen Pressepolitik im Zeitalter der Bismarckschen Reichsgründung (1866–1870/71)*, by Wilfried Radewahn (Frankfurt am Main, 1977), is brilliant in composition; it is lively, clear, and in firm control of the sources. "Bismarck und der Bonapartismus im Winter 1870/71," by Joachim Kühn (in *PJbb* 163 [1916]: 49–100), despite its age, is a work of great insight and understanding in which grace and learning sit easily together. *The Siege of Paris 1870–1871: A Political and Social History*, by Melvin Kranzberg (Ithaca, NY, 1950), is a pedestrian work; with few obvious faults, the book also has few virtues. "Liberals at War: The Economic Policies of the Government of National Defense," by Edward L. Katzenbach Jr. (in *AHR* 56 [1950–51]: 803–23), has much valuable information in it but is more a collection of statistics than a historical narrative. *La défense nationale, 1870–1871*, by Jacques Desmarest (1949), plays old tunes with few enrichments. *The War against Paris, 1871*, by Robert Tombs (Cambridge, 1981), is an accurate and detailed chronicle. *Comment la France est devenue républic-*

aine, les élections générales et partielles à l'Assemblée nationale, 1870–1875, by Jacques Gouault (1954), though overly dramatic in presentation, is still the most illuminating account of its subject that there is. *Berliner Presse und europäisches Geschehen 1871,* by Ursula E. Koch (1978), is important for both the preliminaries of the peace and the armistice.

ARMISTICE AND ELECTIONS. *Bismarck und die Friedensunterhändler 1871: Die deutsch-französischen Friedensverhandlungen zu Brüssel und Frankfurt, März-Dezember 1871,* ed. Hans Goldschmidt (1929), gives a good sample of the pertinent documents and a strong introduction, which is why it is included here and not under the sections dealing with sources. *Gambetta and the National Defence,* by J. P. T. Bury (1936, reprinted 1970) is an entertaining discussion about the legends surrounding its protagonist. *Gambetta dans les tempêtes,* by Georges Wormser (1964), suffers from poor organization and sometimes inadequate source material but contains many substantial and stimulating judgments. *The Beginning of the Third Republic in France,* by Frank Herbert Brabant (1940), is a careful study of the elections for the National Assembly. "A New Look at Conservative Preparations for the French Elections of 1871," by Robert R. Locke (in *French Historical Studies* 5 [1967/1968]: 351–58), is a brisk summary; his book *French Legitimists and the Politics of Moral Order in the Early Third Republic* (Princeton, 1974) is a fine narrative, with politics and biography melded together, but it has been overtaken by Rainer Hudemann, *Fraktionsbildung im französischen Parlament: Zur Entwicklung des Parteiensystems in der frühen Dritten Republik (1871–1875)* (Munich, 1979), a brilliant composition; it is lively, clear, and stocked with anecdotes and penetrating comments.

TREATY OF FRANKFURT. *Der schwierige Weg zum Frieden: Das Problem der Kriegsbeendigung 1870/71,* by Eberhard Kolb (Munich, 1985), is an elegant essay, modest in size though not in accomplishment; it shows how the arrangements for peace in 1871 set a standard for the rest of the century, but it is not a book for the beginner. On the treaty itself: Jules Valfrey, 2 vols. (1874–75), a tract for the times; Gaston May (1909), a book with many merits, not the least of which are detailed maps; and Robert Giesberg (Philadelphia, 1966), a sound piece of scholarship, laboriously based on the sources and persistently dull. Heinz Wolter, "Die Anfänge des Dreikaiserverhältnisses" (in *Die großpreussisch-militaristische Reichsgründung 1871*, ed. Horst Bartel and Ernst Engelberg, 2 vols. [1971], 2:235–305), is long-winded, one-sided, and uninspiring. "The Franco-German Boundary of 1871," by Richard Hartshorne (in *World Politics* 2, no. 2 [1950]: 209–50) is an essay that gives some welcome guidance, but it is written in a professional jargon that should be translated.

THE COMMUNE. Since the events here were part of a civil war that the book does not treat, I list only those that touch on the negotiations between the new German empire and the French provisional government. But I have made an exception for *Bibliographie critique de la Commune de Paris: 1871*, by Robert Le Quillec (2006), which is encyclopedic in scope. Of particular importance is the work by William Serman titled *La Commune de Paris 1871* (1986), a book written with such verve, such detachment, and such mastery of the sources that it is likely to be the last word on the subject. The works by Jacques Girault (2009), David A. Shafer (New York, 2005), Paule Lejeune (2002), and Robert Tombs (1999) attempt to penetrate the deeper significance of the revolution and to connect it, with varying degrees of success, to European affairs. "Der Pariser Commune-Aufstand und die Beendigung des deutsch-französischen Kriegs," by Eberhard Kolb (in *HZ* 215 [1972]: 265–98), is a penetrating essay by the preeminent historian of the diplomacy of the Franco-Prussian war; every word is a peach.

Index

Page numbers in italics refer to figures and captions.

305